LOCAL GOVERNMENT LAW

IN A NUTSHELL

FIFTH EDITION

By

DAVID J. McCARTHY, Jr.

Dean Emeritus & Carmack Waterhouse Professor of
State and Local Government Law, Emeritus
Georgetown University Law Center

LAURIE REYNOLDS

Professor of Law
University of Illinois College of Law

Mat #40064727

COPYRIGHT © 1975, 1983, 1990, 1995 WEST PUBLISHING CO.
COPYRIGHT © 2003 By West, a Thomson business
610 Opperman Drive
P.O. Box 64526
St. Paul, MN 55164–0526
1–800–328–9352

Printed in the United States of America
ISBN 0–314–26489–2

TEXT IS PRINTED ON 10% POST
CONSUMER RECYCLED PAPER

TO MARY E. McCARTHY

D.J.M.

TO JOE, KATY, AND DAVID

L.R.

*

PREFACE

This text will aid students who seek to learn Local Government Law. We hope that it will also assist practicing attorneys who seek an overview of all or part of the subject matter. The relationships among local governments, their citizens, their states and the federal government are so pervasive that choices of emphasis must of necessity be made in a text of this size. Because Local Government Law tends to overlap several other law school courses, the choice in this text was to address at least as many areas as could accurately convey the scope of these relationships and to treat more extensively areas, such as taxation and borrowing, that are not likely to be pursued in such detail in the core courses common to all law school curricula.

The vast scope of the subject inevitably means that individual authors and editors will approach it with differing views of the most interesting and instructive theme and focus. Our choice has been the central theme of delegated power and the limitations imposed on its exercise by law and challenge, the latter because it serves significantly, as intended, to restrain the exercise of governing power. The setting is, perhaps, more practical than theoretical.

Occasionally, throughout the text, comments and queries will attempt to provoke reader reaction (agreement or disagreement) to the status or trend of particular legal principles and of local government policies. Frequent illustrations, many of which have been drawn from actual cases, will be used to assist in understanding the text.

While many cases, articles, books and casebooks were consulted in the preparation of this and preceding editions, we are especially grateful for the assistance provided by the writings of Chester Antieau, Richard Briffault, David Callies, Jefferson Fordham, Robert Freilich, Gerald Frug, M. David Gelfand, Clayton Gillette, Jerome Hellerstein, Walter Hellerstein, Harold Hovey, George Lefcoe, Michael Libonati, Daniel Mandelker, Frank Michelman, Dawn Clark Netsch, Laura Oren, Osbourne Reynolds, Peter Salsich, Terence Sandalow, Sho Sato, William Valente, Arvo Van Alstyne, Judith Wegner, and Robert Williams.

For past editions, Professor McCarthy has expressed his gratitude to several people: to Georgetown's very supportive Dean, Judith Areen; to his student research assistants, Kathryn Kovacs (JD 1995) and David Angeli (JD 1997); and to Georgetown's Office of Administration personnel for their indispensable assistance. Professor Reynolds thanks Jennifer Chavez for her outstanding research and Patricia Estergard for tireless secretarial assistance.

DAVID J. MCCARTHY, JR.
LAURIE REYNOLDS

OUTLINE

OUTLINE

*

LOCAL
GOVERNMENT
LAW

IN A NUTSHELL

FIFTH EDITION

*

CHAPTER I

LOCAL GOVERNING POWER— GENERAL ASPECTS, LIMITATIONS, RESOLUTION OF POWER CONFLICTS AND CHALLENGES

A. INTRODUCTION

§ 1. Basic Questions and Terms

Broadly considered, the study of Local Government Law is the study of local governing powers exercised by entities subsidiary and largely subordinate to the state. A partial understanding of state government and of the roles of governments in the federal system necessarily accompanies the study. When government at any level plans to act, a basic question is whether the proposed activity is an appropriate one for government. "Should government get into the business of owning and operating airports?"

Since all government is restricted within limits constitutionally structured by the people, the next question may be whether the government entity can act as planned. "Can government get into the business of owning and operating an airport?"

When the prospective actor is a government of delegated authority, the question of its ability to act would perhaps be phrased, "Does *this* city, Bigville, possess the authority to own and operate this airport?"

While legislative and judicial attempts to answer these questions may frequently be characterized as unsatisfactory, resolution of the questions is at the heart of local governance. The decision to what extent the local government either ought to or can initiate activity which might be the subject of private action or government involvement at another level is, in the first instance, committed to the local legislative body. The courts often defer to this decision, especially as to the appropriateness of activity. When a judicial decision of appropriateness is made, it may be expressed in a determination whether the activity serves a public purpose, or serves to protect the public health, safety, morality or general welfare. "The expenditure of funds for the purchase and operation of the airport will expedite public travel, will ensure the safety of air traffic operation, will increase local business access to economical commercial routes, will create more jobs, will protect residential areas, and thus will serve a public purpose." Underlying the spoken or unspoken question of appropriateness are basic legislative or judicial views of the importance of centralization or diffusion of power and the consequent protection of individual liberties.

Judicial determination of the local government's ability to act will be the result of reference to the sources of its power. As we shall see, these sources may be constitutional and statutory grants and limitations subject to judicial interpretation. If the questioned power exercise is neither expressly approved nor specifically prohibited, inference of its approval by implication will be tested by the reasonableness of the desired inference and its obvious or attenuated relationship to expressly authorized activities. "The court concludes that the power to own and operate a municipal airport may not reasonably be inferred from the statutory authorizations to regulate traffic and to provide parks and recreational facilities."

It can readily be seen that if the relationship between the asserted implied power and the powers expressly granted is not too attenuated, the determination whether the implication is reasonable may involve a decision, albeit frequently unspoken, that the activity is or is not an appropriate one for local government.

This questioning of the value of action initiated by the local government may also underlie judicial determination of the level of government which should be permitted to act. The question may arise in deciding whether the local government is authorized to act. It may arise because both the state and the local government have enacted legislation on the precise point. It may arise because both have legislated in the area, although not in a conflicting manner. It may arise because the state has attempted to interpose its authority either legislatively or through administrative boards over a matter which allegedly is within the constitutionally protected area of local government.

To illustrate, let us assume that the state legislature has enacted a public disclosure law designed to provide voters with information to make judgments concerning the allegiances and possible conflicts of interest of electoral candidates and public officials throughout the state. Let us further assume that, in the City of Hearing, the local government's legislature subsequently has enacted a local public disclosure law designed to meet the same objectives regarding candidates and officials in the local jurisdiction, but with stricter disclosure requirements. The latter law is challenged in court.

The court may decide that the local government had no authority at all to enact the law. As noted above, if such authority is argued to be by interpretation of express language or implication, evaluation of the appropriateness of the local action may underlie the decision.

The court may decide that without regard to the state's action, the matter of public officials and elections is one committed by the state constitution, or by statute, to the state's purview. Even if, by state law, the local government is permitted to initiate action, without further authorization, on matters of local concern (one form of home rule, as we shall see), the court may conclude that this matter has consequences beyond the boundaries of the locality, and is more appropriately committed to statewide action. Perhaps, then, the question of the local ordinance's validity will turn on judicial decision as to its appropriateness in light of its external consequences, the value of central response over a multiplicity of responses.

The court has additional choices. It may deem the local action authorized and merely supplemental to or in augmentation of the state legislation. Conversely, it may determine that the local law "prohibits what state law permits" in an area partaking of statewide concern and strike it down on that ground. Similarly, it may deem the authorization to demand adherence to procedures as to which it concludes the authorizing legislation is not only directive but truly mandates compliance. Failure to follow mandated steps will invalidate the exercise. Whatever the court's decision, the classification of the activity as "local" or "general" or omitted steps as "directory" or "mandatory" may turn on the appropriateness of both government action and its manner of exercise at the level in question.

Government action is designed to protect the public interest and to preserve the public health, safety, morality and general welfare. This is particularly true at the local level where the desire for services may constitute a primary motivation for the local entity's organization. In promoting such activities, the municipality will have concluded that, for a variety of reasons, government action is preferable to that of the private sector and is to that extent appropriate. Indeed, it may be acting in concert with the private sector to achieve the desired results. As we shall see, the people of many states have in constitutional amendments declared that such activities should be protected against state legislative or administrative incursion. Where such incursion is alleged to have occurred, judicial decision concerning the appropriate government level may call for designation of the questioned local power exercise as either "governmental" (and thus, perhaps, within state legislative purview) or "proprietary." This and other dichotomies arise in part because of the hybrid nature (governor-service provider) of the government entities.

Thus, an exercise of local governing power will be upheld if it serves a "public purpose," if its implied existence is "reasonable," if the matter in question is of "local" rather than "statewide" concern, if the activity is "proprietary" rather than "governmental," or if the manner of its exercise adheres to all steps deemed "mandatory" rather than "directory." The seeming simplicity of the classification process is, of course, deceptive. As in other areas of the law, once the label has been affixed, predictable results corresponding to that label will follow. The much more difficult and unpredictable determination whether to affix a particular label will bring into operation precedent, political theory, and persuasion.

§ 2. Focus and Approach

Our study must accordingly begin with the sources of local governing power, the limitations upon state interference with that power, and the resolution of competing government claims to power priority. Thereafter, with accompanying recognition that citizen challenge serves to restrain abuses of power, we shall engage in a more discrete analysis of the following particular manifestations of local governing power:

a.   The formation of the local entity, alteration, boundary changes, internal operating problems, delegations of responsibility, elections and referenda;

b.   The police and zoning powers, i.e., regulation of citizen conduct, business activity and land use, without compensation, to protect the public health, safety, morality and general welfare;

c.   The acquisition, use and disposition of goods, services and property; and

d.   The acquisition and expenditure of revenues derived from taxation, assessments, borrowing and investments.

Our study will close with a brief view of citizen suits against the local government, seeking damages for injury, or seeking to block or compel government activity.

§ 3.   Local Governing Entities

We have spoken of local governing power seemingly divorced from the entity exercising it. To a large extent, our study will follow that approach. Nevertheless, from the fact that nearly 90,000 government units are in operation, it is evident that promotion or challenge of a particular activity must often involve analysis of the nature of the entity engaging in it. Illustratively, a school district, though it is a unit of local government, may not be able to levy taxes. A city's population may not be of sufficient size to include it within a class to which home rule authority has been granted, or to which the power to act extraterritorially has been accorded. A county may not be able to withstand annexation by an adjoining city. Many of these considerations are relevant to the existence of authority to act or to the manner in which action must be taken. Local governments display wide-ranging variation in terms of the powers they may exercise, the ways in which they are created, their relationships to other units of government in the state, and the manner in which their officials are designated. The resulting multiplicity of local government units can be described with reference to two basic qualities: top-down vs. bottom-up and general purpose vs. special purpose. These features are not fixed categories; each local government entity has features that place it at some point along both spectrums.

Top–Down vs. Bottom–Up

As a matter of basic legal principle, all local governments are creatures of their states, subject to the rules of operation established by those states. Thus, in a sense, all local governments fit the "top-down" description. At the same time, however, local governments display some degree of local representativeness or accountability; where they differ widely is in the extent of their "bottom-up" control.

Most states have divided up their entire territory into counties, which constitute the classic form of top-down government. County structure and boundaries are quite stable, displaying little or no change since the date of statehood. Originally created by the states to discharge state functions locally, many counties have evolved into broader policy-making entities. Urban counties, in particular, frequently provide area wide services and may assume responsibility over regional issues such as mass transit, water supply, and land use planning. Notwithstanding their status as a state subdivision, counties are governed by elected local officials, thus providing an important bottom-up component of local control. In some instances, the county's bottom-up constituency falls out into two discrete segments that reflect the ways in which county services are delivered to two of its constituent groups. On the one hand, counties are responsible for general county wide services, such as the judicial system, which they provide equally to all county residents. At the same time, though, they may provide municipal services such as fire and police protection only to those county residents who reside in the unincorporated segments of the county; county residents residing within municipalities will have their own local services. This dual role may give rise to disputes over the establishment of county-wide priorities, and conflicts between rural county residents and those who reside within the incorporated municipalities in the county.

The municipality, city, or municipal corporation constitutes the prototypic illustration of the bottom-up local government. Though the traditional county government may be adequate to meet the needs of rural areas, denser urban populations need additional regulation and services. Municipalities, in contrast to counties, are typically created by local citizens themselves pursuant to state procedures of municipal incorporation. In addition, and again in contrast to counties, the borders of municipalities change frequently as territory is added or subtracted through annexation and other procedures for boundary change. Most cities are located within counties and subject to county jurisdiction. Though they are created pursuant to citizen initiative (or by the state in response to local petition) and though they are governed by elected local officials, municipalities display some top-down features as well. That is, all municipalities ultimately rely on state law for their very existence and are limited to the exercise of powers authorized either in the state constitution or pursuant to statutory schemes.

Towns or township governments exist in fewer than half of the states and are likely to display a mix of top-down and bottom-up features. They are generally subdivisions of the county created by the state and not by the local population. Similar to counties, they frequently are limited to the exercise of specific powers at the direction of their states. In most of the Midwest, townships perform only a few narrow functions, such as providing some general welfare assistance and road maintenance. In some states, however, towns perform many broad regulatory and service functions. Moreover, the New England town meeting, at which governmental action is taken directly by participating citizens, is perhaps the clearest example of bottom-up activity for all local governments.

General Purpose vs. Special Purpose

Though no local government possesses the broad, inherent power of its state government, counties, municipalities and townships are usually categorized as general purpose governments, because they are authorized to exercise a range of powers and to provide a variety of services. In contrast, the most common and also the most rapidly increasing form of local government, known as the special district, exercises narrowly defined powers in the performance of one or a very small number of functions. Over the last fifty years, the number of special districts has more than tripled, and more than 35,000 are now in operation across the country. And they control an increasingly large segment of local revenues: in comparison to other units of local government, the proportion of spending by special districts has increased two to three times more quickly.

Special districts display enormous variety across a number of basic criteria. In terms of their territory, some are sub-local in scope, others are coterminous with existing municipal boundaries, and still others extend beyond the borders of existing municipal governments to encompass the territory of more than one general purpose local government For revenue raising ability, some have general taxation powers, while others are restricted to user fees or other more specific revenue raising devices. Similar variation is displayed in the manner of creation: some are formed directly by state legislation, some by petition of citizens, and others by voluntary local government action. Their officers may be elected, but they are frequently appointed, either by state or local government officials.

Special districts may be formed for a number of reasons. They may create efficiencies in service provision, by uncoupling service territory boundaries from the artificial barriers created by political borders. By focusing on one narrow function, special districts offer the potential for greater expertise and professionalism in the exercise of managerial discretion. In addition, they allow local governments to engage in regional activities without consolidation or other intergovernmental action that would reduce local independence. Their perceived disadvantages are varied as well. They may be immune from general local government regulations, such as zoning. They may allow local governments to avoid borrowing and spending limitations, since creation of a new unit of government produces an untapped line of revenue raising opportunities. If their officials are appointed, they may be unaccountable and relatively invisible on the local political radar screen. And finally, their narrow focus, though a celebrated source of efficiency and professionalism, also creates disadvantages. That same narrow focus may produce a relentless myopia that gives the officials who direct the special district a single minded drive that ignores the broader community health, safety, and welfare.

§ 4. An Illustration

A further illustration may help to put the foregoing in perspective. Assume that the government of
the City of Allgood wishes to build a stadium in
order to attract major sports teams and sporting
events. City officials think that local business will
be aided by such a venture and that the sports
attractions will provide desirable recreation for the
citizens and will spur the development of athletic
programs for adults and children. In addition, the
possible attraction of major league teams may increase a sense of citizen identification with the city
which will have spillover effects in housing, renewal
and commerce.

Critics raise in opposition the sizeable debts
which may result, the horror stories of other cities'
failures, and the need for expenditure of effort and
funds in areas of higher priority.

As we have seen, the matter will begin with the
question of the city's authority to engage in the
project. Is there express statutory authority for the
city to build a stadium? Is this city within the class
to which such authority has been granted? If there
is express authority, several battles remain to be
fought through the judicial and electoral processes
to enforce the respective public involvement or private sector views.

If there is not express authority, the public-pri-
vate-priority struggle will be engaged on the question whether authority can be inferred from existing constitutional or statutory grants. For example,

can approval be inferred from customary parks and recreation authority? Putting the same basic priority question in another form, "Will the necessary expenditure of funds be for a public purpose, or will the use of the property be a public use?"

Assume that stadium opponents seek the aid of the state in opposition. Does the city's contemplated action conflict with specific statutory provisions or does it enter a field specifically reserved to the state? Does the decision to build and operate a stadium involve such consequences external to the city (economic disruption in other areas of the state, e.g.) that it should be denied status as a purely local matter even if the city's authority is asserted from a position of that type of home rule? If the authority question is answered favorably from the city's point of view, should a state constitutional clause barring state delegation to special commissions of authority over "municipal," "corporate," or "proprietary" affairs prevent supervision or assumption of the matter by the State Board of Economic Improvement? Is this the sort of local benefit that the people, through their constitution, wished to leave to the discretion and judgment of the citizens who formed the city?

Implementation of the plan will bring additional questions concerning the exercise of specific powers. If the land upon which the stadium is to be constructed is outside the city, may the city annex the area? May the land be acquired through eminent domain? If the city is authorized to build, may the power to condemn land outside its boundaries be inferred? Does the city have the necessary power to rezone the land for its prospective use? How will the necessary revenues be raised? Will the city's taxing power support promises to bondholders? Will the city's financial position necessitate creation of a special district, public authority, or other limited purpose government to build, operate, and service the stadium? If there are injuries in connection with the venture, is the activity one which should be protected from citizen recovery? If citizens wish to challenge, who has standing to do so?

§ 5. Comment

The history of local government offers assurance that the stadium project will be challenged through the electoral, legislative and judicial processes in every conceivable way, only a few of which are illustrated above. Clearly the validity of the city's assumption of benefit will play a vital, though frequently unspoken, role in the outcome. Nevertheless, what some hope would be a decision expeditiously implemented may instead be a tortuous exercise in political interplay and public accountability. Such complexity offers to the local citizenry, through referendum provisions, bidding and conflict-of-interest requirements, and debt limitations, some protection against unwise commitments. Such complexity also serves to provide inordinate delay, harassing challenge, sizeable cost increases and manifest inefficiency.

The relative merit of the multiplicity of protections and the prices of inefficiency is but one of the dilemmas facing the student who wishes to assess the value of local government. Others include such questions as what level of government possesses the fiscal power best to support certain government activities and what government decisions are more appropriately decided at relatively local levels.

B. SOURCES OF LOCAL GOVERNING POWERS

§ 1. Local Government and Sovereignty

Whether the City of Allgood can build and operate the stadium, Bigville can own and operate an airport or Hearing can enact a public disclosure law, whether any municipal corporation can act, depends in the first instance upon its authority so to act.

The cities' authority is said to be derivative, necessitating delegation from their states. The states' hegemony over their political subdivisions is in turn said to be plenary. States are described as having inherent sovereignty, some of which they delegated to the federal government in the U.S. Constitution, and some of which they delegate to the local government units they create. While there is some validity to the proposition that local governments are entirely dependent on their states' inherent and plenary authority, it masks a somewhat more complicated reality. Local-state government relations in this country have reflected history, the evolution of corporate doctrine, swings in dominant political and social theory, the allocations of sovereignty in the federal republic, and, of course, the politics of governing power.

History brought such central sovereign's agent entities as counties and townships, necessary because of the geographic impossibility of governing from the center at the center. History brought favor for the state legislature limited by "natural rights" as the entity best able to avoid despotism while exercising sovereign power. History also brought the concept of incorporation, a manifestation of commercial geopolitical centers' long held desire to improve their economies, strengthen their monopolies, and protect both from the whims of centralized sovereignty. Corporate doctrine, now more liberal in recognition of the powers of private, and even public corporations, early on married the strong protections of private and public corporate status to the doctrine that the status and powers thus protected were derived by grant from the sovereign. The corporate charters that produced municipal governments were thus a grant of power from state to local government unit. Corporate doctrine came to distinguish between the property-necessitated protection of "private" corporations and the strong state relationship with "public" corporations.

Political and social theory underscored the relationship between individual liberties and the structure of governing power, whether centralized or diffused among several entities. On the one hand, diffusion of government power decreased the heavy hand of despotism. On the other hand, a multiplicity of political entities interfered with the social contract between the sovereign state and the sovereign citizen; the dominance of that theory brooked no intermediate or competing entities.

Developing federal doctrine attempted to give life to a constitutional structure envisioning a national delegate of sovereign powers and thirteen, now fifty, compacting sovereigns. As will be developed later, the conclusion that there was no federal constitutional warrant for giving status to local governments was probably correct and certainly irresistible given both the complexities of federal-state federalism and the troubled history of nations and city states.

The politics of governing power have manifested the pendular swings between two forces: (1) the state hegemony and concomitant local powerlessness that corporate, political and federalism theory may arguably support and (2) the reality of strong "localism" that reflects a long tradition of local autonomy, the apparent social and economic imperatives for urbanization, and the psychological, intuitive citizen conclusion that closer access to and control of governing power is a necessary predicate to individual social and economic liberty.

In reaction to depredations of corrupt or poorly governed localities, and in enthusiasm for the role of the legislature, in the late 19th century Judge Dillon formulated a strict rule of construction biased against liberal recognition of local power. Judge Dillon's Rule ultimately won out against Judge Thomas Cooley's assertion of an inherent right to local self-government. At the same time, state constitutions were amended to limit local power so as to prevent harmful economic activities. Then, in the 20th century, the pendulum swung again to local autonomy as the home rule movement and prohibitions barring special legislation attest.

Political realities are today more complex. The evolving corporate-authority and local-control theories suggest sizeable local autonomy. Public-choice theorists applying an economic analysis of legal rules assert the importance of a marketplace of numerous local government units, which will compete to attract citizens ("consumer voters") by offering a better mix of services at a better price. The citizens' ability to exercise power through exit (by moving to another local government's jurisdiction) and voice (through exercise of the local vote) should promote efficiency at the local level. Yet, the societal problems in such areas as social welfare and the environment presses for more centralized address, whether by assertion of state power or by regional cooperation of somewhat autonomous localities. The current focus on regional solutions to some major metropolitan area problems has resulted in more metropolitan governance, through intergovernmental agreements and regional special districts, without metropolitan area wide governments. In fact, no major metropolitan area in the United States is governed by a single general purpose regional government. Thus, in the face of doctrinal powerlessness and despite the pressing needs for regional action to abate metropolitan area problems, local independence and autonomy in the exercise of many delegated powers continues to be the norm rather than the exception.

Because local governments have no inherent sovereign power, all local governments actions and regulatory regimes must be based on a valid transfer of power from their state. Local laws are on surest legal footing when the powers they seek to exercise are expressly authorized by state enabling statute, such as when state law authorizes municipalities to own and operate solid waste facilities. But because state delegations of power may fail to anticipate each and every possible local government response to any specific local issue, questions of enabling authority frequently arise. In the absence of explicit authorization, local government powers may be upheld pursuant to one of three modes of state delegation: implied as incident to an explicit grant of power; pursuant to broad state transfer of general regulatory powers to specific local government units, or pursuant to state grant of home rule status to the local government. Each of these sources of state power will be discussed in turn.

§ 2.　Implied Powers from Grants of Statutory Authority

Consider a state statute that authorizes local governments to prescribe "minimum standards to make dwellings safe, sanitary and fit for human habitation." Assume further that the municipality, based on that transfer of power, passes an ordinance that requires hot water in all buildings. Is the

local law valid? The answer will depend on the rule
of construction applied by a court to evaluate the
state delegation. Judge Dillon's Rule, a rule of strict
construction first articulated in the late 19th century, has shown great staying power. According to
that rule, local governments can only exercise powers that are (1) expressly granted; (2) necessarily or
fairly implied from the express grant; or (3) essential, indeed indispensable to the purposes of the
government unit itself. In addition, the rule requires that in a close case, the court should deny
the asserted local power. And in fact, application of
Dillon's Rule to the hot water requirement resulted
in a court's invalidation of the ordinance. Many
states have rejected Dillon's Rule and now apply
more generous rules of interpretation. Other states,
though not abolishing the rule explicitly, have
greatly reduced its importance by granting broad
general welfare power to local governments or by
establishing home rule as an alternative to explicit
state delegation. In some states, though, Dillon's
Rule continues to apply to powers exercised by non-
home rule local government units.

§ 3. General Welfare Enabling Authority

Some state laws have gone beyond the explicit
subject-by-subject delegation of lawmaking authority described in the previous section, and have
adopted general welfare enabling authority, providing a broad transfer of power to local governments
to protect their citizens' general welfare. A state
law allowing cities to adopt all laws "necessary and

proper for the health, safety, and welfare of their inhabitants" illustrates this approach. How should a court interpret this type of statute? In these situations, application of Dillon's Rule becomes problematic, because the generality of the state law makes strict construction difficult. In those cases, one of two results is possible. First, a court may simply state that the state law is fundamentally inconsistent with Dillon's Rule and thus implicitly abolishes the rule of strict construction. Another, less deferential approach would be to conclude that Dillon's Rule applies to produce the result that the general welfare statute does not constitute an independent grant of state power and that local laws must still find state authorization from specific enabling statutes.

§ 4. Home Rule

Home rule evolved in large part as a reaction to the ways in which Dillon's Rule imposed strict constraints on local flexibility to legislate in response to local problems and interests. Beginning with a few late 19th century state trendsetters, by the start of the 21st century home rule had been adopted by more than 40 states. There is no single home rule model from which all states derive their scheme. In some states, home rule is created through state constitutional provision; in others, statutory authority is the source of local power. Statutory delegation of home rule authority tends to include more specific enumeration of powers than the constitutional provisions, yet both tend usually include similar, broad language regarding the transfer of "local" or "municipal" power to the home rule unit. While all home rule states offer home rule status to their large cities, only some allow smaller cities, other small municipal corporations such as villages, and/or counties to take advantage of the discretion and flexibility that home rule provides. In some states home rule status confers unlimited local powers, while in others specific matters are explicitly constrained, frequently in the realm of taxing and spending powers. Although the variation among the states is great, the uniform, fundamental premise of home rule is that local governments do not need to turn to their state creators for authority each time they seek to legislate. Rather, home rule embodies the state's willingness to transfer general local power to local governments, implicitly trusting the local governments to exercise that power to further the welfare of their citizens. Through the adoption of a local charter, home rule units detail their powers and allocate the functions they have assumed among their officials. Upon approval by the voters, the home rule status becomes official.

Broadly speaking, home rule powers fall into one of two general categories–powers of initiative and powers of immunity. By initiative, we mean the ability to undertake actions without specific state authorization; immunity refers to the notion that home rule may be interpreted as imposing a barrier against state intrusion into local affairs. The scope of these two powers will depend in turn on two important factors: the type of home rule model adopted by the state, and the state court's tradition of judicial decisionmaking in the interpretation of the home rule framework. The evolution of home rule powers has spanned two centuries, producing two basic models, the original imperio form and the more modern legislative home rule as proposed by the National League of Cities.

Imperio Home Rule

The earliest provisions granted home rule powers to local governments with respect to "local" or "municipal" affairs. In a 19th century case involving Missouri's home rule framework, the Supreme Court referred to St. Louis as an "imperium in imperio," a "government within a government." The term stuck, and the label continues to be used to describe home rule systems that authorize local control with language that grants power to legislate, for example, with respect to "all powers of local self-government," "all laws and regulations in respect to municipal affairs," or "local affairs and government." In fact, by transferring control over local affairs to the home rule unit, the imperio system appears to erect a barrier against state intrusion—any power deemed exclusively local should be beyond the reach of state intrusion or interference, because the state has relinquished all power over local affairs to its home rule units.

Although the imperio system can easily be interpreted as providing substantial initiative and immunity protection, many state judiciaries were unwilling to relinquish their control over the scope of local powers. The power of the judiciary in interpreting general terms such as "local" and "municipal" resulted in widely divergent approaches to the balance of power between state and local governments in home rule states. Judicial inconsistency in the evaluation of local laws reflected more the consensus of the court about the wisdom of the local action than a principled conclusion that a home rule law was invalid because it exceeded the bounds of "local" affairs.

Legislative Home Rule

As a result of what home rule supporters perceived as undue state judicial meddling, in the 1950s, a nationwide municipal organization proposed new model home rule provisions. The resulting "legislative model" of home rule (also referred to as the "National League of Cities model" or the "National Municipal League model" after the organizations responsible for proposing the reformulation) seeks to reduce judicial power in the determination of the scope of local home rule authority. The legislative label refers, not to the source of the home rule enabling power, but rather to the concept that it is to be the legislature, and not the judiciary, that makes the decisions about the scope of home rule powers. Legislative home rule tends to use language that reflects this shift, along the following lines: "a city may exercise any legislative power not denied by general law;" or "to exercise all powers of local self-government and to adopt and enforce within their limits such police, sanitary and other similar regulations, as are not in conflict with general law." In theory, legislative home rule rests on the assumption that local government has the power to act unless and until the state legislature takes the power away pursuant to general law. Thus, it seeks to enhance the initiative function of home rule status; note, though, that by placing absolute discretion in the state legislature to deny local power by general law, legislative home rule removes the immunity protection established by imperio home rule. In legislative home rule states, state legislatures can prohibit home rule units from exercising any function, including those that would be deemed "exclusively local" and thus immune from state interference in an imperio jurisdiction.

Judicial Interpretation of Home Rule Provisions

Though the two part categorization of home rule schemes as either imperio or legislative is a tidy one on paper, many factors operate to blur the distinctions. For one thing, some state home rule provisions combine elements of both systems. In one state, for instance, home rule units have the imperio-like power to "perform any function pertaining to its government and affairs", but the legislature is able to "specifically" deny any home rule power. Moreover, even in legislative home rule states, judiciaries retain the power to define the scope of local power–a judicial decision that a local law deals with a matter of statewide concern will render the local law invalid. And of course, judges bring very different perspectives on the meaning of local and on the appropriate level of government for the implementation of any given legislative action. These differences inevitably produce different realms for the exercise of home rule power in different states.

Given the broad areas for judicial resolution, it is no wonder that commentators have differed in their assessment of judicial receptivity to home-rule power exercise. In judging the competence of municipal legislation courts, after all, can reject a municipal exercise as not involving a local matter and not otherwise authorized, occasionally because there is no precedent for local government action of this type, or because the court deems the action one beyond the bounds of appropriate governance. For example, Hearing's attempted public disclosure law may have no precursors in other similar localities or may be too intrusive upon privacy rights when balanced against the importance of many of the pertinent local offices.

The courts may decide that the municipal action involves not only the trappings of a local affair but also external consequences which are of such magnitude as to make it more appropriate for government purview at a higher level. Our airport and stadium could present such difficulties.

The courts may find that other provisions of the state constitution seem to confer authority over a matter (such as income taxes) upon the state legislature. They will read the constitutional home-rule delegation in conjunction with the other provisions and reject the local power exercise.

Finally, as noted earlier, the courts may strike down the local ordinance and give predominance to the state legislation because state legislative patterns have indicated preemption of the field or because the court concludes that the ordinance and state statutes are in direct conflict. The decision will more than likely involve a combination of the above, of course.

Conversely, if a conflicting state law is deemed to cover an exclusively local matter in jurisdictions granted local autonomy pursuant to imperio home rule, the state enactment may be deemed preempted by the local enactment. Results in cases involving internal local matters such as civil service, police-power matters such as land use, and local acquisition of goods and services demonstrate that local exercise in the absence of state competition may be deemed appropriate.

The varied terminology of the several home-rule clauses and statutes and inevitable uncertainty attending the local-statewide dichotomy has taxed the ingenuity of courts attempting to resolve conflicts between inconsistent legislation of the state and a home-rule city. For example, one court has interpreted its state's home-rule clause (in a dispute between the state and city not involving a third party) to restrict municipal dominance to the structure and procedures of local agencies and uphold state dominance in substantive social, economic or regulatory objectives unless the law is shown to be irreconcilable with the locality's freedom to choose its own political form. This restrictive reading of the state constitution in an effort to remove the courts from second guessing the state legislature, in what had been a liberal home-rule jurisdiction, may simply have substituted one set of uncertainties for another. Another court has read its state's constitutional clause to permit state legislative preemption (in a local matter) not as to local exercise of all powers of self-government, but only as to local exercise of some of those powers, namely "local police, sanitary and other similar regulations".

In addition to limitations imposed from above by state legislatures, state administrative agencies, and the state judiciary, a local government may find its legislative actions subject to review and rescission directly by its citizens. It is not uncommon for home rule charters to reserve the powers of referendum, whereby citizens vote to approve or reject locally adopted laws, and initiative, whereby citizens themselves directly propose legislation to the citizenry. Both forms of direct voter action can arguably be said to interfere with home rule's guarantee of local autonomy, and challenges have been brought in several states. The Maryland court, for instance, has ruled that its constitutional home-rule clause does not preclude referendum because the elected legislative body of the entity to which home rule was delegated "formulates and approves" the legislative enactment referred to the people. The exercise of voter initiative, however, bypasses the elected legislative body, ruled the court, and is thus inimical to the constitutional delegation of home rule to the local entity.

§ 5. Interpretation and Implication in the Scope of Local Powers

Any time a local government legislates, the action may be challenged as beyond the scope of the government's delegated powers. In this dispute, the scope of local powers will depend on several basic questions. First, what is the source of the local power? If the government is acting pursuant to specifically delegated powers, Dillon's Rule may or may not apply to determine whether the government has the power it claims. In Dillon's Rule jurisdictions, general welfare clauses may not be sufficient authorization for local action, but some Dillon's Rule states find that the general welfare clause implicitly renders Dillon's Rule inapplicable to determining the scope of general welfare power.

If the source of the local power is home rule, a different set of questions arises. What type of home rule system has the state adopted? If it is imperio, the court must determine whether the matter falls within the definition of "local" or "municipal." That inquiry may be wide-ranging, involving consideration of factors such as the extralocal effects of local action, the need for statewide uniformity, and evidence of a state tradition of regulation in the area. Note that by these criteria, most "local" actions may be subject to challenge. Given the interconnectedness among modern municipalities, it is difficult to identify many actions that do not potentially have extraterritorial impacts. A court's unstated assessment of the wisdom of the local law may underlie its conclusion whether the law is local, and thus within the scope of home rule initiative, or whether it impermissibly exceeds the bounds of home rule powers.

The judicial involvement in the determination of the scope of home rule powers should be less in legislative home rule states. There the inquiry starts from the presumption that the local law is legitimate. In the absence of state legislative action depriving home rules units of the challenged power, the state judiciary should refrain from excessive analysis of the nature of the local law, because by definition that task has been left to the legislature. Even in legislative home rule states, though, judicial analysis is inevitable–a state court conclusion that a local law deals with a matter left exclusively to the state is likely to result in invalidation of the home rule ordinance even if the state legislature has not explicitly prohibited the local action. If a local law, for instance, purported to adopt new penalties for crimes committed within its jurisdiction, it is difficult to imagine that a state court would hesitate to invalidate the law even in the absence of state legislative prohibition. Thus, at some level, both home rule schemes require judicial interpretation in the definition of the bounds of permissible local powers; the difference lies in the extent to which each system allocates that power as between state legislature and state judiciary.

Thus, in all instances of local action, unless there is specific state-granted authority for the action undertaken, the legitimacy of the action will depend on interpretation and implication of state intent, even if the government has home rule status. Needless to say, the role of the judiciary in this area is substantial. In addition to the interpretative tasks described above, a restrictive court can strictly limit municipal operation and flexibility by deciding: that the permission to act is an improper delegation of legislative authority by the legislature or that it is not an indispensable attribute of local government.

Legislative History

Legislative documents and charters contain language which is, of course, subject to varying interpretations. Indeed, the political process leading to their drafting, enactment or approval often results in intentional ambiguities designed to achieve support of those who would have to oppose more explicit language. Consequently, the determination whether a power is expressed may eventually involve judicial interpretation of the "legislatively or constitutionally intended" meaning of terms. The reader should not confuse the sources of federal legislative history with the all too common paucity of such materials at some state and most local levels. The flexibility of local power exercise is in the hands of the courts.

Non-delegation Doctrine

The problem of delegation of legislative power is a complex one. To be distinguished are: (i) sovereign delegation of legislative authority to the state legislature in the constitution and the delegation by the state legislature to coequal branches of state government for which the doctrine of separation of powers requires standards governing the delegate's discretion; (ii) policy choices made by the state legislature as constitutional repository of legislative authority with delegation of implementation (administrative) authority for which due process requires standards confining the delegate's discretion; (iii) sovereign delegation of legislative authority directly to municipalities in the state constitution; and (iv) broad delegation by the state legislature of legislative authority to municipalities for which none of the above described standards is required and to which may be applied only the due process requirement of sufficient clarity to avoid arbitrary and capricious enforcement. Thus a state legislature may clearly delegate administration or implementation of state legislation to local governments under fairly general standards. It is by no means equally clear whether a particular delegation qualifies for this description. "All cities of population greater than 500,000 ... may own and operate municipal airports provided that no such airport shall be within five miles of a built-up residential area, and provided that no such airport shall employ tower personnel who are not licensed by the [appropriate authorities].... " Is such a provision a delegation of legislative or administrative authority?

It is also clear that the delegation problem is avoided when the original delegation is made directly by the people to the local governments in the state constitution. Similarly, the constitutional provisions authorizing home-rule delegation would seem to approve the delegation of legislative authority by the state.

Strict adherence to a doctrine of non-delegation would strangle local government. Thus, a practical exception permits the state legislature to delegate to local units legislative power incidental, appropriate or related to municipal affairs or local self-government, with little cavil over what is a local or municipal matter. Local-option legislation which permits local units to accept or reject the application of state enactments in their city (liquor-by-the-drink approval, e.g.) and local opportunity to choose among statutory alternatives of forms of government can and do survive most challenges of improper legislative delegation.

Finally, constitutional provisions may by their terms prohibit delegation of legislative power to certain kinds of local units (counties, e.g.). And courts will occasionally disapprove delegations which appear to violate provisions of the constitution conferring power to act in the matter upon the state legislature. Illustratively a constitutional provision declaring that "the Legislature shall have the power to prescribe the manner of conducting ... elections, the qualifications of candidates for public office ..." might be held to bar a delegation to Hearing of the power to enact a public disclosure law.

The cognate problem of state legislatures' delegating to special state-created commissions the power over certain municipal functions and the vestiges of the doctrine of inherent right of local self-government, though somewhat relevant here, will be discussed in our examination of limitations on state power over municipal affairs.

Judicial decision whether a matter is local (within home rule, for example) or general in nature is theoretically possible whether or not the state has acted and will be discussed infra. As a practical matter, the question will often arise in determining whether existing state legislation preempts, conflicts with or usurps local prerogatives, and will be discussed in that connection.

Essential Powers

Because powers which are essential or indispensable are easily implied from any rationally designed grant of express corporate authority, there has been little need to identify a separate category of powers thus classified. Presumably, providing a meeting place for the city council might be such a power. Removal of "impeachable" officers may be another. Our cities would have no success under this classification regarding the airport and stadium. A more plausible argument, that for the public disclosure law, would no doubt fail as well.

§ 6. Comment

Whether as a general rule courts have been unduly restrictive in reviewing power exercises by local government units, home rule or not, is a matter of some dispute. Some proponents of flexible and powerful local government argue the affirmative. Their position is bolstered by the apparent necessity of some state constitutional amendments calling for liberal judicial interpretation of local laws and by the continued viability in other states of Dillon's Rule as a restrictive device. Others conclude with some support in the cases that, particularly in home rule jurisdictions, courts have been receptive to municipal undertakings. Courts have been expansive in their readings of general welfare clauses and in their evaluations of methods used to implement home rule and Dillon's Rule authorizations. It is one thing to ask the court to approve municipal flexibility and imaginative government in the absence of extraterritorial consequences or state expressions in the area. It is quite another to ask approval despite extraterritorial consequences, or in the face of state activity in the matter, or in the face of due concern by the judge for the separate prerogatives of the state legislative branch. It has been in part the failure of advocacy to assess and attempt to overcome the reluctance engendered by these considerations which has resulted in the "illiberal" decisions. It is arguable that alleged municipal "powerlessness" is more the result of this failure of advocacy and the failure of courage in city hall than of judicial restrictiveness.

It is important to note at this juncture that this section's discussion has been limited to a review of the principles used to determine whether a local law falls within the scope of the power that has been delegated to it by the state. In addition, we have seen how the source of that local power will determine the course of the judicial inquiry, with different analyses applying to evaluate the legitimacy of local laws passed pursuant to explicit delegations of power, general welfare clauses, imperio home rule, or legislative home rule. A determination that the local action falls within the scope of its power, however, does not end the inquiry. Questions may still arise over the extent to which state or federal laws may preempt the local law. Those issues are discussed in Section D of this Chapter. In practice, courts sometimes subsume their analysis whether a law is a valid local enactment within this broader preemption issue; if a court concludes that the local law has been preempted, it matters little whether the law would have been valid in the absence of preemptive legislation. Nevertheless, for ease of analytical clarity, it is helpful to keep the two questions separate.

C. LIMITATIONS ON STATE POWER OVER MUNICIPAL CORPORATIONS

§ 1. "Plenary" Power

As noted earlier, from the federal perspective, it is frequently said that the state possesses plenary power over its municipal corporations and may create, dissolve and realign them, may deny them power and may direct them to accomplish governmental objectives. As a description of the position of a municipality vis-a-vis its state when the municipality seeks a protected status under the federal constitution, where no individual person's rights are at issue, and where its proprietary property is not involved, the "plenary power" description approaches accuracy. Cities have been uniformly unsuccessful in attempts to protect themselves from state power exercise by invoking the individual-or contract-rights protections of the federal constitution. But when the state action affects not only the rights of city citizens as members of the city but also their rights given protected status under the federal and state constitutions (voting rights, creditors' rights, e.g.), the description, though strongly urged, is inapplicable. In addition, there have been occasions, even to the point of suit by the city against its state, when municipalities have successfully withstood normally superior state power because they have been acting under federally conferred power deemed within the ambit of the federal constitution's Supremacy Clause.

Viewing a city's relationship to its state from the state's perspective, one can see that where the municipality is exercising those powers classified as governmental, i.e., where it may be said to be exercising powers which the state might exercise if the city did not exist as its "local agent," state power is superior to that of the city unless the city is insulated by imperio home rule immunity. The state may require the city to act or may prevent city action. Additionally while the state may be barred from meddling in "municipal" affairs, appropriate exercise of state governmental power may be upheld even if it interferes with what are alleged to be the local unit's local affairs, so long as a legitimate statewide interest can be identified. For example, in such matters as environmental protection, coastal zones, and flood plains, state legislatures have directed the adoption of local regulatory ordinances that meet statutory standards. Finally, the state may require its local unit to recognize claims against it which are morally but not legally binding. (Municipal appropriation of funds to pay morally binding claims has been upheld.) The state legislative requirement may be either the waiver of technical defenses (state created) or a directive to pay the claim.

§ 2. State Constitutional Provisions, Generally

We have already seen how home rule provisions limit what would otherwise be the state's plenary power over its subdivisions. State-local relations are further circumscribed by numerous provisions of many state constitutions. Many fall into one of three categories: (a) those which attempt to prevent unwarranted expenditures; (b) those which enshrine certain activities for which there should be local political accountability; and (c) those which serve to create and protect local autonomy.

Most of these amendments in turn have been responses to historical abuses of the late nineteenth and early twentieth centuries. (a) States and cities (with apparent state blessing) engaged in unwarranted and injudicious expenditures involving not only the potential of graft, but also the serious risks of poor investment. Notorious among these were the investments in railroads. (b) As the populations moved to urban density and the impact of cities on state affairs became more pronounced, state legislatures began more and more to meddle in the local units' affairs, often with capricious results. Responsive to constituent and special interest pressures, legislatures would involve themselves with the most menial of local activities. Malapportioned state legislatures (the "rotten borough system") became, in effect, "legislatures of appeals," responding to override local initiative at the behest of those disappointed with the response at the local level and stripping away particular local powers from certain cities ("ripper bills"). (c) As noted earlier, in contrast to the strictness of Dillon's Rule, some courts gave short life to a principle which although now unspoken, has never died: the inherent right to local self-government. Cases are no longer decided on the ground that there is a basic unbreachable right to local self-government, which would serve as a barrier to incremental state meddling. But some state constitutional provisions survive as memorials to the principle's former vitality. And, as some state-constitutional reformation results and attempts to introduce state land use control attest, the doctrine lives on as a practical reality of political psychology.

The present impact of these remedies for earlier state and local excesses should not be underestimated. While judicial interpretation may have in some cases eroded their remedial intent (debt limitations avoided by special authorities, e.g.) and the demands of modern society may have occasionally burst through their apparent inflexibility (urban renewal and private investment, e.g.), they are nonetheless viable limitations which serve occasionally as protections and occasionally as obstacles to municipal or state innovation.

§ 3. Provisions Limiting Expenditures

Illustrative of the constitutional provisions guarding against unwarranted and injudicious expenditures are those which prohibit states from lending their credit to private enterprises or to local units; those which prohibit the state from authorizing its local governments to lend their credit to private enterprises; those which impose ceilings on local government debt; those which prohibit the state and its local government units from paying extra compensation to public officers or employees, increasing public officer compensation during term of office, or paying compensation to public contractors above the contract price; and those which prohibit the payment of unauthorized or illegal claims.

Would these strictures impede the following plan? The state legislature has voted to authorize Allgood (1) to purchase the land and construct the stadium; (2) to pay a generous bonus to the general contractor and subcontractors if the stadium is built on time; (3) to borrow the necessary funds through a bond issue; (4) to enter into an agreement with a nationally known sports management firm whereby the latter will lease the stadium from the city for a number of years, operate it for profit, and pay rental to the city; (5) to use the rental payments to retire the bonds which are to be limited to the rental revenues. We shall be better able to answer these questions after our study of local government revenues and expenditure limits.

§ 4.   Provisions Insuring Local Accountability

Provisions which are intended to insure that certain functions retain local political accountability include: those prohibiting the state legislature from imposing taxes for local units' corporate purposes, and from delegating to special commissions the power to perform, supervise or interfere with municipal or corporate functions; and those requiring local selection of local officers, and local approval of changes in county seats, county consolidations, street railway franchises, and a host of particular subjects.

The special-commission provisions are rarely invoked in this day of complex administrative structures, and regional-state-local cooperation and state take-over of budget matters and school systems. Nevertheless, where they exist, they may prevent state legislative delegation to a commission not sought by, connected to, or acquiesced in by the city, of control over the city's property, funds or functions. Terms such as municipal, corporate, and proprietary may be used. In some states, the courts may give broad protection to the municipality in order to fulfill the perceived objectives of the clause. In others, a statewide-local dichotomy will be used with protection accorded to the latter. In yet others, protection will be accorded to proprietary but not governmental affairs and purposes, i.e., those benefit-promoting services and functions which serve the exclusive interests of the citizen-members of the corporation, and which may have constituted one of the primary motivations for organizing the local unit. Clauses which refer to or are construed as limited to proprietary matters do not bar state activity in connection with the local unit's governmental activities, i.e., the core functions of government in general, basic powers therefore of the state, and responsibilities locally implemented in an "agency" capacity, even though by an incorporated entity. It has previously been indicated that there are substantial numbers of local activities whose placement in one category or the other is highly debatable. For example, should a municipal water and sewage system be "governmental" or "corporate?" The provision of water is frequently deemed proprietary while the removal of sewage is often labeled governmental.

§ 5. Provisions Protecting Local Autonomy

In addition to the home rule schemes discussed in the previous Section, two kinds of constitutional provisions serve to protect local autonomy: those which seek to ban "special," "one-city" legislation, and those which prohibit state imposition of unfunded mandates on local governments.

Special Laws

Prohibitions of "special," "one-city" legislation take many forms. They may require state legislative enactments to be general and of uniform applicability. They may prohibit the passage of local or special laws. They may require that no special law be enacted in any case where a general act can be made applicable. They may in summary or particular detail enumerate the subject matters upon which no special laws may be enacted. Neither the scope of subject matter nor the pattern are uniform among the states and combinations of the above may be found. While their purpose may be to protect municipalities or particular local matters in a municipality from "selected target" attack by the state legislature ("ripper bills"), this may not always be the practical result. Indeed, it would be misleading to convey a picture of the city fighting to prevent state intrusion. Frequently, the "target city" is seeking to obtain the very authorization from the state legislature.

Absent any other constitutional impediment, the state legislature may, of course, enact legislation of general applicability to which the "target city" and others may be required to conform or, under local option, may choose to conform. In addition, unless classification itself is constitutionally prohibited or limited, the state may enact laws which are of general and uniform applicability to a particular class of local units. Such units are frequently classified by population, but may be grouped according to geographic considerations, the presence of facilities (colleges, hospitals, e.g.), financial resources, or the like. Courts often defer to legislative classification but may occasionally disapprove a "grouping" which merely masks a special law. There is no rule of thumb which divides a law of "general" and "uniform" applicability within a class from its converse, the special law. A classification which contains but one municipality and which appears closed to a projected future membership increase is obviously suspect, but in an appropriate case (the only seaport, e.g.) it may withstand challenge. A classification that is not relevant to the law's purpose is also suspect. Some similarities to the classification theories of equal-protection jurisprudence may be noted here.

The provisions that require general laws where practicable afford the additional difficulty of identifying the ultimate arbiter of practicability. In some jurisdictions, the legislature's determination is final. In others, the legislative determination may only be set aside if it is arbitrary, unreasonable, or a clear abuse of discretion. In yet others, the decision is purely for the courts.

Bigville has sought from the state legislature authority to own and operate the desired airport. Allgood hopes for authorization from its state legislature to build the stadium. In the present legislative sessions, the state legislatures respectively enact and the governors sign the following:

"All cities with populations greater than 500,000 ... in which annual commercial gross revenues from intrastate and interstate commerce exceed $100 million ... are authorized to construct, own and operate municipal general business aviation airports...."

"Whereas the City of Allgood is the capital of this state and is the only city whose population exceeds 1,000,000 persons, and is the center of the only major metropolitan area in the state, the City of Allgood may take all steps necessary to construct and operate a stadium...."

Would either of the above withstand challenge based upon state constitutional provisions prohibiting special laws relating to local government units and requiring that laws be of general and uniform applicability? Would your answer be different if the provision in Allgood's state allowed a special law where a general one would be impracticable? Would your answer differ if Bigville were the only city in its state now meeting or in the foreseeable future likely to meet the statutory criteria?

Unfunded Mandates

While special legislation prohibitions and home rule provisions have enjoyed a relatively long tenure as features of local government law, the regulation of unfunded mandates is a newer form of state constitutional protection of local government autonomy. The concern is that mandates impose financial burdens and confuse accountability. They occur when states require local governments to create or expand programs or services but do not provide funds to cover the costs these mandates will generate. In addition to the magnitude of the dollar cost, these mandates have been criticized for blurring the lines of accountability by making it unclear to the public whether the responsibility for the program lies with the state government that created it or the local government that must implement it. Mandates may also create inefficiencies by allowing state legislature to adopt politically popular programs without worrying about how to pay the bills for the program. Local governments may also object to state mandates because they denigrate local autonomy by treating local governments as mere instrumentalities for the implementation of state policies.

Currently, a majority of the states have some sort of requirement that state legislatures must consider the fiscal impact of new programs on local governments. These so called "fiscal note" requirements do not limit state ability to adopt the program, but are based on the assumption that public dissemination and debate of the fiscal impacts of new legislation will lead to more responsible state action. A smaller number of states has gone beyond this procedural requirement; nearly twenty states have adopted laws that require state governments to reimburse their political subdivisions for the costs of complying with new state mandates. Although the primary motivation for these reimbursement requirements has frequently been to limit government spending in general, the result has nevertheless been some increase in the protection of local autonomy.

D. RESOLUTION OF COMPETING POWER CONSIDERATIONS

§ 1. The Allocation of Predominance

Earlier in the text we discussed appropriateness as a consideration in government activity and in the level of government which engaged in that activity. Our discussion of home rule also indicated that various interests would be balanced in resolving the validity of local power exercise. Since government exercise is the exercise of power, one can view the matter from a perspective of predominance, not only as a method of resolving competing and inconsistent power exercises but also as a question of the perception of power. Many allocations of power are accomplished by state and federal constitutions; much, however, is left to the courts. As we have already seen, and whether the government in question be federal, state, or local, one can always question whether the government can act at all with respect to a particular subject matter.

A determination that a local government is acting within the sphere of its own constitutional, statutory, or judicially determined competence, however, is only the first step. Further analysis must be undertaken to determine whether another level of government can also act on the same subject matter, and if so, whether both actions stand. If the actions are inconsistent, the allocation of power and the balancing of interests will lead to the predominance of one. Even if the actions are not inconsistent, the allocation of power and the balancing of interests may so weigh in favor of one level of government that it may be deemed to preempt action by any other level.

In this section, we are concerned about local power and the local government's sphere of competent activity, when viewed in light of state and federal competence and predominance. Of course, in addition to the local matters which the federal (liquor, twenty-first amendment to the U.S. Constitution, e.g.) and state (local officers, e.g.) governments may be constitutionally required to avoid, there are numerous situations in which there is deference to local governing even though the matters are fully capable of general power exercise. Unsurprisingly, courts are repeatedly called upon to reconcile competing claims of predominance.

Illustratively, the airport, public disclosure and stadium ordinances of our cities not only have to be competent actions of those cities standing alone, but also may face, respectively, federal air-traffic noise controls less stringent than those desired by the city, a state public-disclosure statute, and zoning and traffic regulations of the surrounding county inimical to extraterritorial location and operation of the stadium.

§ 2. Competing Federal Power Considerations

We have seen that, in disputes between states and their political subdivisions, the federal courts have not given federal constitutional status to local governments either as government entities or, as in the case of private corporations, as possessors of rights guaranteed by the federal constitution against incursion by their states. Perhaps any other choice would have unduly compounded the already complicated federalism among fifty-one sovereigns, fifty of which have delegated, to the one, the national power and supremacy in its very broad areas of competence. Early development of the federal theory undoubtedly benefitted from the emerging dominance in the states of the plenary power view. The continued vitality of the view that states exercise plenary power over their political subdivisions has in turn benefitted from its uncritical repetition in federal cases. This symbiotic escalation of an overstated principle has blurred the conceptual difference between defining intrastate relationships among a state and its local governments and concluding that, whatever they might be, only the relationship among the federal government and the states qua states is enshrined in the federal constitution.

Resolution of power disputes between federal and local governments, federal and state governments, and occasionally state and local governments reflects the anomalous position of the local government in the federal constitutional scheme. For example, the federal government, in exercising the sovereign power of eminent domain, can take property from neither the state nor its local government without compensation. The state can, however, so exercise its sovereign power of eminent domain to take at least governmental property of its local government without triggering the federal constitution's compensation requirement.

A local government cannot successfully assert the federal constitution's Due Process or Equal Protection Clauses against its state. For the purpose of protecting individual rights (including those of private corporations), local governments are deemed to engage in the state action that is the predicate of liability under the federal constitution and civil rights statutes.

In the exercise of its delegated powers, Congress has enacted regulations, imposed taxes, and tied strings to expenditures, all of which have given rise to challenges by the states. To the argument that the federal constitution's tenth amendment protects the states from direct regulation by Congress in some instances, the U.S. Supreme Court has replied that the constitutional limits on Congress' power directly to regulate the states are structural, not substantive. The states must find their protection in the national political process, not in judicially recognized areas of invulnerability. The Court has left open the possibility of extraordinary defects in the political process that would warrant judicial intervention. It has not defined them, but has suggested such illustrations as a state's being deprived of any right to participate in the national political process or singled out in a way that leaves it politically isolated and powerless. Though the Court has not erected a Tenth Amendment/states rights barrier to federal regulation of state governments, it has accomplished some of the same result through more indirect means. That is, by narrowing Congress's power to legislate pursuant to the Commerce Clause and the Equal Protection Clause, the Court has been able to immunize state governments from a number of federal laws. In some areas, such as the imposition of employment standards and with regard to government antitrust liability, Congress has responded to state and local objections by removing governments the purview of broad federal regulatory schemes.

To the argument that there is a doctrine of intergovernmental tax immunity which protects the states from direct and indirect federal taxation to the extent that the federal interests are protected from state taxation, the U.S. Supreme Court has answered that the sources of their respective immunities differ. The broader federal immunity arises from the Supremacy Clause and is supported by theories of the role of a national government. The narrower state immunity stems from the constitutional structure and desire to protect state sovereignty. Thus, the states are protected against direct, discriminatory federal taxes. Some nondiscriminatory federal taxes can be collected directly from the states even though parallel state taxes could not be imposed directly on the federal government.

The sovereignty of the states nevertheless remains a viable concept that serves to demarcate valid from invalid exercises of Congress' power. For example, the U.S. Supreme Court has held that the tenth amendment leaves the states a residuary and inviolable sovereignty. Whatever its limits, it does not permit the federal government to compel the states to enact or administer a federal regulatory program, either to regulate according to the instructions of Congress, or to take title to radioactive waste, e.g. New York v. U.S. (S.Ct.1992). A choice between two unconstitutionally coercive regulatory techniques is not choice at all, but a commandeering of the state legislative power.

State sovereignty also serves to demarcate valid from invalid exercises of Congress' spending power. The "strings" attached must be of such nature as to coerce state response if Congress' action is to be challenged successfully. If Congress' efforts are, as is more likely, seen to be inducements prompting the desired state response, state challenge will not prevail. Local governments, not sovereigns themselves, will unquestionably be in no stronger position than their states. A financially strapped Congress' attempts to impose its objectives upon the states without the financial inducements—and the states' consequent impositions upon their localities—underlie the efforts to end "unfunded mandates."

One of the attributes of sovereignty has long been immunity to suit unless that immunity is waived. To at least a majority of the U.S. Supreme Court, the concepts of state sovereignty and concomitant state sovereign immunity underlie the federal constitution's eleventh amendment and subsequent court rulings which have immunized the states from suits in federal courts for monetary damages whether federal jurisdiction be premised on diversity (the amendment) or the presence of a federal question (cases). A conceptually difficult exception permits the suits if prospective injunctive relief is sought. The national supremacy of delegated power means that implicit in the federal constitutional scheme is a waiver of immunity by the states in suits by the United States and in suits against each other. The scheme also may be the basis for the conclusion that, if it makes its intention "unmistakably clear," Congress may by its enactments abrogate the states' eleventh amendment immunity when acting in the exercise of its enforcement authority under § 5 of the fourteenth amendment. The abrogation must not be simply a permissible inference from the statute; it must be an "unequivocal declaration."

Sovereign immunity also supports the conclusion that neither the state nor its officials acting in their official capacities are "persons" within the meaning of 42 U.S.C.A. § 1983, and cannot thereby be sued for damages in either federal or state courts under that civil rights statute.

The concept of sovereignty also demands due recognition of the sovereign's regulatory activities within its sphere of competence even if the activities contradict a national policy favoring competition. Thus, the states in their regulatory capacity are exempt from the federal antitrust laws.

The judicial protection of state sovereignty does not extend to the states' political subdivisions. As a result, local governments do not benefit from the Eleventh Amendment immunity afforded to the states. Moreover, the local governments and their officials acting in official capacities are potentially liable "persons" under § 1983. Local government anticompetitive regulations and actions may violate federal antitrust laws unless they are affirmatively authorized by the state. (State supervision is not required. Damages will not be available for violations by local governments. For authorization, it is sufficient if suppression of competition is the foreseeable result of what the new or old statute authorizes.)

Except for the recognition of state sovereignty and sovereign immunity and the absence of status for local governments in the federal constitutional scheme, resolution of federal power disputes with the state and with local governments involves the U.S. Constitution's Supremacy Clause and "dormant" power to block regulatory or taxing activity that unduly burdens or discriminates against interstate commerce. In a dispute between federal and local power exercises, the local government may find its actions regulated (antitrust laws), invalidated (Commerce Clause), or preempted (air passenger enplaning taxes).

It is, of course, possible that federal and state or local actions can coexist because the complementary actions are contemplated by the respective levels of government. When the result is allocation of predominance to the federal exercise under the Supremacy Clause, however, it will be because Congress or duly authorized federal administrative entities have preempted. Preemption must be the clear and manifest intention of Congress and in the federal context includes both conflict and occupation of the field, express and implied. In the absence of an express statement by Congress that state (local) law is preempted, preemption will be the result when Congress intends to occupy the field. This conclusion may be supported by a scheme of federal regulation so pervasive as to leave no room for state and local supplementation, by a finding that the field in question is one in which the federal interest is so dominant that preclusion of state and local laws may be assumed, or by a federal statutory objective and character of its imposed obligations revealing the pervasive or dominant purpose.

Even if Congress has not occupied the field, state and local laws may also be preempted to the extent that they conflict with federal law. This conclusion will follow recognition that compliance with both is impossible, or that the state or local law stands as an obstacle to realization of the full purposes and objectives of Congress.

One area of federal preemption that involves multiple intergovernmental consequences, that of Indian Tribes, deserves special note. The Commerce

Clause draws a clear distinction between states and Indian Tribes. While the Court has construed the clause as being concerned with maintaining free trade among the states even without federal legislation, its function concerning Indian Tribes is to give Congress plenary power to legislate in the field of Indian affairs. That Congress so regulates does not necessarily lead to a preemption conclusion whether the matter be state and local regulation or taxation. Where invoked, federal supremacy combines preemption theory and tribal sovereignty in "Indian Country" (the full extent of which is still litigated) and there are consequent resolutions of predominance when state and tribal power exercises occur. It is clear that tribal reservations are not states and that it is "treacherous" to consider applicable to one notions of preemption that are properly applied to the other.

The legitimacy of state and local regulatory authority over reservation territory, Native American individuals, and the sovereign tribal entities depend on a highly nuanced interpretation of treaty obligations, federal statutory enactments, and judicial determinations. These in turn reflect the stresses and strains of reconciling the "measured separatism" promised in the nineteenth century to help preserve cultural and tribal integrity with the emerging problems of mineral and environmental resource allocations, activities on reservations by non-Indians, (taxation; regulation of gambling, e.g.), and an inconsistency with societal goals of racial integration. The stresses and strains are very real.

For example, congressional requirement of meaningful negotiations between tribes and states that permit gambling, designed to allow the tribes to own and operate gambling facilities, has resulted in friction-intensifying, major endeavors providing very substantial fiscal returns to the tribes, voluntary contributions to the states, and competition with state and local revenue raising.

It was earlier noted that the federal power may play a role in resolving state-local power disputes. Illustratively, by virtue of the Supremacy Clause competent federal exercises of expenditure and licensing powers have enabled empowered local governments to use funds or exercise entrepreneurial powers in a manner contrary to the directions of their "creator" states.

§ 3. Competing State Power Considerations

In many instances both state and local laws will regulate the same subject. The land use development process, for instance may be subject to city, county, and state regulations and permitting procedures. When both state and local laws address the same topic, challenges to the legality of concurrent regulation will require judicial determination whether the local action has been displaced by state law. The question of local power to act, discussed in Section A, is therefore distinct from this Section's discussion of preemption. As in other areas of judicial legal doctrine involving local powers and autonomy, judicial assessment of the propriety of local action and of the wisdom of the social policy it embodies will inevitably inform the court's preemption analysis.

A state may expressly preempt local legislation. If it does so, the role of the court will be quite narrow. Explicit state preemption is problematic only if we are in an imperio home rule jurisdiction and the matter being prohibited is deemed to be "exclusively local." In all other instances, preemption is well within state legislative competence.

If a state and local law are in conflict, in most instances the local law will fall. A clear example would be a local law that purported to decriminalize a state felony. In imperio home rule jurisdictions, of course, a law found to be exclusively local should be immune from state laws, irrespective of the conflict. But beyond that narrow band of immunity, which may exist more in theory than in practice, preemption by state law is always possible, and conflict is the most straightforward type of preemption analysis. Of course, the definition of conflict itself leaves a fair amount of judicial discretion; does a local law that prohibits boating between 4 p.m. and 10 a.m. conflict with a state law that prohibits boating from one hour after sunset to one hour before sunrise? A court seeking to uphold the local initiative, found that the laws did not conflict. It upheld the local ordinance, concluding that the local law was merely supplemental to the state law and did not attempt to forbid what state law had permitted.

The doctrine of implied preemption is exclusively judicial and becomes relevant only in the absence of explicit state preemption. As a preliminary matter, we might ask whether implied preemption is flatly inconsistent with legislative home rule, where local home rule units are granted all powers unless "expressly denied" by the state legislature. Some courts have held that legislative home rule renders implied preemption analysis inappropriate and have concluded that only explicit statutory action can preempt the local unit. Most courts, however, resort to implied preemption analysis, which involves important policy determinations about extraterritorial impacts of local laws, the need for statewide uniformity, and the state's interests in local activities.

Implied preemption analyses typically involve one of two main lines of reasoning: that the local law is inconsistent with some fundamental aspect of the state law; or that the state law is intended to occupy the field. In either instance, a finding of implied preemption means that the court has concluded that the state legislature intended state law to be exclusive, thus leaving no room for concurrent local legislation.

A court may find local inconsistency with state law in a variety of circumstances. It may conclude, for instance, that the state legislature's failure to act to prohibit certain behavior reveals its intent to permit that behavior. It might conclude that a state license implicitly grants the licensee the authority to engage in the activity licensed. In both of these cases, the court would hold that local prohibition or regulation of the challenged activity is invalid because it would be inconsistent with the state's legislative intent to authorize that activity.

Occupation of the field leads to preemption when the court concludes that the subject matter is so completely covered by state law that there is no room left for any local initiative. The greater the alleged state interest in statewide uniformity, the greater the importance of the activity to the state, and the greater the adverse effects of interlocal variation on that state interest, the more likely a court will be to find implied preemption by occupation of the field.

It must be emphasized that, like the federal government, the state must be acting in an area within its competence before it can lawfully preempt local action. If the subject matter is committed by law to local autonomy (a local matter, e.g.), it is the state action which may be rendered inoperative in the particular locality. Not only is there much dispute concerning conflict and occupation of the field, there are also questions whether an ordinance which merely duplicates the state law may stand, whether an ordinance may stand until a state statute is enacted on a matter not deemed local or municipal, and whether in the converse situation the state law is operative until a local law is enacted. The jurisdictions answer these questions inconsistently.

§ 4.   Competing Local Power Considerations

Conflicting power exercises among political subdivisions within a state produce judicial resolutions which have been markedly inconsistent. The dispute arises when two units of local government conflict in the exercise of their lawfully delegated powers and one government entity asserts immunity from the regulations of the other. The cases arise in a wide multiplicity of circumstances–a city seeking to operate an airport on land in the county in violation of county zoning; a county seeking to build a criminal detention facility in a city without regard to city building codes; a state university desiring to construct a student dormitory in an area not zoned for multi-family housing by the city. The conflict in question may be resolvable through state statutory formulae or by intergovernmental agreement mechanisms. If the dispute winds up in court, however, courts have adopted a number of judicial tests. In some jurisdictions, the eminent domain test gives priority to a government seeking to exercised validly delegated eminent domain powers within the territory of another local government. Under the superior sovereign test, the "higher" government will prevail, such as when a court invalidated the application of city historic district regulation to a state office building. The preeminent power test involves judicial determination that one of the conflicting powers is more important than the other, such as when a county, which is required by state law to provide a prison, sought to build in violation of the city's land use regulation. And finally, the wide-ranging ad hoc balancing test, probably the most popular of the tests, requires judicial identification of the competing public and private interests, followed by an intensely subjective weighing of the many relevant factors.

§ 5. Federal and State Constitutional Predominance

The concept of "predominance" might well include the dominant position so allocated to constitutionally protected rights as to invalidate otherwise competent government power exercises that violate the protected areas. We shall see the impact of some of the protections of the federal and state constitutions in subsequent chapters as we study particular uses of local governing power.

CHAPTER II

FORMATION OF THE LOCAL GOVERNMENT, ALTERATION, BOUNDARY CHANGES; SOME PROBLEMS OF ORGANIZATION AND OPERATION—OFFICERS, EMPLOYEES, ALLOCATION AND DELEGATION OF FUNCTIONS, ELECTIONS

A. SOME ASPECTS OF ORGANIZATION AND ALTERATION CHOICES

§ 1. Introduction—Choices for Unincorporated Areas

The objectives which motivate choices concerning municipal organization and alteration run the gamut from aggressive and defensive political considerations to the economics of efficient service management and distribution. For example, even if an area meets the state's statutory criteria for incorporation, the residents of an unincorporated area may choose to remain unincorporated to avoid the tax-supported costs of an additional level of government. The decision to preserve the status quo would probably mean that service needs are few or are met sufficiently by the county and that there is no likelihood or fear of annexation by existing municipalities. The choice to remain unincorporated where incorporation is possible also may denote a strong county, weak existing cities structure, or may indicate a judgment that unmet service needs and the risk of annexation are offset by unwillingness to underwrite the costs of local government status.

If service needs are paramount, the people in the area may choose to purchase services privately or from a government entity, or to avail themselves of the state's procedures for creating a special district. As we noted in Chapter I, this entity may be sufficiently powerful to impose and collect ad valorem taxes and superintend multiple functions, and may often be governed by elected officials. Such an entity would nonetheless differ from an incorporated city because, in the case of a special district, the priority of needs to be served was chosen in its creation. Therefore, it would not possess the city's flexibility to promote the public good or regulate in areas additional to its original purposes. While this government form can provide identifiable, needed services with the least complex government structure, thus allowing our hypothetical unincorporated area to remain close to its original status, it will not likely serve to protect against the possibility of annexation by an adjacent municipality.

If the motives for change include a desire to allow the political process to determine service priorities or to avoid adverse economic, social or political consequences of unincorporated status or of annexation by existing cities, the choice will be incorporation as the broad based, politically accountable governing unit, to the extent existing state classification and related powers legislation allow. "Defensive incorporation" is the term used to refer to an area's decision to incorporate as a municipality so as to prevent annexation by other neighboring cities. To be successful, the incorporation must be initiated first, and state law must protect the newly acquired corporate status from incursion by another municipal government unit. One drawback of such a reactive and protective device is that it may serve to thwart what is seen as the natural growth pattern of the potential annexor. Defensive incorporation might be unnecessary if the state's law requires the affirmative vote of those to be annexed as prerequisite to successful annexation. It will be impossible or unavailing in states that have prohibited suburban fringe incorporations without the consent of the protected city or that have incorporation and annexation mechanisms wherein approvals turn in part on the fiscal effect on other governments.

§ 2. Introduction—Choices for Incorporated Areas

Let us assume that our hypothetical area is an incorporated "city." Its government and citizens may desire to maximize economies of scale in providing services, or may seek to enlarge its tax base (although it will customarily need more than this as justification). It may seek to avail itself of extraterritorial facilities or geographic advantages, or may wish to solve on a broader base a multiplicity of urban problems. A number of choices are available. The city may use existing, or seek state legislative authorization of, extraterritorial powers in its planning, regulatory or utility functions. It may enter into an area-wide council of governments whereby its goals may be reached through mutual planning and discussion and concomitant government actions by the allied independent localities. It may, if authorized, enter into contractual agreements with other municipal entities for provision of services or transfer of functions. It may join in the formation of a metropolitan district, a special district extending across municipal boundaries empowered to perform one or more desired functions (water and sewage removal, e.g.). It may invoke the procedures necessary to annex the adjoining areas. It may enter into one of a variety of government "mergers"–city-county consolidation, federation, or city-city consolidation–to accomplish its goals. All of these choices present in varying degrees the problem of state authorization and the obstacles of geopolitical reality and citizen resistance which may make them difficult or impossible to accomplish.

Citizens of an area within an incorporated city may seek to gain a greater voice in municipal affairs or may desire to "secede" from the city or undo a prior merger. In the former situation, the city may respond by forms of decentralization ranging from local advisory boards to partial functional control within an area by the residents of that area. The "secession" objective, an extremely difficult one, may result in return to unincorporated status or disconnection from one city in order to be annexed to another. There will likely be state legislation governing disannexation or secession.

It should be recalled that the state itself may accomplish any of the above status alterations by legislative direction if not prohibited from doing so by home rule, prohibition of special legislation, or other constitutional limitations.

B.   CONSIDERATIONS COMMON TO STATUTORY INCORPORATION OR ALTERATION PROCEDURES

The political realities of the choices introduced above are self-evident. All changes in governmental structure might have an impact on schools, services, regulation, taxes, entrenched pre-existing government structures and officeholders, and social relations—each politically volatile. During the course of our more specific ensuing discussion, the reader may wish to evaluate the legislatively or judicially required procedures of organization or alteration in terms of their effectiveness in accommodating political realities and in defusing or channeling the virtually inevitable explosion of opposition.

§ 1.   Specific Provisions

There are several aspects common to almost all statutory schemes authorizing organization or alteration with attendant issues requiring the attention of proponents and providing grist for opponents. For our purposes, it suffices to indicate the patterns and the issues for which local law provides the answers.

Some processes involve initial study and recommendations by advisory boards. Equal protection principles may apply to invalidate legislative schemes that limit board membership unreasonably, such as a provision limiting participation to freeholders in the territory.

Many processes begin with petitions. State law will provide the procedural details. In some states, legislative action by the sponsoring local government will be sufficient. If petitions are necessary, or are at least permitted, how many signatures are required? Who may sign, all residents of the area in question or only those owning property? Is a requirement that signers be freeholders unconstitutional? Must the petition not only contain the signatures of a specified percentage of the population but also reflect a specified percentage of real property ownership? When must the petition be filed? How long before the result sought must it be filed? Is there a time period within which signatures can be withdrawn? If the petition fails, when may another attempt be made?

The petitions and the government's initiating or responsive resolutions will customarily be accompanied by required descriptions of boundaries, maps, demographic data and the like. The requirements may insist upon accurate specificity and may even in many jurisdictions call for annexation environmental impact statements.

At several points during the process, it will be necessary to give notice of the proposed action to affected persons. What must the notice contain? What degree of specificity and completeness is required? How is the notice to be conveyed? Dissemination of the notice will customarily involve publication in a newspaper of general circulation at specified intervals. Sometimes, dissemination may be accomplished by mail or by posting signs near the affected area. Do not be misled by the requirement that notice of the pending action be disseminated. Effective notification will almost uniformly require vigilance on the part of the affected persons, because frequently very general forms of notice will suffice. Typically, affected individuals will be deemed to have notice of sign postings on the property affected or of public notices posted in newspapers of general circulation. This constructive notice will be effective so long as the method of notification complies with the jurisdiction's statutory requirements. The closer the issue comes to affecting individual property rights, the closer due process notice requirements come to direct, individual notification.

The proposed action may have to be approved by a county or state board or commission. The approving entity may be a legislative or administrative body. It may be a regular or ad hoc board and may approve or advise. Some processes may require judicial imprimatur, either instead of or in addition to other approvals, such as a general vote of the electorate. The intervention of these government organs may only be necessary in response to a specified number of remonstrances, i.e., protest provisions which may raise the questions alluded to in the above discussion of petitions.

The final result or the matter to be submitted to the electorate will entail the drafting of a document (charter, e.g.) and the framing of the question to be voted upon. Either or both may be set forth in the statutes, and must then conform to the required formulations.

The customary referendum presents numerous questions concerning the jurisdictions whose electorates must be allowed to participate, the limitations, if any, upon who may vote (caveat constitutional implications), the manner of determining whether the question has been approved or disapproved, and sometimes such specifics as the location of polling places.

A host of practical intergovernmental regulatory and economic consequences are reflected in many of the statutory patterns. Where they are not, difficult problems arise. For example, who is to bear the costs of the process? Who retains or obtains title to preexisting government property? How are assets and liabilities to be transferred or shared? What is the tenure of officeholders and employees of preexisting governments? What are the powers of the new entity? What laws govern the new entity? Are power exercises of preexisting government units of continuing validity and applicability? Formulas may be included for necessary intergovernmental agreements.

The state legislation will contain provisions for publication of the results of the process which may frequently envision certification by government officials such as the county board or the secretary of state.

§ 2. Mandatory and Directory

Of overriding concern, as with all state legislative direction, is the intent of the state legislature, as construed by the courts, to require compliance with the letter of some or all of the statutory procedures. Where such intent is found, or judicially declared, failure to comply literally with the statutory steps, thus deemed "mandatory," is fatal to the process. Substantial compliance with other statutory steps, deemed "directory," will be satisfactory; any minimal failure may be corrected during an ongoing process but will not invalidate a completed one.

C.   FORMATION OF THE LOCAL GOVERNING UNIT

§ 1. Incorporation of the Local General Government

We have seen the sources of municipal power and the methods of municipal organization. Statutory patterns such as those outlined above, involving petition, notice, drafting, election and certification procedures, will be followed by citizens seeking to incorporate under home rule power grants or general state legislative authorizations with local unit classifications. Once again, direct grant of a municipal charter by special act of the legislature now occurs infrequently. Most state statutory schemes have been restructured to require citizen initiation and ultimate approval of municipal incorporation.

In addition to strict or substantial compliance with statutory incorporation procedures, certain prerequisites must be met. Constitutional or statutory terms such as "city," "community" or "village," even in those jurisdictions where specific minimum requirements are not set forth in the statutes, have been given meaning by the courts so that everywhere, the area to be incorporated must contain a minimum population and density (often expressed per acre). The territory must be contiguous, must have definitely ascertainable boundaries, must constitute a community (a concept that implies geographic, sociological, economic and political considerations), and must contain only property that is adaptable for municipal uses and that will, at least in the foreseeable future, benefit from existence within the municipality. These prerequisites are not as strictly applied as to require an identifiable "downtown" for the proposed municipality, although some mutual benefit attraction must be present. Land included within the petition for incorporation need not be developed nor platted, but some future benefit other than tax revenues to the city must be predictable. In short, while the state legislature may delegate some legislative authority to the citizen petitioners seeking to form a politically accountable, multipowered local unit, the courts will find the state's power to create such local delegate limited to instances in which potentially benefitted, preexisting communities can be identified.

Also, as we noted earlier, the effect of incorporation on the locality's county or township may be a factor. In jurisdictions where advisory boards assist the courts in approving incorporations, for example, the racial mix of the localities subsequent to incorporation and the need for communities to meet their fair share of low and moderate income housing have been deemed relevant to the desirability of incorporation. Incorporation in suburban areas without the concurrence of the urban local government may be prohibited by statute.

Challenges may be raised to a local unit's legitimate existence, either by the state in the customary quo warranto proceeding, or by persons who hope to avoid a particular power exercise. Where incorporation proceedings were fatally defective and void, such collateral attack by individuals is permitted. But for reasons of stability of the social order, courts do not welcome collateral attacks on the local unit's validity and uphold the government action because of prescriptive exercise of government powers. Frequently, the outcome will be a declaration of the unit's existence as a "de facto municipal corporation." Such status obtains where there is legislative authority for the chosen form of municipal corporation, and where there has been not only a good faith undertaking to organize thereunder, resulting in apparent compliance with the legislation, but also subsequent exercise of corporate powers. Concern for the stability of the social order and practical realities have also motivated frequent curative state legislation validating prior faulty municipal incorporations. Such enactments are uniformly upheld even in the face of special legislation prohibitions. As we shall see in later sections, direct and collateral attacks on municipal annexations may be more liberally viewed by a court than those that challenge municipal incorporation.

Charter amendment and revision may be accomplished by constitutional amendment. Depending upon the original source of the municipality's power, amendment and revision may also be done by general state legislation, state special acts, or action by the local citizens.

The form of the incorporated unit, like the decision to incorporate, will reflect a number of factors: political responsiveness and accountability (e.g., large city council with small constituencies); administrative competence and an appropriate independence from political pressures (e.g., weak executive, appointed manager, and council with non-partisan election); check-and-balance distribution of executive and legislative power or desirability of charismatic leadership (e.g., strong executive and council); or simplicity of governmental operations (e.g., commissioners board, often historically labeled "court," with an appointed administrator or the mixture of legislative and executive functions).

Experience indicates that many local units initially selected forms which later became inadequate to respond to their increased size, complexity or service management challenges. In those instances, state law is likely to detail procedures and substantive requirements pursuant to which a general purpose local government unit may change its classification. The local government may wish to assume a broader range of powers, both regulatory and financial, to respond to the greater complexity. It is not uncommon, for instance, for state law to establish several "classes" of municipalities, each one with a delimited range of powers and revenue raising capabilities. Greater population and urban density will frequently authorize a local purpose government to become a city of a different class, with the resulting enhancement of governmental functions such reclassification brings.

§ 2.   Formation of Special Districts

The formation of special authorities and districts is everywhere governed by statutes which may permit creation by the local electorate or by one or more existing local governments. Many are directly created by state statutes. Boundary ascertainment and referenda may be required in a manner similar to our above legislative patterns.

As we have seen, special districts may be remote from political control or may themselves be subject to the electorate. Divorce from political control is, however, never complete because the district's officials or commissioners may be appointed by elected governments, local or state. Many structures allow for "interlocking" governance whereby locally elected officials serve on the district's board or commission.

We shall see in our subsequent discussion of finances that a special district differs from a municipal administrative department in autonomy, specifically as reflected in the amount of supervision exercised by existing governments. Thus, for example a special district may be permitted to incur debt not aggregated with that of the "sponsoring" city for the purpose of determining the city's position vis-a-vis the constitutional debt limitations. Note, however, that under appropriate state legislation, even "autonomous" special districts' powers may be seized by the state for fiscal and program failures. This has happened most recently with some failed school districts.

§ 3. Comment on the Special District and Other Forms of Decentralization

The availability to existing municipalities of special district forms for accomplishing municipal objectives has been suggested as one method of decentralizing local government. Other proposals for bringing local government control closer to the people have ranged from those which accorded substantial governance authority to small geopolitical areas within the city to those which contemplated the location of "branch city halls" throughout the community. Yet others have used mechanisms that allowed for weighted voting strength. The drive for decentralization has been spawned by the felt needs to revitalize waning citizen involvement and to provide better or more appropriate educational and other services to areas of the city previously underserved for economic or social reasons or to make politically palatable merger, consolidation, or annexation schemes.

The objectives of decentralization have much merit and the felt needs are real. The simpler proposals, such as mini-city-halls and advisory neighborhood councils, have had some beneficial impact on citizen morale and improvement of services. The more elaborate attempts to decentralize, whether under federal community action program requirements or state or local arrangements such as those dealing with schools, have not been notable for their success. Of course, there may have been exceptions. If there were nonpolitical or nonvolatile matters which could be within decentralized partial control, the concept of decentralization could well be a fruitful one. In reality, however, the matters over which decentralized control is sought are emotionally provocative and have a high political profile, because they are matters as to which the geopolitical areas within the city feel growing political impotence. For this reason, the structures of power decentralization may predictably succumb to the crippling chaos and political crossfire which critically undermine their effectiveness. Moreover, the careful mixture of sublocal control and legislative standards necessary to avoid challenge as an improper delegation of authority feeds suspicion that only cosmetic change has been applied to political impotence.

Perhaps the boldest and most extreme form of decentralization is found in citizen attempts to disconnect or secede from the existing multi-purpose unit of government to which they currently belong. State law is likely to articulate strict procedural and substantive prerequisites for disconnection. Nevertheless, the threat of disconnection may itself prompt the centralized and allegedly unresponsive local government to consider sublocal power sharing mechanisms.

Observers await the results of some dramatic recent efforts to decentralize control over public schools and increase educator, parental and community power. Some of the school efforts have responded to perceived need for decentralization. Others, such as charter schools, have been responses to the perceived need to improve the schools. Yet others have undertaken in response to judicial invalidation of both the funding mechanisms and the school system itself. Several major cities, in an effort to reform school performance, approached the issue by focusing on local control and community oversight committees. Results ranged from dramatic progress in Chicago to slow and unsatisfactory improvement in Detroit.

Real power sharing mechanisms raise other questions. For example, New York City's voting-weight-allocation remedies have not survived challenge under the federal Equal Protection Clause or Voting

Rights Act. The U.S. Supreme Court also struck down as a violation of the Establishment Clause a statute that carved out of an existing public school district a new district conforming to the boundaries of an incorporated village exclusively populated by members of a strict religious sect. The new school district concentrated its efforts on the expensive effort of educating the sect's handicapped children; the sect's non-handicapped children continued to attend its private schools. Finally, since a primary objective is to provide an antidote to the frustration of apparent political powerlessness, the politically sterile, indirectly accountable, special district or special authority form may be unsuited to its solution.

D. ALTERATION, BOUNDARY CHANGES

§ 1. Extraterritorial Exercise of Power

Our Chapter I illustrations concerning the domed stadium and the airport alluded to the possible ability of a city to exercise extraterritorial power without expanding its boundaries. Such a possibility raises the question whether extraterritorial power must be express or can be implied. The answer will differ, depending upon the power in question and upon whether the express power giving rise to the inference of implied power is itself extraterritorial in application. If the power under scrutiny is "proprietary," extraterritoriality may be less difficult an implication. For example, city utility storage and sources and the provision of utility services by cities with a surplus to fringe users outside city boundaries have been upheld.

Much more commonly, however, state statutes authorize the extraterritorial exercise of municipal powers, including parks and recreation, airports, utilities, roads, planning, eminent domain and subdivision control and other police powers, in limited areas immediately outside city lines. When an extraterritorial power is thus authorized, powers necessary to its fulfillment will sometimes be deemed included. If Bigville has statutory authority to construct its airport outside its boundaries, would use of the power of eminent domain to obtain the necessary land be upheld?

Courts most rigorously scrutinize attempted extraterritorial exercise of regulatory powers to protect health, safety, morality and the general welfare, looking for express authorization. Where authority to exercise extraterritorial power is not found, the exercise will be ultra vires and reliance upon it by those outside the city will be unavailing. Where authority is found—and it is found in some form in at least two thirds of the states—the legislative motivation may be the probability of eventual annexation, the control of matters which may be indirectly detrimental to governmental responsibilities within the city, recognition of the embryonic "metropolitanism," or provision of services to unincorporated areas. The frequent challenge to "governing without the consent or votes of the governed" has rare success in the face of state authorization, although a different result might be reached where a city has so extended the full panoply of its powers as to have "annexed" the area outside its borders in all but name.

§ 2. Annexation

The statutory methods permitting expansion of municipal boundaries reflect no consistent pattern throughout the United States. The several methods may at one time have been responsive to the demographic facts of life in the particular states. The segmented incorporation patterns of the country's metropolitan areas, most graphic in the megalopolis along the northeast and middle Atlantic seaboard, and the jurisdictions' acceptance of the relative inviolability of local government boundaries, have weakened the municipality's ability to use annexation as a means of solving urban problems by enlarging its territorial base. Although there have been changes to respond to modern needs, there often remain archaic procedures that serve to compound the inflexibilities of annexation. Hence there has been impetus for the exploration of federation and other forms of metropolitanism, although that too has slowed. There remain large areas of the country where annexation is a mechanism to satisfy a municipality's growth needs or to fulfill its expansionist tendencies.

A few states authorize annexation by special act of the state legislature. Absent permitted special legislation, the procedures of annexation, governed by statute everywhere, may at the risk of oversimplification be classified as (a) those which are within the home rule power of the annexing city; (b) those which are initiated by or require the consent of the territory to be annexed; (c) those which require the approval of advisory or administrative boards or local legislatures; and (d) those which require substantive approval of the courts. It should be noted that some classes of cities within a particular state may be authorized to annex in one manner, while other classes may be permitted to do so by another method. Additionally, the annexation methods in several states may combine elements from the above groupings, with consent of the area to be annexed most common.

Unilateral

A few cities have been delegated unilateral power to annex as an attribute of home rule. In the past, the inevitable expansionist tendencies were not troublesome in less dense demographic circumstances. However, one state, notable for annexation by city resolution, found it necessary to circumscribe this unilateral power by statutes authorizing extraterritorial jurisdiction over a limited unincorporated area, restricting annexations generally to land within this extraterritorial jurisdiction, limiting area of annexation in any one calendar year, requiring pre-annexation hearings open to all interested persons, and providing rather liberal judicial disannexation standards for areas not appropriately benefitted by the annexation. Nevertheless, problems in one of the cities, including degenerating services and federal Voting Rights Act challenges to the dilution of minority voting strength, suggest that such circumscription may not be sufficient to stop repeated municipal attempts to annex solely for the purpose of capturing the property tax revenues of the annexed territory. In another state, unilateral annexation authority is accompanied both by rather specific statutory standards with municipal adherence measured by the courts upon residents' appeal, and by required municipal exposition of the services to be provided to the annexed area with mandamus available to assure judicial enforcement of this service commitment.

Consent

Annexation methods involving the consent of the territory to be annexed take several forms. First, the territory may be allowed to petition for annexation with response by the city's government and perhaps subject to referendum. Second, the annexing municipality may be able to accomplish annexation only upon an affirmative vote in the territory to be annexed or affirmative votes in both the city and the territory. Conceivably, annexation might be authorized when the combined total vote of the city and territory approve.

It should be noted that the requirement of concurrent majorities for approval is very common throughout the states, and reasonable classification will withstand equal protection challenge. Most commonly, the territory to be annexed is not an incorporated political subdivision. Where it is, the procedure is normally termed "consolidation" and is governed by a different statutory scheme. Some statutes give additional protection to the territory to be annexed. For example, the annexed territory may be able to establish a community municipal corporation to offset the immediate impact of municipal annexation. Under that arrangement, and existing only for a limited time period, annexed territory may retain some narrow control over matters such as land use, thus temporarily providing some decentralization of the annexing city's governance powers.

Boards

Some statutory annexation procedures require substantive approval of boards or commissions, either the regularly elected entities such as a board of county commissioners, or selected advisory or administrative boards at state or regional levels. The objectives are, of course, not the same. Where a county commissioner's unit is given the approval power, the state is both invoking the regional considerations which may have a positive or negative bearing, and, in order to preserve stronger or at least viable counties, inviting a bias against local expansionism which would alter the power balances. The role of the administrative board, in contrast, is to combine expertise and regional or statewide considerations in the evaluation of the annexation. Such a goal strikes a responsive chord among commentators who believe that the competitive or expansionist instincts of cities and the benefits of annexations to citizens are best handled at the state level with expertise independent of, or somewhat remote from, the local pressures.

Judicial Review

While virtually all methods of attempted annexation can face some review in the courts, there are some which envision full substantive judicial review. Because incorporation and power existence are legislative matters committed to the state legislatures and not delegable by them to their co-equal branches, substantive judicial oversight has presented the inevitable question of improper delegation and violation of state mandated separation of powers. While the challenge has not been entirely unsuccessful, especially in jurisdictions where its imminence has kept the courts from carving out a larger role, the "judicial annexation" jurisdictions' courts have overcome it by reference to legislatively posited standards, however sweeping. Thus, in Virginia, specially appointed annexation courts must determine whether the proposed annexation is "necessary" and "expedient." In this inquiry, they require the annexing government to establish that annexation will produce benefits to the city, to the county losing territory, and to the territory to be annexed. In addition, the municipality must provide detailed data regarding service levels before and after annexation, economic data, and evidence of the environmental impact of the annexation. The courts may approve, reject or modify the proposal, setting terms and conditions for approval. The city in turn, if it does not wish to meet the terms, may abandon the annexation proposal. In an early decision upholding the constitutionality of the judiciary's participation in annexation, Virginia's highest court examined the reality of feasible separation of powers and found some allowable intermingling. The concept barred complete usurpation but not all delegations. Moreover, the fact-sensitive annexation conclusion was seen for the most part as a trial, clearly within the judicial power.

In variations of this idea, other states' procedures permit bypassing such judicial oversight unless a specified number of remonstrances or a citizen-initiated challenge is filed. The courts then undertake to apply legislatively or judicially created standards, some of which result in a thorough judicial review of the annexation. Note that in substantive judicial reviews, the burden of establishing the reasonableness of the annexation may be upon the annexing entity.

§ 3. Dissolution, Division and Detachment

Municipal powers, once properly obtained and vigorously exercised, may nevertheless lie dormant at some point in time, thus making the conditions ripe for municipal dissolution. More frequently, as noted earlier, economic considerations, changed geopolitical conditions, the unconstitutionality of special voting arrangements, or failure to realize annexation benefits may bring about a desire to secede from a municipal unit and return to unincorporated status, reincorporate, or join another municipality, or to oust a section of the existing municipality. Each of these objectives may be achievable by the local area pursuant to statutory procedures often accompanied by advisory bodies and a substantial role for the judiciary. Of course, each of these objectives may also be achieved by the state legislatures if no state constitutional limitation intervenes. Under appropriate legislation, states may assume the local government's powers, especially in cases of fiscal failures. State power must of course observe the protections of constitutionally guaranteed individual rights. For example, state legislated detachment of sections of a city which resulted in the local disenfranchisement of almost all of the city's black voters was held to be a violation of the fifteenth amendment to the U.S. Constitution.

Dormancy of the municipality's total powers alone will generally not accomplish dissolution although there are a few statutes so providing. In other instances, termination of the municipal corporation can be accomplished in one of the following ways: with the permission of the state legislature, either by officially surrendering its corporate status or by state legislated dissolution; by voter petition or election; or by judicial or state decree and certification.

Division of a municipality whereby its territory is divided between it and another may be accomplished by appropriate state legislative enactment or by adherence to state legislative procedures for disannexation followed by annexation. For example, where changing conditions would seem to indicate that a particular area was in fact becoming part of a community other than the one in whose boundaries it was located, some jurisdictions allow disannexation from the latter and annexation to the former with the consent of the governing municipal bodies. The courts will scrutinize the withholding of consent by the "loser," allowing it to be voluntary and more than ministerial but rejecting arbitrary or unreasonable recalcitrance.

Again, outright detachment, severance, ouster or disannexation of an area from the municipality may be accomplished by state legislative enactments or under procedures envisioning judicial or administrative agency determination that the area in question is not now receiving and will not in the foreseeable future receive municipal benefits. In those cases, municipal retention is deemed unreasonable, motivated solely for revenue purposes. Disannexation, we have seen, is sometimes provided where expected municipal benefits have not materialized within a specified time period.

Statutes frequently provide for adjustment of assets and liabilities when such municipal contractions occur. In addition, courts will occasionally make adjustments. In the absence of such, the original municipality retains all of its original powers and real property within its revised boundaries, and all of its personal property. It also remains solely liable even for its preexisting debts.

§ 4. Political Realities and Constitutional Implications

An annexation must be authorized, and the annexed area must be contiguous and suitable for

urban services and development. The annexation
must not have a discriminatory purpose or, under
the federal Voting Rights Act, a discriminatory impact. Unquestionably, then, the political realities
and constitutional implications of boundary alteration are a significant and constant source of difficulty and challenge. For example, let us assume that
our illustration cities, seeking to construct an airport and a domed stadium, envision annexations of
the projects' respective locations some miles outside
the cities. Neither city intends to annex sizeable
portions of the intervening areas, which are largely
populated by low income members of minority
groups living in service-poor conditions. Assume
that the annexations must either be initiated by or
receive the consent of the areas to be annexed. Our
cities' plans would be vulnerable because the territories sought are arguably not contiguous. They
might be thwarted by defensive incorporation of the
areas in question. The price of consent may be
inordinate. The plans may face serious challenge
under the federal constitution and laws.

Contiguity

It is a requirement of both original incorporation
and annexation, except apparently in one state, that
the territory to be annexed be contiguous. Some
statutory exceptions exist. For example, problems
arise when the desired area is only contiguous if
certain geographical factors are ignored or if the
requirement is satisfied by a connecting link of
minimum dimensions. Statutes and courts have

sometimes resolved the former problem in favor of annexation, thus approving the joining of areas on two sides of a railroad, or a river. Such favorable result is by no means certain, however.

The judicial reaction to "corridor annexation" is much less favorable, though far from consistent. Local government lawyers refer to "strip," "barbell," "balloon," "stem," "spoke," "shoestring," or "flag" annexations to describe the shapes that result when a city or landowners use narrow corridors of land to link the annexing city to relatively distant areas seeking to be annexed. State courts are divided over whether the statutory contiguity requirement is satisfied by technical contiguity. Some courts limit their inquiry to confirming that the dictionary definition of contiguity, that the city be "physically touching" the parcel of land to be annexed, is met. Others apply the requirement not only to support the desire that municipalities be the corporate reflection of real communities, but also to prevent revenue expansionist tendencies motivated by the acquisition of desirable areas and the avoidance of those more needing municipal services. Similarly protective are requirements that the area be suitable for urban development and services. Here a standard of reasonableness is commonly applied.

Defensive Incorporation

Because, as we have seen, annexation is generally not permitted where the territory to be annexed has separate incorporated status, perhaps the most effective line of resistance for opponents of annexation is a separate municipal incorporation. Because the proceeding first begun takes priority, the community on defense will race to begin incorporation steps before annexation steps have begun. While it is possible that the area will not qualify for incorporation, statutory standards and judicial requirements are likely to be so minimal as not to constitute a major barrier. Accordingly, a state legislature which seeks to foster effective local government realignment must set more stringent standards for incorporation. Since it is rarely difficult to determine which proceeding began first, litigation will more likely constitute an attack on the degree of adherence to statutory provisions by the entity that acted first. These seemingly hypertechnical disputes and procedural haggling, of course, mask the underlying causes of resistance: unwillingness to be subjected to predictably increased taxation; maintenance of original escape from urban problems; fear of racial, ethnic or economic integration; undesirability of the annexing city's school policies on such matters as sex education, textbooks or corporal punishment; protection against unwanted land use controls; limitation of improperly motivated urban expansionism; and retention of the historic or traditional character of the territory to be annexed.

It is worth noting here the phenomenon of balkanization, that is, the problem of urban strangulation resulting from a multiplicity of nearby municipal corporations, many of them defensively organized for the above enumerated reasons. In this instance, some courts have been willing to scrutinize the external consequences of municipal power exercises particularly in the control of land use.

Urban strangulation has motivated commentators to urge government restructuring more in line with geopolitical reality and power realignment more reflective of supporting revenue sources. Some have urged abolishment of local government—an impossible objective, although in this country's newest states, and for complex historical reasons, Hawaii and Alaska have with much success avoided many of the pitfalls of corporate multiplicity. The fear of such strangulation has prompted legislatures in several states to forbid incorporation within specified suburban areas without the consent of the protected cities.

Price of Consent

From the annexing city's point of view, the cost of a territory's consent to annexation may be so great as to outweigh the benefits of annexation. We have seen that state legislation may authorize temporary mini-municipal corporations with near veto power in matters such as land use in order to protect annexed areas. We have also seen that annexing municipalities may be required to observe pre-annexation service commitments or to extend to annexed areas within a specified time services commensurate with those throughout the original city.

Even more costly may be the negotiated quid pro quo for consent, involving tax considerations, additional services, waiver of some financial obligations, undertaking of promotional activities and the like. Similar "hard bargains" are sometimes necessary where the area to be annexed is largely controlled by a developer or subdivider, not within the extraterritorial control of the annexing city, and ostensibly resistant to annexation.

Challenge Under the Federal Constitution and Laws

Annexations and boundary changes involving general municipal governments as well as special districts have been challenged under the federal constitution and laws. We shall note later that the fifteenth amendment prohibited a redrawing of municipal boundaries that disenfranchised the city's black voters. Customary, state authorized, municipal exercise of extraterritorial power has been unsuccessfully challenged under the Due Process and Equal Protection Clauses. Boundary decisions—for example, inclusion in a special assessment benefit district of property unable to be benefitted and not contributing to the problem—may be attacked as unreasonable and confiscatory under the Due Process and Takings Clauses.

More frequently, however, challenges arise under the Equal Protection Clause. Classifications here must be reasonable. Decisions or actions by the government which implicate protected classes or fundamental rights require much more demanding judicial scrutiny and persuasive government justification. Many equal protection challenges to annexations focus upon electoral impact and will be discussed in a later section. Boundary decisions may include school districts or service districts challenged as being discriminatory. While proof may be circumstantial, successful fourteenth amendment, equal protection challenges will require proof of discriminatory purpose. Intentional discrimination is unlikely to be proved by individual legislators' statements of what may have motivated their votes. It may well be demonstrated by a composite of discriminatory school district, land use, housing and regulatory decisions by interlocking local government bodies.

Classic equity powers of the courts implement the remedy, limited to, or as extensive as the scope of the problem even if multi-jurisdictional. Where limited to a single jurisdiction remedy, a court that approved such inducements to extraterritorial, voluntary involvement as well financed magnet schools supported by state funds and increased taxes with state tax limits enjoined was deemed to have exceeded its remedial authority. Once racial imbalance caused by de jure segregation has been remedied, the school district may not be obligated to remedy imbalances caused by demographic factors, and the federal court then has discretion to relinquish jurisdiction. A court's end purpose is not only to remedy the violation to the extent practicable, but also to restore control to state and local authorities.

Federal statutes implementing the constitutional guarantees in such areas as housing, employment and voting will customarily be triggered by evidence of discriminatory impact irrespective of intent. In covered jurisdictions, annexations are subject to specified federal court or executive preclearance under the Voting Rights Act as having neither discriminatory purpose nor discriminatory impact.

Our illustration cities' plan not to annex poor, minority areas while annexing other areas that serve their purposes might somehow meet contiguity and reasonability requirements, might not face defensive incorporation, and might not change the minority areas' present status, thus having no discriminatory impact thereon. Nevertheless, the decision not to annex, though itself not illegal, might well be some evidence of a discriminatory purpose that would affect the validity of the other actions by the cities.

§ 5. Cross–Boundary Cooperation; Consolidation and Federation

As has been mentioned, a number of other alternatives are available to citizens and local governments desiring to adapt to meet changing economic, geopolitical and social conditions. These involve intergovernmental cooperation, intergovernmental agreements, and sharing of power in a variety of ways.

Contracts and Compacts

In all states there is likely to be authority for contractual arrangements among municipalities for the accomplishment of certain objectives. There is a great number of such intergovernmental arrangements throughout the country covering information exchange, sharing of facilities, mutual aid, provision of services by one government for the other, transfer of functions by one to the other, and the like. These agreements are said to facilitate the maximum utilization of expensive or unique facilities, to achieve economies of scale, to provide services which a particular locality is too small to provide for itself, and to allow mutually beneficial development of specialized resources by local government members of the joint enterprise.

These arrangements may involve the interlocal contract authority, now nearly everywhere available, for one municipality to purchase services or utilities from another, or for two or more entities to engage in a joint enterprise to achieve the objectives mentioned above. In the absence of interlocal cooperation statutes, it will be left to the courts to determine whether all participants need contract authority (yes), and whether more than the actual provider need service authority (likely yes) and extraterritorial powers (mixed).

If the contract transfers functions from one government to another, authority to engage in the transfer will be essential. While it is not always clear when a transfer of functions has occurred, when one government effectively surrenders policy determination in an area wherein it can competently act to another competent government, it has transferred the function. The conclusion may be circumstantial, inferred, for example, from a service contract of unreasonable duration thus constricting government policy decisions. The courts will generally demand more particular state authorization than rather generic contract or interlocal cooperation authority, especially because transfers of functions may, by state law, require electoral approval. Transfers of functions will sometimes occur vertically, such as occurs when a county charges a fee to perform certain municipal functions for one or more of its cities.

For geographic and economic reasons, the interlocal services or joint enterprises may involve an interstate area. The result of interstate cooperation will be akin to a metropolitan district (noted infra); it will be a public corporate instrumentality of both (all) participating states. The agreement will be an interstate compact, an arrangement raising its own set of issues such as: (i) the U.S. Constitution's requirement for congressional approval, but only if the compact tends to increase the political power of the states at the expense of federal supremacy; (ii) effect of one participant's laws on the compact entity (binding if the compact itself so states; binding if they cover external operations of the agency clearly implicating that state's regulatory powers, say some; binding if accompanied by complementary or parallel legislation in the other state(s), say others); and (iii) interplay with home rule (almost certainly involves regional, not local, concerns).

Discussion of the eleventh amendment in Chapter VI briefly notes the importance for immunity purposes of classifying state entities as arms of the state. The issue is also relevant for interstate compacts. The U.S. Supreme Court has ruled that the answer is not uniform. The Court will presume that the compact entity does not qualify for eleventh amendment immunity unless there is good reason to believe that the states structured the entity to enjoy the special constitutional protection the states themselves enjoy, and that Congress concurred in that objective when it approved the compact. Illustratively, in denying immunity to one interstate compact entity, the Court said: "A discrete entity created by constitutional compact among three sovereigns [two states and the approving federal sovereign], the Port Authority is financially self-sufficient; it generates its own revenues, and it pays its own debts. Requiring the Port Authority to answer in federal court to injured railroad workers who assert a federal statutory right, under the FELA, to recover damages does not touch the concerns—the States' solvency and dignity—that underpin the Eleventh Amendment." Hess v. Port Authority Trans–Hudson Corp. (S.Ct.1994).

"COGs"

Regional councils of government officials were originally fostered in part by federal grant planning requirements. These groups consist of the chief elected officials of the region's local governments (sometimes of interstate regions), who with the assistance of staff concern themselves with many and varied areawide problems. While the COGs cannot compel local government action, COG-developed plans, policies and solutions will often be fol-

lowed by concomitant government actions of the
independent municipality government members.

Metropolitan District

One or more functions or services for which an
area's municipalities may be individually responsible could perhaps be more economically or effectively managed on an areawide basis. Hence, municipalities will take advantage of state legislative
authorization to create a special metropolitan district for this purpose, governed by a board often
consisting of some of the elected officials of the municipalities or their appointees.

Consolidation

Imaginative consideration of the concepts of interlocal agreements and metropolitan service districts has led to study of the possibilities of metropolitan government in a broader sense. Local
governments have long been authorized to merge
with one another, thereby creating a new entity.
Not all states have satisfactory consolidation procedures, but in many, the authorization for, and
details and results of, city-city consolidation are
very specifically set forth.

Merge With County

Although its importance has been downplayed in
some states, the county can be a resource in dealing
with metropolitan problems in several ways. It may
provide services or functions through intergovernmental arrangements. It may be the shell for inter-

governmental tax base sharing. It may serve as the vehicle for merging the metropolitan area. At the risk of some oversimplification, ventures in broad metropolitanism that involve counties have taken one of what might be classified as two forms: federation or city-county consolidation.

Although they are frequently concentrated in smaller urban areas, some major metropolitan areas have been involved since consolidation began in 1805. While proponents say that substantial success seems to have outweighed political upheaval and such other problems as constitutional challenges, increased service expectations and cost savings which did not meet projections, ardor for these mergers seems to have cooled. Many proposals have therefore been rejected; yet there have been approximately thirty city-county-consolidations in the U.S.

Federation, as the term implies, envisions the creation of a multi-purpose metropolitan area government, which then assumes the responsibility of performing many of the functions that were previously the responsibility of the federated localities. In addition, the metropolitan government is charged with many regional policy and planning functions with power to compel local unit compliance. The metropolitan county will have sufficient power to be a functioning central government. Yet the local units will retain some independence and their identity. Difficulties include choosing between or reconciling competing county and local power exercises.

It can readily be seen that this metropolitan remedy is politically difficult (e.g., for the reasons supporting defensive incorporation) and probably requires a metropolitan condition in which the suburban communities must see the center city or cities as important to their continued growth or existence. Such precondition may be affected by decisions to transfer commerce and industry to the suburbs or to remain in or return to the city.

Other city-county arrangements have included the creation of a city by the merger of counties. Different results occurred where the city was entirely within its county. Several cities were allowed to achieve independent status leaving the balance of the county to continue its separate existence. In some instances, the major city through a form of consolidation with the county undertook to perform some of the county government functions, although other intra-county localities remained in existence. In some jurisdictions such consolidations occurred long ago. Nevertheless, it is this method of creating a general metropolitan government by centralizing major functions while permitting retention of local identity which has been recently undertaken in some large metropolitan areas. This method utilizes a traditional governmental unit to which there has long been citizen "allegiance," or at least some sense of belonging, as a shell for the creation of the metropolitan central government. But it is faced with the same political and practical realities. Thus, for example, the new "unigovernment" may have to create two service districts, a general one embracing the entire county area, and an urban service district consisting of the total area of the principal city. Similar consolidations may be proposed for cities and their townships.

The consolidation may have been pressed to improve the city's deteriorating tax base (indeed, in one case under pressure by the major employer) with resulting disagreements among area voters. Challenges to the procedure for voter approval and to the failure to reorganize services which affect certain groups of neighborhoods may also accompany the venture.

E.   SOME PROBLEMS OF ORGANIZATION AND OPERATION—OFFICERS, EMPLOYEES, ALLOCATION AND DELEGATION OF FUNCTIONS, ELECTIONS AND REFERENDA

§ 1. Introduction

Incident to the organization and basic to the operation of local government units are the internal structure, the relationship of subordinate functionaries, the allocation of power within the unit, the ability to enact and implement legislation, and the involvement of the citizens in ongoing regulation, in effectuating political accountability or in overseeing government activity. A complete examination of the myriad details of employment relationships, typical offices, the legislative process and council meetings, methods of daily operation and the specific jurisdictional election and referendum differences is beyond the scope of this text. Nevertheless, certain significant matters deserve attention. For example, we shall briefly explore policies designed to assure proper motivation and integrity in government, and attempts to protect government employees and applicants from discriminatory treatment.

Earlier in this Chapter, the various alternative forms of local government's executive and legislative structures were mentioned. While there are apparent mixtures of classic governing roles, we shall see that there are policies designed to preserve the identity of the legislative, executive and administrative or judicial processes even where all are exercised by the same entity.

Frequently, for reasons of political protection or citizen involvement, private citizen roles in the governing process will raise suspicion that power has moved from publicly accountable officials to unaccountable private citizens who may act arbitrarily. Yet, as we shall see, some "citizen delegations" of power are approved by the courts.

Finally, at many points in the governing process from officer election to ordinance referendum the necessity of, scope of, and limitations upon the elective process must be paramount considerations in the exercise of local governing power.

§ 2. Employee Profile

In several cities most employees are in classified service. In others, a substantial number of the employees are by this means protected against the adversities of changing government administrations. In yet others, few employees are in classified service. Of course, municipal creation of a civil service requires state authorization unless recognized as an attribute of home rule. Frequently, government employees may be classified on a statewide basis; in those states, state legislative or administrative efforts in conflict with local policies involving local employees produce the inevitable preemption questions, particularly in home rule jurisdictions.

A municipality which has created a government employee cadre protected from the political vicissitudes may consist of the following: elected officials who are not in the classified service; a number of appointed officials whose positions are excepted from the classification system because their duties involve professional relationships, confidential relationships with elected officials, or functions that are viewed as necessarily or desirably politically accountable; civil service appointees who are chosen because of qualifications suitable for a particular position but who are not on a career competitive ladder with expectations of promotion; and employees in the career service, selected on the basis of their performance on a standardized exam and competing for merit system promotions and greater responsibilities.

The civil service and career service components of the merit system will likely be accompanied by appropriate and reasonable classification of positions and specificity of job descriptions, pay standardization for parallel positions and classes of positions, methods of selection and promotion including examination of pertinent skills and certification of results, provision for armed service veterans' preference in selection, selections in order from lists of eligible candidates, limitations on avoidance of the merit system by municipal contracts for services with outside concerns, provisions governing discharge and reduction in force, and retirement provisions (sometimes including pension fund, investment protections and policies).

§ 3. **Officers**

When the employment position is a public office, excepted from the merit system, the duration of the officer's entitlement to hold office is generally fixed by constitution, statute or charter. The incumbent may continue to hold office validly until a successor qualifies. An officer, elected or appointed, may be removed for cause through procedures set forth in existing legislation. There is authority supporting a common law power of local governments to remove for cause.

There is considerable variation among the jurisdictions in denominating particular positions as offices. Typically, the attributes which distinguish an office from an employment position are powers conferred by law, a fixed or specified term, tenure in office (including the right to receive the emoluments of office), personal liability, bonding, and the authority to exercise sovereign governmental functions. For example, one acting as legal officer of the city, representing it in court actions, and drafting or approving legal instruments to which the city may be a party, has been held to be invested with elements of the sovereign power of the city government. This distinction becomes necessary when cities attempt to create positions additional to those authorized by statute or charter in a manner neither expressed nor implied in their sources of power. The distinction may also be significant in interpreting the intent of prohibitions of dual officeholding.

§ 4.   Devices to Protect Against Conflicts of Duty and Interest

Certain constitutional, statutory, charter or ordinance provisions are designed to ensure that public officials, and in many instances government employees as well, serve in the pertinent office motivated solely to perform its functions for the public good. These provisions seek to avoid the complications inherent in dual officeholding and conflict of the public interest with the officeholder's personal financial interests or allegiances to a relative, patron, political party or foreign power. Such provisions may invite citizen vigilance by including public disclosure of personal finances, public disclosure of campaign finances, public meeting requirements of public bodies (extending, for example, even to state university faculty meetings), and some popular access to legislative and administrative proceedings and records. All such protections have been the basis for much litigation in which personal rights of the individual come into conflict with what is asserted to be the public interest. Thus, freedom of association and privilege against self incrimination, protections found in the first and fifth amendments to the U.S. Constitution, have limited overreaching government attempts to "guarantee the loyalty" of government employees.

Dual and Plural Offices

Constitutional, statutory, charter, or ordinance provisions or the common law itself may support a prohibition against dual officeholding. The common law doctrine is limited to "offices," although legislation may be more inclusive. The prohibition is intended to avoid the incompatibility which results from a conflict or inconsistency in the functions of offices held by one person where one government office is subordinate or subject to the supervision or control of another, or where the duties conflict, motivating the incumbent to choose one obligation over the other. Illustratively, a state legislator was not prevented by the common law doctrine from holding simultaneously a local position as township attorney, even though the township was entitled to lobby to seek or prevent state legislation. The court upheld the dual offices because neither the decision to lobby nor the duty to carry it out were necessary responsibilities of the attorney's office. In jurisdictions that consider avoidance of a conflict of interest an additional rationale for the doctrine, these facts might have created a violation.

Because the common law prohibition was limited in application to incompatible offices, and thus not applying more generally to prohibit plural office-holding, more inclusive state constitutional or legislative prohibitions have been adopted. Many states now regulate the ways in which the holder of one office may seek another. The prohibition of incompatible offices generally results in the forfeiting of (or "resignation" from) the first upon assumption of the second. The ban on plural offices generally presumes the holder of the first ineligible to hold the second. Specific provisions may identify offices that cannot be sought while the candidate holds another office. As in so many other areas, the question of equal protection of the laws can arise in classifying which officers must resign to seek another office and which may retain their present office until their quest for another is successful.

The incompatibility or simultaneous holding of an office subordinate to another need not always result in vacation of one of the incumbencies. Frequently when the superior office becomes vacant, the subordinate officer assumes its duties in a de facto, acting capacity under the applicable law. This does not violate the rule. Moreover, in jurisdictions where the common law rule is recognized, there exist numerous statutory authorizations of such situations as city councilors serving as special district board members. Where legislative approval exists, the common law rule is inapplicable.

Related to provisions presuming resignation or ineligibility are, of course, term limits. Whether they are viewed as ballot access limitations or as qualifications to run again or to hold office, office-holders at local, state, and, perhaps, federal levels face an eruption of efforts—indeed, have themselves adopted measures—to limit the number of consecutive terms they may serve. The consequences to the powers that turned on seniority and to the role of unelected staffs have yet to be measured. Limits applicable to local and state offices have been upheld by the courts. The U.S. Supreme Court has held that state-imposed term limits on that state's congressional delegation violate the federal constitution.

Conflict of Interest

The efforts to guard against conflicts of interest giving rise to potential improper motivation have support at common law and are manifested by numerous provisions invalidating municipal action and penalizing officers and employees who act in such circumstances. The common law and legislative provisions have raised a number of questions to which the jurisdictions give differing answers in this highly fact sensitive area. For example, can a prohibited conflict arise indirectly, or in non-financial circumstances, or in a matter from which the officer has withdrawn, or to which the pertinent body has given assent by an overwhelming majority? We shall see conflicts of interest again in our discussion of municipal contracts.

Related is the increasing adoption of ethics codes covering official appointments, relations with lobbyists and others while in office, and employment after leaving office.

Campaign and Personal Financial Disclosure

The subtleties of conflicts of interest are such that many critics deem the traditional protections insufficient at best. National, state and local governments have faced a formidable crisis of credibility and trust with the electorate. As a result, governments at all levels through legislative action and the people of several states through popular initiative have enacted laws designed to purify the electoral process. Illustratively, these laws require disclosure of campaign contributions and expenditures, limit contributions and expenditures, and require disclosure by public officials and candidates of personal financial information. The common goals of these laws are to publicize sufficient detail to permit citizen vigilance and to prevent improper influence by the threat of public disclosure and penalties for failure to disclose including disqualification for office.

Despite this laudable purpose and the overwhelming evidence of the necessity for additional protection, the "first generation" of these laws was frequently found too intrusive. On a policy level, critics are not unmindful of the fact that many of those who serve government at all levels have valid reasons to keep some of their financial circumstances private. Would the loss of these people to government service be too high a price to pay for the unproved benefits of public disclosure? In many instances, the courts found other "prices" too high. Personal finance disclosure requirements were invalidated as constituting an overbroad intrusion upon the right of privacy and thereby an unconstitutional restriction upon the right to seek or hold public employment or office. Required disclosure of campaign contributions and expenditures would be found wanting under the U.S. Constitution's first amendment if minor parties, their supporters and those doing business with them could suffer official and private harassment as a result of such disclosures. While the state's interest has supported strictly defined limitations on individual and group contributions, "first generation" limits on expenditures and the use of personal funds ran afoul of the first amendment. Strict scrutiny under the Equal Protection Clause and due process requirements of specificity in penal clauses (especially in light of the first amendment implications) resulted in invalidation of offending provisions. Laws that were held to impose additional eligibility requirements to those set forth in state constitutions for constitutionally enshrined offices were consequently invalidated. Here, as in other areas, state constitutions may offer more protection than the federal constitution. Of course, localities attempting to improve upon state law risk the preemption problems discussed earlier.

Hearing's attempted public disclosure law requires not only appropriate authorization but also careful drafting to avoid the substantial constitutional problems. Its authors must carefully assess the objectives to be achieved. Similar strategy governed the drafting of the "second generation" of these laws. Legislatures and legislative drafters reduced their expectations and attempted to devise laws that more closely met constitutional objectives, that reflected the first amendment interests, that were aimed only at substantial potentiality of conflict, that were more elastic in the categories of personal details to be disclosed, and that were designed to relate more specifically to conduct within the government's regulatory powers, vulnerable positions, and pertinent information. The "second generation" has been more successful in surviving challenges under heightened scrutiny. The Supreme Court ruled, by a narrow plurality, that the Federal Election Campaign Act's limitations on certain political party expenditures does not violate free speech or freedom of association guarantees. Heightened scrutiny was satisfied because the law was found to be closely drawn to match the sufficiently important government interest of combating political corruption. The ruling may indicate a similar fate for challenges to legislation aimed at banning otherwise unregulated "soft money," corporate and other large donations for funding electioneering communications.

§ 5. Residency Requirements

Some offices and positions in government are circumscribed by many other provisions of law which, like the foregoing, are designed to insure proper motivation and the appearance thereof, the absence of favoritism, full attention to duty and the use of government positions for their intended purposes. Illustrative are restrictions on nepotism, on outside work and on political activity. Of course, there is the frequent requirement that one be a bona fide resident in order to be eligible to vote or hold office. Other common provisions, designed to improve local knowledgeability and responsiveness, include three discrete residency requirements, each one serving a distinct goal. The first two may be characterized as prior residency requirements; the third, as a requirement of continuing residency.

The first requirement, applicable to all voters in a jurisdiction, demands a period of residency as a prerequisite to registration and voting. It is designed to ensure voter knowledgeability. Although such residency periods were at one time substantial, they have been sharply limited, though not completely outlawed, by the courts. One of the limitations' effects has been the enfranchisement of college students in the jurisdiction of their college residence.

The second type requires that persons who seek to be candidates for public office (and, perhaps public employment as well) reside in the appropriate jurisdiction for a specified time prior to the election. It is designed to ensure that potential public officers are locally knowledgeable. Judicial receptivity to lengthy requirements has been mixed, and especially inhospitable where the local demographic facts suggest that the prior residency requirement may discriminate against minorities.

The third may affect both offices and employment. It requires that, in order to hold a public position, the person in question either be a resident, or take up residence within the particular jurisdiction by a specified time after election to public office or entry upon employment. In addition, the individual must maintain resident status for the duration of the position. Its premise is that more responsible and responsive government will result when government officials and employees are themselves members of the community being governed. Continuing residency requirements have been held not to implicate an asserted constitutional right to travel, and where reasonable, i.e., where there is a reasonable link between the residency and the position for which it is required, will successfully withstand challenge under the federal constitution. They may occasionally be invalidated under state constitutional or statutory provisions but are more likely to be the subject of political rather than legal dispute. In urban communities, the push for more stringent official and employee residency requirements with particular attention to teachers, welfare personnel and police has confronted the necessity for communities to relax their requirements where the local cost of living was felt to be a hindrance to effective employee recruitment and retention.

§ 6. Challenged Employment Practices

The expanding scope of challenges to government employment practices includes assertions of federal constitutional and statutory protections against discrimination and unequal treatment in obtaining and retaining positions, assertions of federal first amendment rights in connection with restrictions on political practices, and dismissals from government employment.

Traditional hiring, job assignment and retention, and promotion policies have come under attack. Challenges have included position availability, entrance examinations, educational requirements, height and weight minimums, examination achievement levels as a condition of continued employment, physical skill, strength and endurance tests, job assignments and non-rotation policies harmful to promotion possibilities, merit promotion examinations, pay classifications, and maternity leave policies. These policies have been challenged for the allegedly discriminatory effect on the basis of race, ethnicity, alienage, age and sex in violation of equal protection or federal statutory provisions prohibiting such discrimination.

Equal Protection

The results of federal constitutional challenges to state and local action may be somewhat unpredictable because the U.S. Supreme Court has held that the equal protection clause only protects citizens from purposeful discrimination. Intent must be proved. Results will also depend on the level of scrutiny. The courts will engage in strict scrutiny and demand compelling justification where race or other suspect classifications or fundamental rights are implicated. Note, though, that the right to public or publicly funded private employment is not "fundamental" for equal protection purposes although the latter may be in an application of the Privileges and Immunities Clause protections. The courts may instead engage in intermediate scrutiny demanding substantial justification where important rights are involved and enhanced judicial solicitude is warranted. In other matters, rational justification of the classification will be sufficient, although the need for more persuasive "rational justification" may arise in some cases and not in others.

Race is a suspect classification involving a discrete and insular minority. A similar status befalls lawful aliens. The U.S. Supreme Court's treatment of lawfully resident aliens illustrates different levels of scrutiny. Generally, state or local legislation that discriminates on the basis of alienage will be sustained only if it withstands strict scrutiny, that is, if it can be defended as advancing a compelling governmental purpose. Examples of compelling state interests are relatively rare. However, courts are more tolerant of classifications based on alienage when the criterion is used by the state or local government to protect a legitimate and substantial interest in establishing the form of government and in limiting the right to govern to those who are full fledged members of the political community. Thus, while restrictions on lawfully resident aliens that primarily affect economic interests will be strictly scrutinized, a lesser standard of review will apply to evaluate exclusions of aliens from important elective and appointive positions involving duties central to representative government. Are the classifications tailored to the legitimate interest, or are they under-or over-inclusive? Is the classification applied to persons whose duties "go right to the heart of representative government"? Courts have nullified laws excluding aliens from eligibility for the admission to the bar, the competitive civil service, the practice of civil engineering, and the opportunity to serve as notary public. In contrast, they have applied the "political function exception" to uphold various citizenship requirements for police, public school teachers, and probation officers.

Statutory Challenges

It is important to note again that state constitutions and laws, if not preempted at the federal level, may offer greater public employee protection than is available under federal law. So too, federal statutes may provide protection where the constitution would not, by protecting individuals from actions with discriminatory impacts. Thus, countless cases have arisen under the federal civil rights statutes, particularly those involving age discrimination, pregnancy discrimination, the Americans with Disabilities Act, and employment discrimination under Title VII. The judicial decisions have produced a body of case law that is sufficiently substantial to be largely beyond the scope of this text. A good illustration may be employment discrimination challenges, as affected by the Civil Rights Act of 1991. The challenges to public employment actions may allege disparate treatment of the challenger, i.e., intentional discrimination because of protected status, or may assert a disparate impact upon a protected group.

In a disparate treatment case, the civil rights plaintiff must present evidence prima facie sufficient to prove that his or her protected status (race, gender, e.g.) played a motivating part in the employment decision, even if there were other motivating factors. The burden of production then shifts to the defendant, who may attempt to show that, without the discriminatory criterion, sufficient business reasons would have motivated the same employment action. The plaintiff, in turn, may show the justification to be pretextual. Business necessity is not a defense to a claim of intentional discrimination. But if the defendant's showing that it would have taken the action anyway is persuasive, the court may grant declaratory and injunctive relief and attorney's fees and costs directly attributable to the discrimination claim, but may not award damages or issue an order requiring any reinstatement, hiring, promotion, or back pay.

In a disparate impact case, the plaintiff is seeking to show that, even if the challenged practice (or the entire decisionmaking process if its elements cannot be separately analyzed) is fair and neutral on its face, it causes a discriminatory impact on the basis of race, color, religion, sex, or national origin, upon an identifiable, protected class of workers. In an indirect, circumstantial case, by a statistical showing, the proper comparison is between the racial (or other protected status) composition of the challenged jobs and positions and that of the qualified population of the relevant labor market, or equally probative alternatives. When the plaintiff has established this prima facie case, the defendant must demonstrate that the practice is required by business necessity or does not cause the disparate impact. If the defendant fails so to demonstrate, or if the plaintiff responds to a practice shown to be required by business necessity by offering a different, available employment practice with less discriminatory impact but with equal value in serving the employer's legitimate interests, and the employer refuses to adopt such practice, the plaintiff has carried the burden of proof.

Seniority systems are given special treatment under Title VII. In a government's employee reductions because of a financial exigency, established seniority systems may prevail over court-ordered, minority hiring goals to remedy Title VII violations. So too, when a seniority system is not the result of an intention to discriminate, its operation will not be an unlawful employment practice even if there are some discriminatory consequences. Thus, when seniority systems or changes therein are challenged under disparate impact theory, the challenge must be accompanied by proof of a discriminatory purpose. The adoption of a seniority system for an intentionally discriminatory purpose is an unlawful employment practice when an individual becomes subject to the seniority system or when a person is injured by its application. Application to local gov-

ernments of federal statutes prohibiting employment discrimination is not barred by assertions of
state sovereignty under the tenth amendment.

Remedies and Reactions

Shaping the appropriate remedy against a defendant government employer is difficult and politically volatile. The courts have required not only future
good conduct but back pay and remedial efforts to
make amends for past discrimination. Thus, a civil
service commission might be ordered to make a
new, non-discriminatory examination available to
all applicants; to place successful minority exami-
nees who had failed past examinations in a priority
pool, if otherwise qualified; to create a second pool
of eligibles from among those not identifiable as
discriminated against; to certify to requisitioning
police departments eligibles from the two pools on a
formula of one from the priority pool to every one to
three from the second pool. Or, a city might be
ordered to hire as many African American teachers
for the forthcoming school year as is necessary to
attain the racial ratio that existed before discriminatory in-service testing and minimum achievement
requirements were instituted. In another case, a
fifty percent minority promotion requirement imposed to remedy an equal protection violation in the
state police force was permitted under the fourteenth amendment.

After the finding of a constitutional or statutory
violation by the defendant government or agency,
there often follow remedies like the above specified

in a consent decree. Persons not the subject of orders or decrees may wish to challenge them. The 1991 Civil Rights Act, which has its own provisions affecting remedies, also covers these challenges. The Act provides that practices within a consent decree or court order may not be challenged by a person who, prior to the entry of judgment had notice and reasonable opportunity to object, or by a person whose interests were adequately represented by another who had previously challenged the decree or order.

State and local governments and agencies have not only complied with court orders, they have also voluntarily engaged in affirmative action. Non-minorities and males whose dismissals, hirings and promotions have been implicated in the implementation of the plans have challenged them under the federal constitution and statutes, alleging "reverse discrimination". The Supreme Court has decided that employment decisions based on race must be strictly justified even in reverse discrimination cases. But when the challenge is constitutional, only a bare majority of the Court has agreed that statistical comparisons must be of the number of minorities in the relevant pool qualified to undertake the positions' tasks, if they demand special qualifications. The Supreme Court has held that a plan to remedy minority or gender employment disparities must be justified by a compelling government interest and the means chosen must be narrowly tailored to achieve the plan's purpose. Remedying past discrimination by a state action is a sufficiently weighty state interest to warrant the remedial use of a carefully structured affirmative action plan. It may not be necessary to have a contemporaneous finding of past discrimination by the government as long as there is a "firm basis" for believing that remedy is warranted. If demonstrative evidence of a statistical disparity is to be used, the evidence must compare the percentage of qualified minorities now employed with the percentage of qualified minorities in the relevant labor pool before it can establish the required predicate to an affirmative action remedy under the fourteenth amendment. Thus, specific bona fide requirements or training will be taken into account when determining the relevant labor pool.

A majority of the Court has applied similar reasoning to "reverse discrimination" challenges (asserting that the employer improperly took race or gender into account) under Title VII. When the plaintiff establishes a prima facie case that race or gender has been taken into account in the employer's decision, the burden of production shifts to the employer to give a nondiscriminatory rationale for the decision. An affirmative action plan may provide that legitimate rationale. The burden of production then shifts back to the plaintiff to show that the plan is invalid and the rationale is pretextual. While the employer may be expected to offer evidence in support of the plan, the burden to demonstrate its invalidity is on the plaintiff. The plan will be valid even without an admission of past discrimination by the government employer if the following requirements are met: if it is based upon a manifest imbalance in a traditionally segregated job category (using the relevant labor force statistics described above); if it avoids unnecessarily trammeling upon the rights of non-minority or male employees or creating an absolute bar to their advancement (race or sex one of several factors, e.g.); and if it is intended to attain, not maintain, a balanced work force (a specified, limited duration for the plan's operation, e.g.).

First Amendment

The matter of dismissals has other constitutional perspectives involving the federal first amendment and due process requirements. Among the many first amendment concerns incident to local government employment are those related to patronage and those asserted in challenging dismissals or failures to rehire. While the dimensions of the full practical impact have not yet been realized, the federal first amendment rights have been held to predominate over traditional patronage considerations where retention of the government position in question requires allegiance to a particular political party (although coercion to join another party need not be proved), unless such political affiliation is proved to be an appropriate requirement for the effective performance of the policy making or confidential duties of the specific position. Re-employment, promotion, transfer and recall after layoff based on political affiliation or support are likewise prohibited because of the scope of public employees'

First Amendment rights. The Supreme Court has also extended this protection to independent contractors who supply services and materials to the government.

When a local government employee challenges the government's dismissal or failure to reemploy as an improper decision implicating first amendment rights, the challenger faces a considerable burden of proof. It must be shown that the employee's actions were constitutionally protected and were a substantial or motivating factor in the dismissal or refusal to reemploy. The government must have a reasonable and good faith belief as to the substance of the employee's speech before disciplining the employee. If the government employer can then show by a preponderance of the evidence that the same decision would have been reached even in the absence of the protected conduct, the employee's claim will fail. The employee's freedom of expression may, of course, be limited by appropriate time, place and manner regulations. The government employer may argue that the employee's speech has been disruptive of the operations of government. Police officers and firefighters may be, as a practical matter, more limited in their ability to speak on issues of public import than other local government employees because restraints are permissible when the employee's views are inconsistent with the mission of the employing agency and with the employee's role in the agency. Public employees retain their first amendment right to speak on matters of public concern even if they have a personal stake in the controversy. Criticisms of officials and official practices may appropriately result in dismissal if they do not involve matters of public concern, given their content, form and context. Dismissal or other challenged action may also be upheld if, in balancing the individual's and state's interests, the speech was found to be sufficiently disruptive of the defendant's efficient provision of services to warrant the action, which was then motivated to preserve the state's interest, not to punish protected speech. The cases apply the balancing test with considerable divergence. Finally, the government's action may be upheld if it would have occurred for legitimate reasons notwithstanding the contemporaneous exercise of free speech.

Due Process

Procedural due process implications in dismissals from public employment have expanded well beyond the vestigial theory that no one has a right to government employment. Explanations for discharge must be given and opportunity to respond must be afforded in the appropriate contexts. In order to invoke procedural due process rights at dismissal, the public employee must prove a "legitimate claim of entitlement" to the position, either pursuant to existing laws or a specific provision in the employment contract. Where a position is by law terminable only for cause, such a claim may be asserted. Where it is terminable at will, the claim is unavailing. The full extent of the "entitlement" test is evolving. For example, courts have refused to dismiss summarily an assertion by a non-tenured teacher (normally, no entitlement) that in the absence of an official tenure system at the public institution, he had relied on the security of de facto tenure earned after term of service. Applicants who successfully achieve positions on hiring or promotion eligibility lists have been held to have no claim of entitlement to appointment or promotion. Whether there is a claim of entitlement in any case will be decided by reference to state or local laws or contract. What process is due will be a fact sensitive conclusion of federal law, not necessarily cabined by the process set forth in the relevant state or local laws. The circumstances will require a pretermination hearing and will determine its scope; effective notice and an informal opportunity to be heard usually suffice.

The fourteenth amendment's Due Process Clause protects liberty interests. Even where there is no entitlement constituting the requisite property interest, due process considerations may be relevant. Thus, for instance, an employee may be granted the right to a name clearing hearing if dismissal would not only damage the person's chances of future employment, but would also stigmatize the employee by public dissemination of the damaging information said to be the cause of the dismissal.

§ 7. Public Employee Unions

The National Labor Relations Act does not cover state and local government employees. Their labor relations are covered by a mixture of the common law, numerous state statutes, and local ordinances. There is enormous variety, and local laws must be consulted.

Unions

The constitutions' protection of individual freedoms undergirds employee associational rights. The necessary balancing of government and individual interests, however, may tolerate appropriate limits. Thus, for example, in some states public employees will not be permitted to join a union that also represents private employees. In others, certain strategic employees (management, e.g.) may not be members of inappropriate bargaining units or, perhaps, of unions at all. There is substantial interstate variation on this point; consider, for instance, the union of school principals in New York City.

In the absence of statutes, the constitutions' protections, of course, do not require the government employer to listen or to agree to deal with government employee unions. Thus, given its right-to-work laws and other traditions, a state may choose not to authorize recognition of any union as bargaining representative for government employees. More likely, state statutes may authorize recognition after proper representation elections. If the union can be recognized as bargaining representative, has the employer been authorized at least to meet and confer or meet and discuss? Authority, if not express, may occasionally be implied; a finding of implied authority is more likely in the case of employees performing services and functions deemed proprietary rather than governmental. Note that, while the full extent of meet-and-confer authority may not have evolved, it does not include the requirement that the government enter into an agreement with the union.

Collective Bargaining

If collective bargaining is authorized, it would seem necessarily to imply that a labor agreement must be reached, although it must be noted that some government employer-bargainers, such as officials of a dependent school district, may not have full budget authority to execute a binding agreement. Wage agreements may then be subject to budget action at another level. Statutory authorization is always required and is available in many forms in several states. Government employers may be permitted but not required to engage in collective bargaining, may be permitted to bargain only on some subjects, may be required to bargain (mandatory bargaining) on some subjects, or may be generally authorized but specifically prohibited from bargaining on certain subjects. There may be particular laws covering such selected groups as teachers, police and fire personnel. "Sunshine laws" may require that some of the negotiations sessions be public.

Certain premises have long acted as counterweights to the development of public employee labor relations and indeed have underlain the many restrictive interpretations of the common law. Collective bargaining, and especially employee strikes, are a surrender or denial of government sovereignty; bargaining and associated techniques change the appropriate role of government from unilateral regulation to bilateral agreements; and collective bargaining agreements and their dispute resolution mechanisms bind the government to exercise power in a predetermined way. Thus, they are subject to the criticisms that they improperly tie the hands of subsequent governments, and that they constitute an improper delegation of power into politically unaccountable hands. The counterweights are sometimes reflected in a judicial search for authority to bargain and sensitivity to apparent statutory preemption, in judicial attitudes toward arbitration, and especially in judicial and public reactions to public employee strikes.

Statutory Interpretation

To determine whether the matter at issue is a subject for bargaining, some courts are flexible, recognizing the evolutionary development of collective bargaining. Other courts, in contrast, are strict in their search for state authorization in interpreting the inevitably vague, ambiguous, or generic terms of the statutes to determine whether the matter at issue is a subject for bargaining. Does it involve working conditions or managerial discretion? The courts may seek to decide whether the agreement on the matter is the permitted exercise of government discretion or the prohibited surrender of it. The state's labor laws and other legislation may speak to the matter. Which statutory terms govern? Does the statute impose standards that limit discretion or prohibit its exercise in a certain way, or does it merely set forth procedural requirements for the decisionmaking process? Does the statute enable bargaining on the matter or mandate it? Has the statute set forth minimum requirements and permitted discretion beyond the minimum or has it preempted bargaining and set fixed terms?

Arbitration

Early judicial and legislative reluctance has given way to approval of at least some kinds of arbitration to resolve disputes. Arbitration may be voluntary or compulsory, and binding or advisory. Resolution of disputes during the bargaining process may involve mediation and interest arbitration. The latter, generally voluntary, is likely to be compulsory as to some classes of employees, such as those whose sensitive positions may be accompanied by strike prohibitions. Grievance arbitration to resolve disputes during the collective bargaining agreement's implementation period is least vulnerable to judicial interference when the results are deemed advisory. When grievance arbitration is binding, the courts can play a role in determining whether the dispute is arbitrable under the agreement, whether the result is governed by or subject to additional legislation, or whether the agreement's promise to arbitrate this sort of issue is invalid as contrary to law. It has been suggested that courts sitting in industrial states may be more comfortable with labor relations techniques customary in the private sector.

State Labor Board

The alleged failure to negotiate or other problem may be the subject of complaint to the state labor board. Exercising its administrative expertise and authority under the labor statutes, the board will make the initial determination whether there has been an unfair labor practice.

Strikes

One of the most volatile issues in public employee labor relations is employee use of the strike weapon and related job actions. So called "sick-outs" and "work to rules" actions, where employees strictly follow the letter of all rules applicable to their jobs, thus slowing down the process of government, are similarly controversial. The counterweights mentioned above, and the need both to protect against coercive paralysis of essential services and to preserve government's ability to determine budget needs and priorities have led to the prohibition of strikes by legislation and at common law. Enforcement of the prohibition may include injunctions and the contempt power, such sanctions as fines, jail sentences, suspensions, dismissals, and forfeiture of bargaining representational status. Even private damage actions have been explored.

Despite the potential penalties and in the face of overwhelmingly negative public sentiment, public employee strikes and job actions abound. Courts and legislatures in an increasing number of states have concluded that there are sufficient alternatives to safeguard the public interest and that blanket prohibition of public employee strikes is both unworkable and unhelpful to a sound negotiation process. At least one court reached this conclusion in applying the continuing, evolving common law. Removal of the prohibition has been heavily circumscribed by such limitations and conditions as: unavailability for essential services directly related to public health and safety; use only in disputes during negotiations, not for grievances; injunctions when strikes' durations or targets constitute a serious danger to the public health and safety; and the requirement that employees first exhaust carefully prescribed bargaining or dispute resolution processes before filing for judicial relief.

Civil Service–Collective Bargaining Conflict

Civil service statutes and statutes dealing with public employee labor relations present conceivable conflicts between the merit system and the objectives of permissible collective bargaining. The states which have attempted statutory resolutions seem equally divided among such responses as absolute priority to the civil service laws in all matters; absolute priority to the civil service laws on certain, specified matters; or dispute resolution left to the discretion of the local government employer. The majority of states, however, have attempted no legislative solution and hence have left to the courts the difficult task of defining the appropriate applicability of the two sets of laws.

Agency Shops and Non-member Dues

Public employee unions have sought to have "union shops" in which all employees in the particular bargaining unit must join the union or, at least, the more common "agency shops" in which the employees need not join the union but must contribute union dues. Agency shops that have resulted from agreements by the government employer, and the frequent additional agreement for dues check-off by the employer as pay is distributed, have brought to the U.S. Supreme Court the confrontation between dues payers' constitutional rights and unions' use of some dues proceeds for political purposes. The Court has approved the agency shop concept but has demanded that such a plan draw a careful line between dues and political contribution portions. A constitutionally adequate plan must minimize the risk of even temporarily impermissible use of non-members' contributions, must provide adequate justification for advance deduction of dues, and must furnish to non-members a reasonably prompt opportunity to challenge the use of dues and the portion so used before an impartial decisionmaker.

Union Issues

State and local governments' labor relations involve a multiplicity of issues common to labor relations generally. Some, however, may be peculiar to public employees because their employer is the government. Illustrative are three areas of concern to public employee unions: drug and disease testing;

voluntarily adopted comparable worth plans; and privatization.

Drug and Disease Testing

Government testing of testing of blood, urine, and other bodily-fluids may arise in a variety of contexts. The government may be interested in screening for drug use or disease, and may seek to impose a process that is either widespread or localized, mandatory, universal, or random. In this context, the government is, of course, a state actor whose actions must pass constitutional muster in light of search, privacy, self incrimination, and due process rights. Federal civil rights statutes, state constitutions and laws, and collective bargaining agreements may be involved and may provide stricter protections than the federal constitution. While the final chapter on this matter is far from complete, and while there is divergence among the courts, that some guideposts are developing may be illustrated by the search and seizure issue. Under classic federal fourth amendment jurisprudence drug and disease testing constitutes a search and therefore must meet requirements of reasonableness. Are the employees in a position of diminished expectations of privacy? Was the search justified at inception by an interest other than general law enforcement, and was it conducted in a manner reasonably related to the matter justifying the search? Was there individualized reasonable suspicion to search the government employee? Reasonable suspicion requires a combined showing of quantity of information and indicia of reliability of that information, but it sets a lower threshold than probable cause as required in criminal cases. Absent reasonable suspicion, drug and disease testing is impermissible unless there is a "special need" to conduct suspicionless testing. That standard has been interpreted as meaning that the government has an interest in preventing substantial and real risk to the public safety, and that the interest is distinct and apart from the interest in law enforcement generally. Chandler v. Miller (S.Ct.1997); Ferguson v. City of Charleston (S.Ct.2001).

The courts differ on whether a random testing program is akin to administrative, warrantless searches in the enforcement of building and housing codes. Where allowed at all, random searches without reasonable suspicion will be closely scrutinized, and the individual's privacy expectations must be balanced against the government's interests to determine whether requiring a warrant of individualized suspicion in the particular context is impractical. Random testing generally will only be approved where privacy interests are minimal, the government's interest is substantial, and safeguards are provided to ensure that the individual's reasonable expectation of privacy is not subject to unregulated discretion. Courts differ on the nexus required to justify suspicionless random testing. Some courts require a showing of causal connection between the employee's duties and the feared harm, e.g., drug use by drug-interdiction agents. Some courts, rejecting the analogy to administrative searches, say that the reasonable suspicion has to be individualized to the person targeted for the testing. Others require only that a nexus exist between the risk posed (drug-using employee) and the evil sought to be prevented by the testing, regardless of whether the employee's job duties relate to the proffered evil. Under this formulation, regular office workers in a sensitive government building could be subjected to random testing to protect substantial government interests.

The U.S. Supreme Court has upheld federal regulations imposing drug testing, without a warrant or individualized suspicion of misconduct, on customs employees who sought drug-interdiction positions or who were required to carry firearms, and on railroad employees involved in train accidents. In those cases, the Court concluded that the searches were reasonable in light of strong government interest in a drug-free work force in sensitive law enforcement and safety positions. It is worth noting that the Court has also emphasized the importance of governmental concern, together with reduced expectations of, and negligible intrusion upon privacy, in upholding random, suspicionless urinalysis testing of public school student athletes. In contrast, the Court rejected suspicionless tests of all candidates for state office for the sole purpose of demonstrating the state's commitment to the struggle against. drug abuse.

Comparable Worth

Comparable worth efforts are designed to remove the vestiges of gender discrimination in assigning pay levels to positions traditionally held by women. Comparisons of these positions with others determined by studies to be comparable in training required, skills and challenges may demonstrate significant pay differentials that may be or have been the result of gender discrimination. So long as they fall within the applicable statute of limitations, past differentials and the costs of pensions and other fringe benefits may be included. Thus, the remedial costs may be very high. Litigation under federal equal pay and non-discrimination laws has not been notably successful, because courts have not been persuaded that the laws applied or that discrimination was proved. Nevertheless, public employee unions have negotiated carefully sequenced, multi-stage plans to achieve comparable worth pay status in the public work forces of some states and cities.

Privatization

"Privatization" is the term given to contemporaneous efforts to turn to private industry for a wide range of government's "governmental" and "proprietary" services. Among the services most frequently subject to privatization efforts are jails; hospitals; transit; waste collection and recycling; street and traffic light operation; vehicle towing and storage; ambulances; utility billing and meter reading; emergency medical treatment; legal services; labor relations; paving; sewers; snow removal; parks, buildings and grounds maintenance and security; vehicle maintenance; printing; data processing; insect and rodent control; payroll; public relations; tax assessing; personnel services; and secretarial services. Some cities contract for such services. Others also make city departments bid in competition with the private sector. Yet others divide service areas among private contractors and city departments.

The proponents argue that privatization is more efficient and helps to "reinvent government." In addition, they allege, it decreases the administrative burden on governments, enhances the government's opportunity to focus on policy, improves accountability and cost benefit judgments, and increases competition driven productivity within city departments. From a financial perspective, privatization is praised for its ability to reduce city personnel commitments from civil service longevity to the duration of the contracts with the private sector.

Opponents—with public employee unions in the lead—argue that there is no conclusive evidence of greater efficiency. Privatization masks unwillingness to reform government services. If there is less efficiency in government, it stems from labor policies that ought to be applied to the private sector or discontinued. They warn that privatization is frequently a subterfuge for the curtailment of services. The poor will suffer because service will not be economical. Private contractors will bid low and later raise prices when the city has abandoned its capacity to provide the services. Privatization, they say, will serve to resurrect widespread contractor patronage.

§ 8. Restrictions on the Exercise of Executive, Administrative, Legislative and Judicial Functions

An earlier section alluded to the variety of executive-legislative forms available to local governments. The evident possibility of a board of commissioners or council exercising legislative and administrative functions raises the specter of the doctrine of separation of powers. For example, the board of commissioners could enact the basic governing building code, and could thereafter be the entity which grants or denies permits or considers appeals from grants or denials. The mayor may be a voting member of the legislative body, may execute legislation and may be the magistrate who adjudges violations of local ordinances. The possible combinations are limitless.

Separation of Powers and Functions

It is often said that the doctrine of separation of powers is not applicable to local government. If the doctrine is understood to mean separate powers exercised by separate co-equal entities, with checks and balances, the statement is correct. It does not mean, however, that the functions which are classified as legislative, executive and judicial are so blurred as not to be separately identifiable. Even where one entity seems to possess powers in all classifications, the rules governing their exercise will help to identify the separate functions and the results which accompany such exercise.

Local Legislature—Ordinances and Resolutions

The distinction between ordinances and resolutions may illustrate this. Where statutes and general ordinances are silent concerning the mode in which a municipal governing body may implement the powers conferred on it, the governing body may express its will by either ordinance or resolution. Again, where a statute confers numerous powers, some by provisions expressly requiring enactment by ordinance, others by provisions silent as to the mode of enactment, the municipality may implement the latter powers by either ordinance or resolution. The choices are subject to the qualification that resolution enactments must reflect decisions that are "administrative" as opposed to "legislative" in nature. To draw this distinction, it is necessary to examine the scope and purpose of a given enactment. An enactment is "legislative" to the extent that it provides a permanent rule of government or conduct designed to affect matters arising subsequent to its adoption. An enactment is "administrative" to the extent that it deals with temporary or special matters and involves only a factual determination that conditions necessary for the operation of a statute or general ordinance have been met. Accordingly, where the appropriate statute or general ordinance is in effect, a municipal governing body may enact resolutions to grant permits, sell particular parcels of municipal property, build bridges, establish nurseries to supply parks, order removal of specific buildings, among myriad other acts.

The most likely circumstances to be considered "legislative" and to require the more time consuming and expensive ordinance form are those where, under the rule of "equal dignity," the council seeks to amend or repeal an ordinance, or where the council seeks to regulate the conduct of persons or the uses of property and to impose a penalty of fine, imprisonment or forfeiture for violation.

The determination whether a given enactment may be implemented pursuant to ordinance or resolution is of critical importance to the municipal council. If the council is exercising legislative power, its action may be subject to mayoral veto, if permitted. If the council is exercising legislative power, it may only do so in legislative session or on days designated by its charter as legislative. Its action may be petitioned to referendum by the electorate. The determination whether a matter is legislative or administrative also underlies the ability of the electorate to initiate legislation in those jurisdictions where popular initiative is permitted.

To enhance the electorate's ability to oversee legislative activity, such exercises may be required to be taken at public meetings, after legislative hearings, with appropriate notice. While regular meeting days may be set forth in the charter, notice of special meetings or special subjects may be required not only for council members but also to accommodate the jurisdiction's open meeting requirement. Legislative enactments will likely require a number of readings before final passage and appropriate publication thereafter.

It should be noted that municipal councils may be allowed to hold emergency legislative sessions with resultant short circuiting of the various requirements. The jurisdictions are split over who has the final say in determining the existence of an emergency, the council or the courts.

Conversely, if the council's power exercise is deemed "administrative," it may be taken in executive session. The matter will not be subject to popular referendum. There will be no mayoral veto. The hearings, if any, may be investigatory. The council sessions need not be public and the enactment will not require several readings before final passage.

To illustrate, let us again assume our hypothetical public disclosure law. Its councilmanic proponents may fear a mayoral veto. They may also worry that a properly filed citizen demand for referendum may result in suspension of the law as well as substantial time and expense. The number of signatures needed to invoke the referendum process may be within reach of a consortium of influence interests, political opponents and persons who are sensitive to the law's privacy implications. Accordingly, and as a result of these factors, further suppose that the law has been enacted in executive session. To the power source, preemption and constitutional challenges illustrated earlier in this text, the council has now created the possibility that opponents may attack the resolution or ordinance as improperly enacted. It may in fact be easier for the opposition to mount a court challenge than it would be to produce the necessary votes to win a referendum.

If a court subsequently invalidates this power exercise—a most likely result although councils continue to try this route—there may then be a long delay before the next charter specified "legislative session" of the council. It will be necessary for councilmanic proponents to obtain the necessary, probably charter indicated, quorum majority to declare the need for an emergency legislative session in order to avoid the delay. The limited time allowed by the charter may be insufficient to accomplish the necessary, open, legislative process so that the council may be left with no alternative than to declare an "extension" of the last "legislative day."

Once again, the council may have afforded opponents the opportunity to test in court the validity of the emergency designation or the failure to adjourn so as to extend the limits. And still the opposition has not yet had to confront the law on its merits.

If one assumes that the councilmanic proponents of the many actual attempts which resemble our illustration were not poorly advised, or that the legislative-administrative characterization of the contemplated action was not really debatable, one is left with the question whether a power exercise in which so much is risked to avoid popular reaction is worth council approval. And if one believes that the council should take a leadership position despite possibly adverse constituent reaction, are not the benefits of popular education attendant upon a well run referendum worth the risk of failure and better in any event than the "back door" approach?

Local Executive and Courts

The local executive possesses only such powers as are conferred by statute or charter. In some forms of local government this may include independent powers such as administrative department supervision, or the power to veto legislative enactments of the council subject to override.

Two further considerations of power separation should be mentioned. Inevitably, the courts will be separate even at the local level. They will customarily be subject to the supervisory authority, or be actual components, of the state court system. Occasionally, the functions of magistrate will be blurred.

Even where the separate functions intermixed in one entity are surrounded by safeguards such as the above, there may be circumstances in which an individual's constitutional right to due process is affected by the compelling intermingling of responsibilities and allegiances. Illustratively, the U.S. Supreme Court invalidated a traffic offense conviction imposed by the city's mayor sitting as authorized as judge in traffic court, not because the union of executive and judicial power in him was wrong, but because his responsibilities for the city budget and revenues to which his court's fines substantially contributed, and his participation as tiebreaking voter on the city council, placed him in a situation of virtually irresistible temptation. He was officially charged with inconsistent duties, one partisan, the other judicial. The inconsistency necessarily risked a lack of due process, which the Supreme Court held deprived the offender of a trial before an impartial judicial officer.

§ 9. Delegation of Implementation Authority

It is said that the local government is the recipient of appropriately delegated state authority and cannot re-delegate it to its subordinate agents, whether they be government employees or private entities. The statement must be qualified in several ways. While the doctrine of non-delegation among co-equal branches of state government may be rooted in state constitutional concepts of separation of powers, due process measures appropriate delegation of local legislative power by the state to its local governments and delegations by legislatures at both levels of administrative and adjudicative powers. What must distinguish the legislative discretion that cannot be delegated from implementation of policy choices legislatively made are standards sufficiently restrictive of administrative or adjudicatory discretion to prevent arbitrary conduct. The involvement of private citizens does not necessarily indicate an improper delegation because the citizens may have reserved to themselves (either by state constitution or local charter) a role in the legislative process (directly through initiative or referendum), or because their role in implementation of the legislative power is sufficiently circumscribed by standards.

Illustration—Legislative vs. Administrative

As noted, the determination whether delegated discretion is legislative or administrative will frequently turn on the adequacy of the standards governing the delegated authority. Courts are inconsistent in the strictness with which they view such standards. Generally, courts are likely to be stricter when power is delegated to private citizens, fairly rigorous when "governmental" powers are at issue, and least demanding when the matters are "proprietary." Inconsistency may reflect judicial recognition of the practical realities of day to day government. It may also be based the court's recognition of the negative consequences of strict enforcement of the standard. After all, local legislators are frequently part-time and meet only periodically. As a result, in many instances, courts are likely to affix the administrative label to delegations by local governments that are based on a general rule with adequate standards to guide the delegate in the rule's implementation. In this regard, courts may be sympathetic to the arguments that the problem occurs too frequently for the legislative body to pass upon individual instances, or that the generic legislation is amenable to case by case implementation upon a determination of specified factual prerequisites by the delegate. To illustrate, compare legislation which delegates to the chief of police the authority to set speed limits and parking regulations in the downtown business area (invalid) with legislation authorizing the chief of police to reduce speed limits to ten miles per hour and to impose parking bans when, during stormy weather, major downtown commercial events or rush hour, traffic conditions become hazardous (valid). The adequacy of the delegation will be affected by such factors as the frequency of need to cope with minimally different factual situations, the need for emergency response, the social usefulness of the conduct regulated, judicial experience with local administrative responsibility, the competence and qualifications of the public official, and the inherent limitations of the language to express adequately the variations to be foreseen.

Citizen Involvement

The roles of private citizens in the exercise of local government authority have several dimensions. In many jurisdictions, by constitution, statute or charter, the local government's citizens are accorded a legislative role in the exercise of initiative (enactment of legislation by the voters), referendum (approval or disapproval by voters of legislation enacted by the local government), or recall (mid-term removal of local officials upon vote of the citizenry). All processes involve similar notice, petition and election steps with attendant questions discussed elsewhere in this text. Recall may have specific requirements limiting the target offices and necessitating statement of reasons. The responsive roles of the local government during and after the processes may be specified in order to avoid the necessity of the election, if possible, and to protect the results from immediate reaction. It is important to note that by initiative or referendum, the people cannot accomplish what the local legislative body could not achieve, whether the limitation be the authority of the local government to act on the matter, preemption of otherwise appropriate action at another competent but predominant governmental level, or predominance of such other constitutional clauses as home rule or of constitutionally protected rights. The exercise of such popular roles, if otherwise appropriate, is not an improper delegation of authority. In fact, it may not be deemed a delegation at all, but rather, in the words of the Supreme Court, "a power reserved by the people to themselves."

In other contexts, local governments have attempted to allot to private citizens localized roles in the exercise of local governing powers. Municipalities have given effective control over a regulatory scheme to private citizens for a multiplicity of reasons. It may be because the city government lacked the political courage to regulate in the face of citizen protest, because the matter in question could better be handled by those in the pertinent expert discipline, or because the municipality deemed it more effective to decentralize or to involve the affected electorate in the ongoing regulation. Thus, for example, municipalities have attempted to allow building lines to be determined by the owners of neighboring properties, to ban billboards and gasoline service stations unless property owners within the affected area consent to their construction, to require substantial neighbor consent in the affected

area for the construction and operation of philanthropic homes for the aged or children in a residential zone, or to involve the rental property owners
themselves in the setting of rent controls.

The rule against re-delegation of legislative authority and the necessity of adequate standards are
the operative factors incident to such apparent delegations of discretionary authority to private citizens. For example, where adequate standards were
coupled with the direct involvement of municipal
officers (factors governing and limits upon rent
control; mayoral appointment of appeals board, e.g.)
and no power was given to the private citizens to
adopt or amend any ordinances, involvement of the
owners of rental property in the implementation of
rent control laws was upheld as proper. Where,
however, delegation to private citizens of the authority to impose restrictions on the use of others'
property is not coupled with adequate standards to
control discretion, there is a high risk of arbitrary
and capricious exercise. The courts have not invalidated the delegations simply because the delegates
are private citizens not politically accountable.
Rather, the apparent total discretion thus delegated
is deemed to constitute an invalid delegation of
legislative authority because the use upon which
restriction may be placed, itself valid and not restricted or prohibited by the city, is a matter over
which the private citizens have complete sway. Restriction of the use, then, becomes a matter of whim
in the absence of controlling standards, and the

private group substitutes improperly for the elected council.

There have been mixed results when the local government has imposed restrictions and the power delegated to private citizens is the removal of those legislatively adopted standards. The judicial inquiry in a challenge to this type of delegation of power will focus on the interests of those given the right to remove the restrictions. If the power of consent is held by those who would be most directly affected by the restrictions' removal and by those who have a property interest near the area affected by the restrictions, a court is less likely to see the potential of arbitrary and capricious decisionmaking. As a result, it is more likely to uphold the delegation as proper.

The interests of nearby property owners in permitting a restricted use may not always be an adequate substitute for explicit standards, however. The nature of the delegates' interests may itself bar the delegation. For instance, where churches and schools were granted the power to prevent the award of liquor licenses for premises within a specified area, the delegation to those private entities did not merit the deference normally due a legislative zoning judgment. Because it replaced reasoned government action with standardless authority that could advance religious objectives, the delegation entangled the churches in the processes of government. On that basis, the Supreme Court invalidated the local law under the Establishment Clause of the federal first amendment.

§ 10. Elections and the Fourteenth Amendment

Having decided to tackle the thorny issues related to local governments' elections for local offices or to the exercise of initiatives and referenda, the U.S. Supreme Court and the lower federal courts developed to a substantial extent the dimensions of the dictates of the fourteenth and fifteenth amendments to the U.S. Constitution. In doing so, the courts confronted the myriad forms of local government, the occasional responsiveness of those forms to local needs, disparities of voting strength, and limitations frequently favoring rural interests, long-term residents, the white majority, or owners of real property. Some referenda had historically been designed on other than a simple majority basis, excluded some people from participation where their interests were not as great as others', and were limited to certain legislative subject matter. Historically, popular approval or rejection of government legislation might sometimes occur only if an extraordinary majority voted to do so. Historically, the property tax played so large a role in local revenue that property owners were accorded the exclusive right to reject municipal debt that would have a direct effect on their property tax or values. Historically, on some matters referenda were mandatory; on others referenda might be conducted at the behest of the government unit or of a specified number of citizens.

The courts' development of applicable principles has led them to analyze questions ranging from ballot access to the issues in referenda, from poll taxes to party governance, and from reapportionment to gerrymandering. Elections for elective offices had to be distinguished from discrete, "single-shot" electoral exercises, such as referenda and initiatives. In brief, the results may best be seen as answers to three questions: What is the subject matter of the election? Who may vote? How is that vote to be counted?

What Is the Subject

There are local government structures that envision appointed members. The courts have reviewed election mechanisms where the governments have determined to have elections. They have not substituted their judgment for that of the local entities on whether offices shall be elective or appointive. The subject matter of a regular election to elective offices necessarily includes who may be on the ballot and the pertinent role of political parties. The courts have scrutinized laws governing write-in voting, ballot access by minor parties and independent candidates, and term limits. They have also dealt with challenges to laws proscribing party endorsements in non-partisan elections, which in turn are often the results of earlier reforms to make local governments less subject to partisan pressure. Several interests are relevant to the judicial balance. First, the state has a legitimate interest in assuring that items on the ballot have sufficient local support, so as to avoid ballot confusion. The state might also be concerned about preserving the political independence of local government offices. Second are the constitutional rights of the individuals subject to the limits to speak freely or associate for political purposes. Third, the court may factor in a concern for the rights of qualified voters to cast their votes effectively. And finally, depending on the case, some federal interest may weigh in the balance, such as the power of Congress to judge the qualifications of its own members. Strict scrutiny and compelling justification are involved when the right to vote is severely restricted. In other cases, heightened scrutiny demanding substantial justification is directed to the nature of the injury, the interest asserted by the government, the effect of one on the other, and the necessity for imposing the burden rather than a less onerous alternative. Note the analogous free speech evaluations of campaign contribution limitations.

There are elections to choose among candidates for what may be called "one-shot" boards, such as a board to design a plan for reorganization of a city and county which will subsequently be presented to the electorate. Longstanding laws may limit membership to freeholders. Referring to election and referendum cases, the U.S. Supreme Court unanimously invalidated such a limitation as not rationally related to the purposes of the board, and thus did not address whether strict or heightened scrutiny was needed.

In "single-shot" electoral exercises, subject matter is often a constitutionally determinative factor. Where local law authorizes popular approval or rejection on some issues and not on others, the alleged disproportionate impact of subject matter of the referenda may be the focal point of the election challenge. The fact of the referendum, we have seen, is not an improper delegation of legislative authority. But like the legislative enactments thereby reviewed, it is subject to constitutional limits. Where the referendum's availability is not a constitutionally improper classification disadvantaging "discrete and insular minorities," making it more difficult to enact legislation on their behalf (local fair housing ordinances, e.g.), then the fact that referenda are permitted or required on some issues (public housing, zoning for land use, e.g.) does not offend equal protection. Likewise, states may not limit the availability of initiatives or referenda in a way that disadvantages a particular group. Accordingly, where a state statute prohibited any legislative action, including initiative or referenda, designed to protect individuals from discrimination on the basis of their sexual orientation, the Supreme Court found the law to be violative of the Equal Protection Clause, and without rational relationship to a legitimate state interest.

Referenda and initiatives also involve issues of ballot access—for the subject matter. Laws that regulate the process for qualifying referenda and initiatives significantly affect subject matter ballot access for particular individuals and groups. The first and fourteenth amendment principles have led courts to invalidate laws that limited petition signers on the basis of their ethnic, party, or property-ownership statuses. Similarly, concerns about freedom of speech have led courts to invalidate laws that proscribed the use of paid signature gatherers. Similarly, the Supreme Court ruled that a state statute requiring that initiative proponents report the names, addresses and amounts paid to each circulator violated the First Amendment's free speech guarantee. Laws regulating subject matter ballot access may also be challenged as granting or limiting ballot access on the basis of wealth. One state court upheld an act that would render a referendum on funding a public sports stadium null and void unless the team affiliate entered into an agreement with the State to reimburse the state and counties for the cost of a special election. Even if the team affiliate had gained access to the ballot based on wealth, the court reasoned, the people had an alternate means to place a measure on the ballot through the petition process.

Who May Vote

Substantially assisted by constitutional provisions and statutes, the courts rather early cleared away such obstacles to exercise of the voting franchise as improper residency requirements and prohibitive poll taxes. A state constitutional provision disenfranchising persons convicted of enumerated felonies and misdemeanors, including crimes of "moral turpitude," was invalidated under the Equal Protection Clause because, while facially neutral, it was adopted with racially discriminatory intent and operated in accordance therewith. Found unconstitutional under the federal fifteenth amendment was an attempt to reconfigure municipal lines thereby disenfranchising minority municipal voters. In addition, persons who were not municipal residents were not permitted to assert their inability to vote to invalidate municipal exercise of extraterritorial powers, although there was some suggestion that extraterritorial powers might at some point be so expansive as to amount to annexation in fact if not in name. The failure to extend the franchise would then be more successfully attacked.

Courts have invalidated state statutes that have attempted to control in detail the structure and processes of political parties or to override party determinations of who may vote in party primaries. The judicial invalidations have found violations of the members' speech, associational and voting rights. Note that such rights, however, did not insulate party limitations that themselves violated equal protection. Consider, for instance, the "white primaries" mandated by a Texas statute commanding that "in no event shall a negro be eligible to participate in a Democratic party primary election." Even where the political parties were simply invested by the state legislature with authority to limit membership, beyond the will of the party, the parties were found to be governmental instruments and thus subject to principles of Equal Protection. Nixon v. Condon (S.Ct.1932).

When the local government has determined to fill an office in a regular election, to fill a temporary office, or to engage in popular legislative initiative or review by elections, then persons cannot be denied the vote by classification inconsistent with the demands of equal protection. The right to vote is fundamental. Denial, therefore, must be compellingly justified. Where the asserted distinction of interests is deemed insufficiently compelling, government attempts to limit the vote will be invalidated. On that basis, for example, courts have invalidated a provision that limited voting rights in school board elections to people who owned property, leased property, or had a child attending school in the jurisdiction. Similarly invalid was a provision limiting a vote on government issuance of bonds to property owners and a provision limiting a local vote on the location of an airport to those who lived in the city, thus denying the franchise to those living near the improvement. Where, however, the franchise is extended to all who are disproportionately affected by the operations of a special purpose, local government unit of limited functions, in an election designed to give greater influence to the constituent groups found to be most affected by the government unit's functions, such extension is not a denial to other potential voters. In an electoral challenge seeking to exclude voters, the challenger must show that the statute's extension of the franchise is wholly unrelated to the election's purpose.

A related group of cases suggests that where a franchise need not be extended, but is, objections to the extension may not be successful. Consider the issue of "dual resident voting"; in some states, local governments have been authorized to extend the vote to nonresident property owners. This area of franchise law is particularly relevant considering the rapidly increasing number of older citizens who move to warmer climes for several months during the year, as well as the growing phenomenon of second and third vacation homes. Courts have rejected challenges from the permanent residents that extension of the vote to nonresidents impermissibly diluted the strength of the residents' vote.

Decennial redistricting responsive to the interests of minority voters has resulted in the creation of minority representational districts. The Supreme Court ruled that use of race as a factor in redistricting is permissible as long as racial considerations did not predominate over race-neutral districting principles. However, since racial classifications (benign or otherwise) are presumptively invalid, the U.S. Supreme Court has held that white voters who demonstrate that they were assigned to a district because of their race may assert equal protection challenges to such newly created congressional districts. Subsequent examination of the districts has led the Supreme Court to invalidate a district when the challenger showed that race was the predominant factor in its creation.

How Counted

When the right to vote is not denied, there remains the complex balancing process demanded by assertions that the impact of the vote of particular persons or groups is diluted by lines which have been improperly drawn under equal protection analysis. Dilution of the vote can take many forms. For instance, more votes may be needed to elect one representative than a comparable group needs to elect an equal representative. More votes may be needed to uphold local government legislation than to reject it, or the converse. Concurrent majorities in areas of unequal population may be required. Where voting units are aggregated to determine the ultimate result, counting outcomes solely as dictated by majority votes in each unit may dilute majorities or minorities in any of the individual units. For political purposes, local government entities may be so structured that equal votes are accorded to duly elected representatives of areas having widely disparate populations. The impact of minority votes may be diffused by the structure of the electoral districts.

Article I, § 2 of the U.S. Constitution has been held to require that congressional districts be so apportioned as to provide equal representation (subject to state lines) for equal numbers of people, permitting only the limited population variances that are unavoidable despite a good faith effort to achieve absolute equality, or for which a demanding standard of justification is met. Under the fourteenth amendment, the command of "one-person-one-vote" applies to apportionment for state and local legislatures but permits minimal population deviations that result from legitimately respected state and local interests, such as county lines. Local interests must yield, however, when they collide with the objectives of Article I, § 2 in congressional apportionment.

The fact that extraordinary majorities may be required in referenda is not ipso facto unconstitutional. If there are neither improper exclusions, nor disadvantages to identifiable, protected minorities, the referendum structure can validly make it more difficult to promote or prevent government action by requiring electoral approval or disapproval only upon the vote of more than a simple majority. As above suggested, the principles designed to guard against vote dilution in the election of representatives are not as fully applicable in "single shot" referenda where a popular voice in local legislative enactments is to be given limited play. The referendum puts a discrete issue to the voters, and if its adoption or rejection has a disproportionate impact upon an identifiable group, courts can decide whether it is appropriate to limit the franchise to that group or to give its votes special weight. Requiring the affirmative vote of concurrent majorities of each group is one method of giving votes of the smaller group special weight. Concurrent majorities may be upheld where there is a "genuine difference in the relevant interests of the groups," group attributes which are pertinent to its stake in the outcome. In elections on issues such as restructuring of governmental units involving consolidation or annexation, for example, a requirement of concurrent majorities among unequally populated subelectoral groups (e.g., those annexing and those to be annexed) in a referendum does not amount to invidious discrimination. Dilution of majority and minority votes in the aggregation of unit votes by treating each unit as if it had voted only the way its majority voted is invalid, however, in representational elections.

Even though the structures may have been approved by the voters and their representatives duly chosen in elections wherein their votes had equal weight, local government structures, such as the New York City Board of Estimate and a regional school district formed by several municipalities in Massachusetts, which gave equal votes to representatives of districts having widely disparate populations, have been held unconstitutional. Because the problem is the indirect effect of a structure that accords weight to representatives' votes not supported by population comparisons, it may be necessary for the challengers to demonstrate that the board engages in legislative activity in order to connect the original vote to the alleged diluted effect (obvious in a direct dilution case).

An election scheme or structure may not be designed with the intent to minimize or cancel out the voting strength of racial minorities in the population. This aspect of vote dilution is a diffusion of minority strength. What is impermissible is such diffusion as constitutes denial to a minority group of meaningful access to the political process. The object of equal protection here is to assure minority voters a fair chance to elect candidates representing their interests, not to entitle them to an election district in which they can control the election.

When the electoral single, multi-member or at-large districting scheme is thus challenged as a violation of equal protection requirements, intent to deny access to minority groups must be shown, and the court must consider the issue in historical contexts, with "an intensely local appraisal of the design and impact."

Judicial recognition of the justiciability of malapportionment, racial gerrymandering, and vote dilution almost inevitably led the U.S. Supreme Court to recognize the justiciability of political gerrymandering, especially that which follows the decennial census. The Court continues to recognize the justiciability of political gerrymandering claims, but disagrees as to the standards that should govern the claim. In one case, a plurality, noting that districting is intended to have substantial political consequences, stated that unconstitutional discrimination would occur only where the arrangement consistently degrades a voter's or a group's influence on the political process as a whole. The Court has made clear, however, that political gerrymandering to protect incumbency is not subject to strict scrutiny.

The Voting Rights Act

Dilution of voting strength is not only a fourteenth amendment issue, but, like many of the matters in this section, is covered by the federal Voting Rights Act as well. There, a discriminatory impact will trigger remedies even if the intent required for the constitutional violation cannot be

proved. The Act, in § 2, forbids state or local government imposition or application of any voter
qualifications, prerequisites, standards, practices, or
procedures in a manner that results in denial or
abridgement of a citizen's right to vote on account
of race, color, or membership in a language minority group. Section 5 of the Act establishes a statutory requirement of judicial and executive review of
alleged local vote abridging or retrogressive changes
in specific, covered jurisdictions. The challenged
procedure may be precleared only when both the
purpose and the effect of denying or abridging the
right to vote on account of race, color or religion are
absent. The Act does not cover changes other than
those affecting rules governing voting; thus it did
not apply to invalidate a reduction in newly elected
minority county commissioners' authority. Nor does
the Act support a challenge based on the size of
government authority (i.e., single-member rather
than multi-member commission).

Under the Act, as in equal protection circumstances, electoral single, multi-member, or at-large
districting schemes may be challenged as impairing
the challenger class' ability to elect representatives
of their choice. The court will engage in the intensely local appraisal and will undoubtedly be faced
with statistical evidence. For example, to succeed in
attacking multi-member districts, the challengers
must meet several high evidentiary burdens as a
"necessary precondition" to bringing such a claim.
They must show that the minority group is sufficiently large and geographically compact to be a

majority in a single-member district; that the minority group is politically cohesive (and the inference may be drawn from past election evidence that an aggregate of different minorities form a single cohesive group for this purpose); and that the majority sufficiently votes as a bloc to result usually in defeat of the minority candidate. Only after the threshold showing is met will the court determine from the totality of the circumstances whether the challenged system impedes the ability of the minority to elect its chosen representative.

The dilution problem is not only relevant to legislative bodies; it may affect judicial elections as well. For instance, the Voting Rights Act has been held to require preclearance of an ordinance consolidating multiple judicial districts into a single countywide municipal court. The issue may also involve the indirect effect of annexations or other boundary adjustments even including presently vacant land. Impermissible purposes under § 5, for example, it has been held, may relate to anticipated as well as present circumstances. It should be noted that the courts may not forbid all municipal boundary expansions that dilute the voting power of particular groups. They may, however, insist upon modifications to the subsequent electoral plan designed to neutralize adverse impact on minority political participation.

Decennial redistricting too has raised questions under the Voting Rights Act such as those based on a failure to achieve maximum minority political influence (improper vote dilution may not be inferred therefrom); those challenging the creation of minority-dominated legislative districts (not necessarily a violation); and those placing minorities as significant voting blocks in majority-dominated districts (not necessarily a violation).

CHAPTER III

REGULATION OF CONDUCT AND THE USE OF LAND

A. THE POLICE POWER

§ 1. Relation to Zoning Power

Perhaps the most pervasive and basic power of local government is the police power. For our purposes, we shall define the police power as the exercise of government power to limit, regulate or prohibit personal and business activity and property uses without government compensation in order to protect the public health, safety, morality and general welfare.

Conceptually, any such definition of the police power may be seen to include zoning. However, the municipality in question must be authorized to exercise its powers in one of the variety of ways we have earlier discussed and, traditionally, police power authorization is separate from zoning enabling legislation. Some municipal governments possess the former authority but not the latter. Many courts will emphasize that the two, although intimately related, are not coterminous. In that regard, they note that zoning power objectives have been customarily considered less inclusive, limited to ends peculiar to the municipality's fundamental land use program, rather than directed to a general problem common to the community at large. The dividing line of this theoretical separation is not readily discernible, especially since land use is frequently the subject of limitations originating in both the police and zoning powers. We shall explore land use regulation specifically in part B of this chapter.

§ 2. Challenges to Police Power Exercise

The state authorization of municipal police power may, of course, relate to a specific object to be regulated. Many such detailed authorizations exist. Commonly, however, police power authority is primarily delegated by the state in rather generic terms and much support is found in the general welfare clauses of power delegations. Except where the question involves possible extraterritorial application of the challenged city action, conflict with or preemption by state legislation or exclusivity, or the particular mechanics of implementation, framing of a power challenge in terms of lack of authority is uncommon. As will be discussed infra, such a challenge is more likely to be framed in terms questioning whether the object of the municipal power exercise is a proper one for invoking the police power. We shall return later to challenges to the mechanics of regulation: licensing, prohibition, nuisances, enforcement, investigations and penalties.

Through individual challenges, abusive government regulation may be checked by the constitutional and statutory doctrines designed to protect individual rights, to structure a nation of states, and to promote government accountability. As we have seen, an individual deemed to have standing may challenge the government's regulatory exercise as unauthorized, as in conflict with, or preempted by, federal or state law, as disfavored over other interlocal exercises, and as improperly enacted (outside of legislative days, not in public meetings, e.g.). The challenger may argue that the regulation violates the Due Process and Equal Protection Clauses of the federal fourteenth amendment and similar state constitutional provisions, and may raise such incorporated express and implied fundamental rights as freedom of speech, freedom of expressive and intimate association, privacy, free exercise and non-establishment of religion, travel, reasonable search and seizure, and double jeopardy. Other federal constitutional provisions may be the bases for challenge: the Impairment of Contracts, Commerce, Privileges and Immunities, and Takings Clauses. The regulation may implicate state constitutional clauses not replicated in the federal constitution. It may allegedly violate such applicable statutes and regulations as those implementing constitutional provisions. The constitutional challenges may be facial or as applied, and in the latter instance may include additional attacks upon licensing, permits, inspections, declarations of nuisance, prosecutions, and other matters related to enforcement.

To illustrate, let us assume that a municipality has enacted an ordinance declaring that door-to-door solicitation at private residences for the purpose of soliciting sales orders is a nuisance and as such is punishable as a misdemeanor. This type of regulation, commonly called a "Green River Ordinance," was first enacted by the town of Green River, Wyoming in 1931 and became popular across the country during the following decade. The ordinance has been challenged on behalf of door-to-door salespersons for national news and opinion magazines, perhaps as a defense in a prosecution for a violation. In addition to the questions we have already seen, viz., whether the city is empowered to act, whether the enactment conflicts with or is preempted by state legislation, whether the city council met in proper legislative sessions observing the appropriate notice, hearing, readings and quorum requirements, and whether the enactment is in proper form, there remain such questions as:

(i) Whether preservation of the residents' privacy or their protection from uninvited solicitation when in their homes is an object for which the police power may properly be invoked;

(ii) Whether the means, declaring door-to-door selling to be a punishable nuisance, bear a real and substantial relationship to the desired objective;

(iii) Whether the ordinance impinges upon the magazine publishers' rights of free speech, or freedom of the press;

(iv) Whether the terms of the ordinance are so vague as to allow arbitrary enforcement;

(v) Whether the inclusion of door-to-door sales-persons and exclusion of other sales approaches constitutes an improper classification so that the group is denied equal protection of the laws;

(vi) Whether the ordinance unduly burdens interstate commerce;

(vii) Whether state delegated authority to regulate for the public welfare includes the power to prohibit otherwise lawful business and whether such prohibition is confiscatory;

(viii) Whether enforcement of the ordinance is guided by sufficient standards so that delegation of enforcement powers is appropriately one of administrative authority; and

(ix) Whether imposition of criminal penalties is authorized.

It is readily apparent that many of the questions raised about a police power exercise are intertwined, and in fact are simply different focuses upon the same underlying problem. For example, an improper classification may indicate that the means chosen are not rationally related to the end sought. A provision that violates due process requirements because it is so vague as to allow arbitrary enforcement may at the same time be void under the federal first amendment requiring precision of regulation because the ordinance is overbroad in its impact upon free speech. It may similarly violate the federal fourteenth amendment because it has classified according to the content of the communication. Delegation of authority to implement a vague provision may also be challenged as an improper delegation of legislative power because there are not sufficient standards to limit enforcement discretion to administrative bounds. One might argue that the object to be achieved is not properly within police power purview because it inhibits exercise of constitutionally protected human activity. If the regulation affects the challenger's property or a state created claim of entitlement, it may constitute: an unconstitutional taking of property without procedural due process (hearing, confrontation, etc.); an unreasonable or confiscatory violation of substantive due process (courts may query whether substantive due process is applicable to claims of entitlement); or a taking for which compensation must be paid in order to avoid a violation of the Takings Clause (a regulatory taking).

While we shall return to regulatory takings in our study of land use regulation and of eminent domain, full exploration of all of these challenges is beyond the scope of this text and only some will be further described here. Nevertheless, it is important to be aware of the nature of each of these interrelated challenges. Effective advocacy, judicial assessment and careful drafting require precision of target.

§ 3. Due Process—Appropriate Objects for Police Power Exercise

Is the object of the ordinance one for which the police power may properly be invoked? At the outset we should note that political reaction is likely to influence the boundaries of regulation. Political opposition may surface as an adverse reaction to overly solicitous government intervention in the lives of its citizens, or as an effective alliance of disparate centers of self interest, or as a general desire to engage in the conduct that is beyond government's competence to overcome. The opposition may limit the government through exercise of the referendum power, political pressure, or disobedience so rampant as to overwhelm enforcement capability. Thus, in a real sense it serves to circumscribe and limit the reach of the police power. Witness public reaction in some jurisdictions to strict residential use codes, local gun control efforts, or public area smoking bans.

The courts, of course, may reflect such political reality in their evaluation. Generally, though, they respect the "separation of powers" because the state legislature has committed to the municipal legislature the primary regulatory responsibility. This respect is manifested by the courts' willingness to entertain the presumption that a challenged ordinance is reasonable and legitimate. To the challenger then falls the task of demonstrating unreasonableness, and if there are reasonably conceivable facts to support the power exercise or even if the matter is fairly debatable, the challenger will lose. The challenger thus faces the heavy burden of negating every reasonable basis which might have underlain a legislative determination that there was a reasonable need for the enactment.

The range of permissible police power exercise defies accurate description. The scope can perhaps be illustrated not only by the efforts we shall see later in this chapter but also by the following. Municipal efforts, frequently successful, on behalf of the public health and safety have included: attacks on air, water and noise pollution and smoking in public places; smoking reduction measures; restriction of the sale of drug paraphernalia; limitation of the impact of video arcades on children during school hours; restriction of headphone use while running in public streets; firearm registration and handgun prohibition; traffic-safety regulations; scientific-research laboratory controls; sanitation measures such as disease control, food quality regulation and trash disposal; closing of businesses on Sundays; banning dangerous animals; removal of slums and blight; school discipline and demonstration regulations; reducing crime potential (early closing hours of certain commercial establishments, e.g.); riot control and prevention; and adult and juvenile crime prevention and punishment.

On behalf of the public morality, municipalities have restricted gambling and the availability of liquor, attempted to eliminate temptation to immoral activity by banning massage parlors and prostitution, and banned the display or offering of obscenity on stage, film or in publication, particularly in connection with its impact on juveniles.

Consider the following representative sampling of municipal initiatives to protect the public welfare. Municipalities have sought to advance aesthetic considerations throughout the community by such measures as sign control. They have attempted to provide additional support to local property values by restricting uses in specific zones, by specifying the location and dispersal of adult entertainment establishments, and to promote peace and quiet through such methods as loudspeaker control, door-to-door solicitation regulations, and limitations on telephone solicitations. Their interest in protecting the public's purse (though often deemed to be a matter of statewide concern) has led to measures such as price-sign requirements on gasoline pumps; regulation of auctions, pawnbrokers, second-hand dealers, loan businesses and fortune tellers; requirements concerning scales and food weights and measurements; control on vending machines; regulation of solicitation of funds; prevention of fraud and deceptive practices; regulation of employment agencies; rent controls; landlord tenant regulations; rate-making; and franchise controls. And finally, they may seek to protect the civil rights of citizens through public accommodation laws, human rights laws regulating what once were private clubs, enhanced punishment for bias-related crimes, and ordinances designed to guarantee fair housing opportunities and to control block-busting, panic selling and other real estate problems.

The courts' receptivity to the extent of government regulation, however, is not unlimited. When the ordinance seeks in effect to impose "one person's morality" on the general public, or seeks to accommodate "one person's aesthetic sensitivities" by requiring public observation thereof, the courts are prepared to find that the object is not one for which the police power may properly be invoked.

In the last analysis, the city's competence to act depends upon the reasonableness of the action. There is a point, difficult to articulate in the abstract, when the reality of what is being done or the speculative or highly personal nature of what is sought to be prevented overcomes the presumption of reasonableness. In those cases, the customary judicial reluctance to intervene in the legislative process will disappear.

Some courts have attempted to illustrate this scope of municipal power in reviewing regulation of businesses and occupations. These can be categorized for present purposes as follows: ordinary vocations that are pursued on private property by private means; occupations that are useful but involve under certain circumstances social or economic evils offensive to the public health, safety, morality or general welfare; and businesses that involve claims of a private right in, or extraordinary use of, public streets or parks. All three categories are regulated to some degree. Obviously, the scope of municipal regulation is greatest in the last situation and certainly is sizeable in the second category. There, though, regulation is accompanied by the danger of imposition of personal morality or sense of the general welfare in the municipal determination of social and economic evils. This danger is most real in connection with the first category where regulation may tend to expand beyond control of external consequences to enforcement of private morality.

§ 4. Due Process—Relation of Means to Object

Integrally related to the determination whether the matter is a proper subject of regulation is the question whether the means chosen are also reasonable, i.e., whether they bear a real and substantial relation to the ends sought. Thus, for example, moving beyond the question whether other constitutional protections have been ignored, one might ask:

(i) Whether control of incinerators and oil burning equipment is rationally related to prevention or material reduction of air pollution;

(ii) Whether reduction of phosphates in detergents will materially reduce pollution of local water sources;

(iii) Whether requirement of deposits on drink containers or additional taxes on high tar cigarettes will reduce litter or prevent smoking of the more harmful substances;

(iv) Whether closing commercial establishments on Sundays is rationally related to promotion of a day of relaxation and recreation;

(v) Whether a curfew of any use of the streets after certain hours or the closing of certain untended establishments (laundromats, e.g.) at certain times is rationally related to restoration of civil order or reduction of the potential of crime;

(vi) Whether prohibition of the administration of massages to persons of the opposite sex or of licensed taverns' hiring female bartenders is rationally related to prevention of consequences detrimental to the public morality or protection of the status of women;

(vii) Whether prohibition of "for sale" or "sold" signs on residential property bears a real and substantial relation to the prevention of racial block-busting, panic selling and the promotion of fair housing goals;

(viii) Whether commuter, on-street parking bans and the imposition of commercial parking taxes will reduce traffic and promote the use of public transportation;

(ix) Whether prohibition of the possession of bludgeons, switchblade knives, brass knuckles, sawed-off shotguns, Molotov cocktails and operative handguns will reduce accidental and intentional death and injury;

(x) Whether restrictions on group occupancy of residences advance the municipality's interest in preventing overcrowding, and in promoting traffic control, aesthetics and property values;

(xi) Whether the requirement of two attendants on duty at self-service gasoline stations is rationally related to fire prevention;

(xii) Whether prohibiting or restricting the sale or advertising for sale of implements which are known or can reasonably be known to be intended for use with law-controlled substances (drug paraphernalia) will serve to reduce illegal drug use; and

(xiii) Whether allowance of on-site, outdoor commercial advertising and prohibition of off-site, outdoor commercial and non-commercial advertising on fixed structures (billboards) or the banning of all off-site advertising are rationally related to the elimination of pedestrian and traffic hazards and to the preservation and improvement of the city's appearance.

Again, in the absence of other defects, reasonableness will be presumed. Nevertheless, courts vary widely in their willingness to uphold the regulations illustrated in the previous list.

An ordinance may be also attacked as a violation of the constitutions' due process clauses on the grounds that it is confiscatory or vague. (We shall refer later to procedural due process requirements in its enforcement.) The ordinance may be confiscatory. If it is a rate regulation enactment, it is not the nature of the business whose rates are regulated but the impact of the regulation that is at issue. The rates will be invalidated if they are so restrictive as to be prohibitory or confiscatory, thus in effect constituting an unreasonable termination of an otherwise lawful business.

Police power regulation may also be confiscatory if the cost of compliance amounts virtually to a taking of property of the persons being regulated. Note the cognate assertion under the Takings Clause. There is no clear line between proper police power regulation and a regulatory taking requiring compensation, and several health and safety ordinances which were understandably alleged to have crossed the line have nevertheless been upheld as valid police power exercises.

An ordinance will also be deemed defective under due process requirements where it either fails to give a person of ordinary intelligence fair notice that contemplated conduct is forbidden or encourages arbitrary and erratic enforcement, or both. For example, a curfew ordinance which prohibits loitering or remaining on the street and excepts those whose business requires being there (firemen, policemen, e.g.) may be upheld, while a similar ordinance with a blanket prohibition will fail to comport with reality, is incapable of total enforcement, and will both fail to define appropriately the forbidden conduct and encourage arbitrary enforcement.

§ 5. Other Constitutional Limitations

As noted above, the due process question of the rational relationship of the means chosen to the end sought will not be answered by a presumption of reasonableness where the ordinance denies first amendment freedoms or imposes discriminations based upon race, color, religion or ancestry. Moreover, the presumption is rebuttable and the reasonableness of the means is rarely divorced from other constitutional considerations. Under federal constitutional jurisprudence the justification for the local power exercise must move beyond reasonableness to compelling persuasion where the implicated right is one of the fundamental rights incorporated as applicable to the states through the federal fourteenth amendment or where a suspect class is regulated.

State constitutions contain declarations of individual rights and other provisions which may serve directly to limit police power exercise. Indeed, these limitations and state due process requirements tend to be more strictly applied by state courts than the federal restrictions are invoked by federal courts. The somewhat less intrusive judicial review operative at the federal level stems from federal courts' adherence to the principle that the police power has been reserved to the states and should not be interfered with unless the balancing of the federal constitutional protections with the legitimate goals of state police power so dictate. Thus, for example, while there is federal authority upholding the Green River ordinances, the majority of state courts has invalidated them as too prohibitive. Similarly, under federal precedent, a community may limit the number of unrelated people living in a home; only when the ordinance tries to distinguish between related family members in its definition of permitted occupants will the federal constitution be implicated. Similar state court opinions, however, have interpreted state constitutional provisions to invalidate restrictive municipal definitions of family in residential zones. Note, though that constitutional challenges must be distinguished from those raising similar concerns under the federal Fair Housing Act and the Fair Housing Amendments Act of 1988.

Commerce Clause

An attempted regulation (such as the Green River ordinance, a law limiting phosphates in detergents, or one that regulates the interstate transportation of garbage or sewage, e.g.) may be challenged under the federal Commerce Clause. Under its express commerce power, Congress will, as noted earlier, be permitted to regulate the channels and instruments of interstate commerce, to protect instruments and persons moving in interstate commerce even from intrastate threats, and to regulate matters that substantially affect interstate commerce. Where Congress so acts in an area in which the state or local government may also act, but asserts its predominance under the Supremacy Clause, the issue is one of preemption. Distinguishable are congressional acts that regulate the conduct of municipalities where the issue is then violation. For example, while the Clayton Act damages remedy is not available against municipalities, they may be subject to injunctions for violation of the Sherman Act (antitrust) unless their anticompetitive activities have been deemed affirmatively and clearly authorized by their states, which are exempt. The old or new authorizing statute will be sufficient if the suppression of competition is a reasonably foreseeable consequence of its enactment. Another illustration is the local government's liability for hazardous substances and clean-up costs under the Comprehensive Environmental Response, Compensation, and Liability Act, 42 U.S.C.A. § 9601 et seq.

Even if Congress has not acted, Commerce Clause objection may be raised when on balance, the putative police power gain is outweighed by the undue burden which impedes the free flow of interstate commerce, when then there are less risky alternatives, or where the enactment discriminates against interstate commerce in favor of local commercial businesses. The so-called dormant Commerce Clause is said to implicitly divest states of that power to regulate interstate commerce which is positively granted to the federal government. Individual states are prohibited under the Clause from discriminatory action aimed directly at interstate commerce, from enacting state regulations that, while facially nondiscriminatory, unduly burden interstate commerce, and from regulating those aspects of commerce that by their unique nature demand cohesive treatment. Pursuant to its Commerce Clause power, though, Congress may expressly authorize state and local laws that would otherwise be invalidated by application of the dormant Commerce Clause. Note also that the challenge under the dormant Commerce Clause extends to local government exercise of regulatory or taxing powers, but will not apply to invalidate the government's actions when it has entered the market as a participant. The market participant doctrine permits a local government to place conditions on a discrete, identifiable class of economic activity in which it is a major participant, if the conditions imposed by the government entity do not have a substantial regulatory effect outside of the particular market.

First Amendment

An ordinance may be challenged as violating rights to:

(i) freedom of speech (bans of labor picketing near schools and all residential picketing; censorship of films, plays, student newspapers, and books; prohibition of exit polling, immediate post-catastrophe solicitation by adjusters, airport activities, "for sale" signs, political signs in residence yards; off-site outdoor advertising; permit systems for parades and other public displays, e.g.);

(ii) freedom of association (curfews, admitting women to men's clubs, vagrancy laws, e.g.);

(iii) freedom of religion (Exercise: fund solicitations, home schooling, home visits, loudspeakers; Establishment: Sunday Blue Laws, city hall Christmas creches and other displays of symbols, religious invocations at games, liquor-license veto by churches, e.g.); or

(iv) the right to travel (population limitations in land use laws, municipal moratoriums on new housing construction, durational residency requirements, e.g.).

As cases involving the freedom of speech illustrate, federally preserved rights are not absolute but will yield to the legitimate demands of the police power. The degree of recognition of the police power depends upon the balance struck between the gravity of the evil sought to be avoided and the importance of the right (clear and present danger as against free speech, e.g.). Does the regulation ban speech or conduct? If it is clearly directed to conduct that is not a substitute for speech, then it will be upheld if it is benign and within the legitimate interests of government. It will be sufficiently justified if it is shown to be within the constitutional powers of the regulating government, if it furthers an important or substantial government interest, if that government interest is unrelated to the suppression of free expression, and if any incidental restriction on first amendment freedoms is no greater than is essential to achieve that interest.

If speech or conduct related to expression is regulated, is it protected or unprotected speech? For example, obscenity as defined by the courts is not protected. Regulation of protected speech, however, must be content neutral. For example, the government may not choose to punish "fighting words" involving racial bias but not others.

If the speech is protected by the first amendment, what method of regulation is involved? Prior restraint is always troublesome, but freedom of speech does not mean "free to say anything, anywhere, at any time." There is a heavy presumption against any form of prior restraint. If the regulation grants unbridled discretion to the restrainer and fails to provide for a swift and predictably scheduled decision followed quickly by court review, then it involves prohibited prior restraint.

The issue may involve the place of the speech. What is reasonable may depend on whether the place is a traditional or designated public or partially public forum or a private forum. If the regulated speech involves a public forum or is beyond the limits of a partially public forum, appropriate regulation must be compellingly justified and use the least restrictive means if based on the content of the speech.

There may, however, be appropriate time, place, and manner regulation. To be appropriate, the regulation must be content neutral. Content neutrality includes several important components. First, the regulation must be justified without reference to the content of the implicated speech. On that basis, the Supreme Court upheld regulation of adult theaters and bookstores because the local law focused on the uses' secondary land use effects and not on the content of the material. Second, the law must be narrowly tailored to serve a significant government interest, but need not adopt the least restrictive or intrusive means of doing so. And finally, the law must leave open ample alternative channels for communicating the information.

Regulation of speech may be characterized as overinclusive or underinclusive, concepts that also are relevant to equal protection challenges to regulation. In first amendment contexts, if the regulation is overinclusive, it may regulate too much speech (prohibit almost all signs on private property, e.g.) and fail the "narrowly tailored" requirement. If it is underinclusive, it suggests a content basis.

Due process concepts of vagueness are involved in first amendment issues as well. If the regulation exceeds the limited area of its competence, it is subject to arbitrary implementation. For example, the community may have a legitimate interest in regulating the use of sound trucks or to avoid inflammatory parade activities to protect public health, safety and welfare. At the same time, though, total prohibitions, and requirements for permits that may be enforced in a selective or arbitrary manner, will be invalidated as undue encroachments upon first amendment rights.

The first amendment applies, though with somewhat less rigor, to commercial speech. To be protected, commercial speech must concern lawful activity and must not be misleading. The restrictions must directly advance substantial government interests and may be no broader than necessary to serve those interests. Again, the least restrictive means of regulation are not required. If the goal of the regulation is consumer protection, for instance, there must be a reasonable fit between the legislature's ends and the chosen means, taking into careful consideration the costs and benefits of the burden imposed. In some cases, local regulations amount to a blanket prohibition of truthful speech about a lawful activity. Relevant cases include a ban on advertising liquor prices, and a prohibition of advertising smokeless tobacco or cigars within 1,000 feet of a school or playground. In these cases, strict scrutiny will apply, and the regulation will likely be found to be unrelated to the valid end of consumer protection. Such a prohibition on speech will be deemed violative of the First Amendment unless the expression itself is deceptive, related to unlawful activity, or otherwise flawed in some way.

Equal Protection, Contracts, and Privileges and Immunities Clauses

While the government's role as a "market participant" may deflect a Commerce Clause challenge, it remains subject to the Equal Protection Clause. Moreover, if its efforts affect fundamental interests of nonresidents, the government will need substantial justification to avoid violation of the Privileges and Immunities Clause in Article IV of the U.S. Constitution. In an important case involving a city's preference of local residents in awarding municipal contracts, the Supreme Court rejected a claim of impermissible infringement of the right to work under the Commerce Clause. At the same time, though, if concluded that the city's conditions on its expenditures for goods and services as a marketplace participant must be based on a substantial justification to withstand challenge under the Privileges and Immunities Clause. The Court did not decide the issue but rather remanded for trial on the substantial justification issue. Other resident preferences for government employment are also frequently the subject of litigation. Durational residence requirements, such as those requiring an employee to have lived within the jurisdiction for any length of time in order to be eligible for government employment, are generally invalid. Prospective, ongoing residency requirements for public employment, however, are frequently upheld where the goal and means to improve local government are legitimate.

The constitution's prohibition of impairment of contracts is not absolute. Contracts are subject to police power exercises that are reasonable and necessary to serve an important public purpose.

Equal protection considerations will invalidate improper classifications. Essential to determining whether the ordinance is reasonable, whether its requirements bear a real and substantial relation to the evil to be cured, is the question of the propriety of the law's coverage. The class of individuals or entities subject to the regulation may not unreasonably be segregated from others to whom the ordinance does not, but ought to, apply. For example, an ordinance prohibiting a person from giving a massage to a patron of the opposite sex in massage parlors, health salons or physical culture studios, but not in barber shops, beauty parlors, YMCA and YWCA health clubs, was declared invalid because the class was structured arbitrarily, without rational relation to the evil attacked which could have as easily occurred in the unregulated entities.

Compare a different type of municipal classification in which the equal protection challenge was unavailing. One city adopted an ordinance that permitted only municipal residents to park within the

municipality. Denying the nonresident's equal protection challenge, the court found that denying
parking privileges to nonresidents rationally reflecting commuters' heavier contribution to local traffic
congestion and air pollution.

Here again, the courts are willing to invoke a
presumption that the ordinance's classification is a
reasonable one, with the burden of establishing the
contrary on the challenger. Where the class is defined according to race, religion, color or other
suspect criterion, or where the regulation applies
only to some people and impacts upon a fundamental right (classification by content and freedom of
speech, severe restriction of voting rights, e.g.), the
presumption is inapplicable and the burden is on
the government to show a compelling state interest
justifying the classification. Local government affirmative action regulations have not been justified in
the absence of past discrimination demonstrable
either by explicit government admission or by comparisons of the composition of the targeted businesses or workforce with the racial composition of
the relevant qualified business or workforce population. Even where rational justification is the test,
there is evidence that the courts may tend to give
more scrutiny when the ordinance frustrates other
important state policies. Some heightened review
appears to have been the basis for state court
opinions invalidating laws that excluded group
homes for retarded children; limited education for
children of undocumented aliens; or reduced services to the home-bound disabled while preserving

services for those in placement residences. Note again that state courts may more strictly apply state equal protection and cognate clauses.

Frequently, the challenger (perhaps with some basis in fact) will allege that the class was determined in a discriminatory manner as a result of improper city council motivation. For reasons ranging from separation of powers to the difficulty of competent proof, courts are loathe to look into the question of legislators' motivations and will frequently say so. Nevertheless, the assertion that government action has discriminated against a suspect class requires a showing of intentional discrimination and necessarily will focus upon legislative motivation. In addition, the effect of that motivation may itself be so arbitrary as to be invalid. The cognate equal protection violation charge of intentional or purposeful discrimination in the administration of an otherwise nondiscriminatory law will be discussed later.

Another judicial response should be noted in situations in which challengers have been unsuccessful in their attempt to use the equal protection clause to invalidate a law's classifications. Occasionally, the court will find that the evil sought to be cured is particularly pernicious with respect to the specific class sought to be regulated. Nevertheless, the court may conclude that even though the municipality could have expanded the scope of the evil and thus included a larger class, the narrower classification will stand. The judicial rationale will be that the local legislative body need not correct all the evil at once, but may attack it step by step. For example, in upholding a fair housing ordinance applicable only to owners of five or more dwelling units as a valid step in attacking some of the evil, the court justified the classification on the ground that an owner of five or more units who would attempt to discriminate purely on the basis of race, creed, or color in the sale or rental of such units is potentially a more dangerous threat to those who would be hurt than a similarly biased owner of four or fewer units.

§ 6. Regulation and Prohibition

There are additional considerations relating to the enactment and implementation of police power ordinances. One of the most persistent obstacles to the form of the regulation is the strict interpretation which many courts give to the state's delegation of the power to regulate, holding that the power to regulate does not include the power to prohibit. Inevitably, this strictness creates an incentive for local governments to regulate as severely as possible without crossing the line to impermissible prohibitions. As a result, many challenges have alleged that the confiscatory nature of the regulation is so severe as to rise to the level of prohibition. These challenges have had some success.

For example, our illustrative Green River ordinance may be seen as a prohibition of solicitation of subscriptions by house-to-house canvass without invitation. Or it may be seen as regulation of subscription solicitation limiting it to radio, television, periodicals, mail and local agencies. In the sense that all regulation limits, the limitations make all regulatory legislation prohibitory to some extent.

§ 7. Licenses, Permits, Fees

Regulation of activity and land use under the police power is frequently accomplished by delegating to administrators the power to approve or withhold licenses and permits, pursuant to legislatively adopted standards. Without the license or permit, the activity cannot be undertaken. State delegation of the power to regulate will usually be held to include the power to license for regulation and to impose reasonable conditions and qualifications upon the grant or renewal of licenses and permits. Just as is the case with other regulatory ordinances, license and permit requirements are subject to the improper delegation, preemption, and constitutional challenges previously discussed. For example, an ordinance which permitted churches and schools, in effect, to veto the issuance of liquor licenses for establishments within a 500–foot radius of their location was viewed as a delegation to private entities of a power normally exercised by government agencies, and held not to be entitled to the deference normally accorded a legislative zoning enactment. Because the valid objectives of the ordinance could have been achieved in other unobjectionable ways, and because the substitution of the standardless church judgments for reasoned public decision-making appears to have the principal effect of advancing religion, the ordinance was deemed to have risked political fragmentation along religious lines, an entanglement held unconstitutional under the Establishment Clause of the federal first amendment.

Fees are customarily exacted for the award or renewal of licenses and permits. While one might conceptually demonstrate that the costs of regulation are expenses of government like all others and that methods of obtaining revenues to pay government expenses constitute taxation, the power to exact license and permit fees has been considered to be within the penumbra of the police power, not needing authorization to tax. As a result, such fee exactions must be carefully tailored to recouping the cost of the permit and its regulatory structure. Fees found to be intended as primarily a revenue raising device will be invalidated. As we shall see in Chapter V, in order to license for revenue, the municipality must be empowered by state delegation of the taxing authority, which will be evaluated under the legal principles applicable to local taxation efforts.

Regulatory license fees nevertheless provide sizeable amounts of money (witness the income from parking meters), largely because of judicial liberality in applying the governing standards, viz., that the fees be reasonable and not regularly or largely in excess of the municipal expense of policing the function and administering the license program. Such expenses include the costs of investigating the applicant, expenses incurred in issuing the authorization, costs of all supervision and investigation insuring that the licensee conforms to the applicable rules and regulations, and, frequently, other police charges reasonably related. Where public property user permit fees are set within the discretion of the administrator who may then respond to content-based stimulus, not surprisingly, the first amendment is implicated.

In our study of land use regulation, we shall see that local governments have imposed upon subdividers and developers fees in lieu of land contributions, as well as impact fees that attempt to assess the development's transportation and education impact on the existing community. In addition, some communities levy linkage fees, which attempt to quantify the impact of high intensity development on the local demand for housing. In those communities, large scale non-residential development may be subject to a fee that requires those whose development will bring in many new employees to contribute to the supply of affordable housing for those employees. In many instances, these fees have been exacted under the police power (as a means, for example, of meeting the locality's "fair share" housing burden), although some courts classify them as taxes and demand authority. In some states, they are specifically authorized by statute.

§ 8. Nuisances

Where the municipality is deemed empowered to prohibit, prohibition of occupations or activities noxious to the public health, safety, morality and general welfare may be accomplished by declaration that they constitute nuisances. The city's nuisance declaration is not impervious to challenge, however. The designation must be reasonable and constitutional. The list of valid municipal nuisance designations is limitless. Some are of such longstanding and universal applicability as to be considered "nuisances per se." The courts, however, have the final determination whether the activity, condition or structure is in fact a nuisance. Only then can the activity be prohibited through the exercise of the police power.

The nuisances in question are public in nature. Their detrimental impact must sufficiently affect the public or a portion thereof to warrant prohibition. The ordinance, of course, is often general, leaving to administration the determination that particular activity or land use falls within the generic class. Abatement of the particular nuisance will then be sought under such locally available procedures as court decrees or administrative cease and desist orders, with costs charged to the person or entity in question. Under appropriate standards, emergency summary abatement (destruction of disease-ridden or unsafe buildings, e.g.) may be allowed, so long as the citizen has an available, though subsequent, hearing to challenge the specific nuisance designation. Recovery against the public official and the municipality may be had for wrongful abatement, in the latter case because summary destruction, where improper, will be deemed a taking requiring compensation.

§ 9. Investigation, Enforcement and Penalties

Enforcement of the police power ordinances also allows municipal investigation and supervision to assure compliance; revocation of abused licenses and permits under applicable standards of reasonableness, and appropriate procedural due process; and civil and criminal penalties for violation.

Inspections

Frequently, regulatory investigations may authorize areawide, multi-building, internal inspections. The U.S. Supreme Court has held that where such inspections involve entry into private dwellings or the private areas of commercial establishments, the federal fourth amendment requires that entry be conditioned upon judicial issuance of a warrant. Probable cause for issuance even for areawide inspection will exist if reasonable legislative or administrative standards, varying with the municipal program to be enforced, are satisfied with respect to a particular dwelling or private area. Probable cause standards will not, however, require specific government knowledge of the condition of that particular private area or dwelling. The Court's rulings were not intended to imply that commercial areas may not be inspected in many more situations than private homes, nor were they intended to affect licensing programs requiring inspections prior to operating a business or marketing a product, to which inspections the licensee may have consented in advance.

There are warrantless searches. Some, involving drug and disease testing of public employees, have been discussed in Chapter II. Others do not involve the type of search and expectation of privacy that triggers the constitutional protection (aerial observation from a helicopter, e.g.). Yet others involve "closely regulated" businesses. There, if required substitutes for the purposes served by the warrant are present, the search will be valid even in aid of a law that both regulates and punishes. There must be a substantial government interest that informs the regulatory scheme pursuant to which the inspection is made. The inspection must be necessary to further the regulatory scheme. The statute's inspection program, in its certainty and regularity of application, must provide a constitutionally adequate substitute for a warrant by fulfilling its two basic functions: advising the target that the search is being made pursuant to law within a properly defined scope; and limiting inspector discretion.

One-stop inspections raise similar questions. Sobriety checkpoints, for example, may be held not to violate the fourth amendment where the balance of the government's interest in preventing drunken driving, the extent to which the checkpoint system may reasonably be said to advance that interest, and the degree of intrusion upon individual motorists who are briefly stopped, weighs in favor of the program. In examining the degree of intrusion, the fear and surprise engendered in law-abiding motorists by the nature of the stop, not the fear of discovery, are relevant. Compare roving patrols on lonely roads with visible stopping points.

Violations and Penalties

The power to impose penalties for violations of police power ordinances must be delegated, and it is settled that the power to designate misdemeanors may appropriately be delegated to municipalities. Some state authorizations prescribe the penalties for violations of municipal ordinances, and the prescribed penalties may be exclusive. There may be other state legislation, applicable to various classes of municipalities, or authorized charter provisions which make certain misdemeanor or offense penalties available for violation of a municipality's laws. A municipality may denominate the violation an "offense" or a "misdemeanor" and thus invoke the applicable penalty contained in these separate general provisions. Sometimes the local ordinance itself specifies the penalty.

Clearly, a penalty that exceeds the state delegated limits is invalid. Clearly, all violation proceedings are subject to the fundamental fairness requirements of procedural due process. Equally clearly, constitutional rights to counsel, jury, indictment, specificity of charge, confrontation of witnesses, and other due process questions involving discovery and burden of proof, and constitutional protections against double jeopardy, self incrimination, and illegal arrest and search must be afforded and observed in appropriate municipal criminal proceedings. Exploration of each of these rights and protections is beyond the scope of this text. Of significance here is the fact that absent state or charter restriction the municipality may in many jurisdictions enforce its ordinance by resort to either "civil" or "criminal" process. Accordingly, not all municipal violation proceedings are criminal in nature; in civil proceedings, the rights and protections surrounding the criminal process need not be provided.

Ultimately, it is for the courts to decide whether a given "civil" or "criminal" designation is proper. Some courts have decided that virtually all municipal violations are in the nature of misdemeanors. Others retain the traditional civil classification for some and deem others criminal. In their analysis of this issue, the courts have looked to the extent and kind of the relief and punishment sought, the degree of outrage associated with the conduct allegedly amounting to the violation, and whether that conduct is punishable under general laws of the state. Generally, as the severity of the permitted punishment increases, as the conduct for which the action is brought grows more outrageous, and as the conduct prohibited by the ordinance more closely approximates conduct prohibited by general laws, the courts with increasing likelihood will designate the proceeding "criminal." Conversely, as the relief sought more closely resembles the relief obtainable in traditionally civil actions and as the conduct for which the action is brought more approximates conduct actionable by private parties in civil suits, the designation will more likely be deemed "civil."

Whatever designation a court decides to be proper in a given instance, the consequences that follow that decision are by no means clear. While substantial authority requires observance of basic elements of due process, the various courts have inconsistently answered questions concerning the applicability and availability of the broad range of rights and protections above mentioned. Lengthened lists of rights considered to be absolute, the evolution of concepts of procedural due process, and the courts' creation of more rules responsive to the demands of fairness have contributed to a blurring of the distinction between civil and criminal.

§ 10. Discriminatory Enforcement

Inevitably, not all those who violate municipal police power ordinances are penalized. Comparisons between the groups of violators, that is, comparing those who are charged and prosecuted with those who are not, may lead to a charge of discriminatory enforcement. This charge arises when the alleged violator suspects that political or other arbitrary considerations motivated the enactment or enforcement of the ordinance. The courts willing to consider the charge do not deem it a defense to the allegation of violation. Rather, it is a reason for dismissal on constitutional grounds.

Intentional discrimination in the administration of an ordinance violates equal protection. But success in this challenge is rare. Selective enforcement—the fact that other offenders have not been prosecuted—is not in itself a constitutional violation. One who alleges discriminatory enforcement must meet the heavy burden of establishing conscious, purposeful discrimination on impermissible grounds or an intentionally pursued pattern of discrimination. Illustratively, an operator of an adult movie theater and an adult bookstore alleged, inter alia, that the county improperly enacted a zoning ordinance making the operations unlawful in their present locations, and prevented their status as non-conforming uses by delaying action on needed permits prior to the rezoning. Although the county had permitted several businesses to bring themselves into voluntary compliance by obtaining permits, it sought to shut down the plaintiff's adult establishments. The complainant alleged discrimination on the basis of the character of the business involved, and asserted a violation of his first amendment rights. The complainant's ability to recover, however, was conditioned on his ability to show that he was treated differently from those who demonstrated his level of chronic delinquency in seeking permits.

§ 11. Estoppel

We saw in Chapter II and shall see in Chapter IV that local governments may not bargain away such governmental power as the police power. As a corollary it is frequently stated that local governments cannot be estopped to exercise their police powers. It would be more accurate to say that estoppel will be rarely applied. But the doctrine is available under traditional principles to one who is victimized by inequitable police power application. For example, where a landowner postponed his application for a particular land use permit at the behest of the city legislators who were at that time quietly preparing to rezone the area in question, the court held that it would be inequitable to permit the municipality to deny the use to which the landowner could have obtained a vested right prior to rezoning had he not accommodated the very legislators who then rezoned.

The question of estoppel often arises because a citizen has relied to his or her detriment upon the approval given by a ministerial officer. The municipality asserts that the permission was improperly granted and beyond the scope of the officer's authority. It argues that the officer made a mistake of fact or acted in contravention of applicable ordinances. Of course, if the official was without authority to issue a permit or approval at all, or if there was evidence of misconduct or deceit, there would be no estoppel and the city could validly revoke the approval. But where the official had the authority to issue the necessary permit or certificate, where there was no evidence of bad faith, where there were substantial expenditures and change of position in reliance, courts have held the city estopped from arbitrary revocation. Estoppel has been awarded even though the official's interpretation of the applicable ordinances and regulations may have been a questionable one, as long as the previous standards were met.

B.   REGULATION OF LAND USE

§ 1.   Functional Components of the Land Regulatory Process

No area of local government operation is more the subject of public reaction and political sensitivity than land use regulation. At the outset, it will be helpful to identify the participants in the land regulatory process and outline briefly the functions each performs. There is a great variety from state to state and thus the following will be typical rather than uniformly applicable.

The state legislatures delegate to certain political subdivisions authority to enact zoning ordinances, to create various boards and commissions, and to regulate the uses of land in myriad ways ranging from subdivision controls to such police power exercises as housing and building codes. The federal government also has an impact on land use regulation. For instance, strings attached to federal grants motivated increased state attention to such matters as regional planning. Other federal initiatives, particularly in the area of wetlands regulation, have provided an incentive for state efforts to reclaim some control of the land use regulatory functions. State efforts, whether they resulted in state level regulations or state participation in local land use processes, have raised the inevitable political outcry that land use is appropriately a matter for local control. This opposition, led by local governments and citizens alike, has been very successful. Nevertheless, recent efforts have produced more attention to statewide planning and regulating land use in environmentally sensitive areas.

Regional or local planning agencies, departments, or commissions are the repository of local and, where possible, state legislative delegations of power. Sometimes the planning functions are also performed by the municipal legislative body, but this is becoming increasingly infrequent. The planning commission, most commonly appointed by the local legislative body, will customarily be responsible for development of the area's master plan, for implementation of subdivision controls and of the necessary oversight of planned unit developments. Applicants seeking approval of subdivision or comprehensive design plans, and frequently, those seeking rezoning, will be required to obtain the approval of the planning commission. The commission's functions are advisory (to the municipal council), adjudicative, and administrative.

The municipal legislature will have responsibility for enacting police power ordinances. Customarily, the council will also be delegated the zoning authority, although some state statutes delegate zoning authority directly to zoning commissions, district zoning councils, and the like. These entities may simply be the municipal legislature acting under another name, or may draw just a part of the membership directly from the municipal legislature. The council (or zoning commission) will have the responsibility of enacting the zoning ordinances, officially adopting the master plans and official maps, delegating administrative implementation functions to planning commissions, zoning boards and other administrators, and enacting amendatory zoning ordinances (rezoning). To be valid, the delegations must of course be accompanied by appropriate standards. Applicants seeking rezoning will apply to the council. Their application may first have to be considered by the planning commission, either upon referral from the council or through procedures requiring rezoning applicants to file first with the planning commission.

Applicants who seek to use land in accordance with the zoning ordinance or who wish to obtain exemptions from its requirements for a number of reasons will be required to seek permits, variances, or special use or exception status from an administrator, often the city building inspector. This administrative entity is also commonly charged with the responsibility of compliance inspection and enforcement.

Appeals from administrative action concerning permits and requests for variances and exceptions will be considered by a board, often called the board of zoning appeals or board of zoning adjustment, created by the municipal legislature pursuant to state enabling legislation. Sometimes the city council itself will serve as the appellate entity.

The courts play a substantial role in the process. Under customary local procedures, persons with appropriate standing who are disappointed with the action of the planning commission or the board of zoning appeals may seek review of those decisions in the courts. Persons with appropriate standing who are disappointed with the city council's amendment of the zoning ordinances (rezoning) or its rejection of the proposed amendment may challenge the amendatory ordinance or the failure to amend in the courts. In the latter case, challenge to the denial of rezoning may take the form of challenging the reasonableness of the original ordinance.

Implicit in the above descriptions is the matter of hearings, notice, and the due process requirements that must be observed. While there may be no federal constitutional requirement of an adversary hearing before legislative action of the council or quasi-legislative actions of the commission, state constitutional clauses and statutory procedures deemed mandatory may contain pervasive hearing requirements. Since many of the hearings required are likely to be deemed administrative, the strictures of judicial due process beyond those necessary for fundamental fairness and substantial justice may not be applicable.

The rules may be slightly different in those jurisdictions where voters may participate directly in the local government regulatory process, either through the initiative or referendum process. In some jurisdictions, courts have held that the specific legislative method of enacting or amending zoning ordinances was meant to be exclusive. A growing number of jurisdictions, however, permit zoning ordinances or amendments to be enacted by initiative, or to be approved or rejected by referendum. As noted in Chapter II, the initiative and referendum processes are subject to the constitutional limitations that affect the legislative power, however exercised, and are available for legislative, not administrative, matters. Thus, the Maryland court found initiative, but not referendum, inconsistent with Maryland's delegation of home rule legislative power to the local legislature. In Oregon, with some following elsewhere for a time, judicial views of small-spot rezoning led the courts to classify it as adjudicatory or administrative, not available for initiative. Some state laws may explicitly prohibit referral of some issues. Under New Jersey law, for example, local redevelopment and housing ordinances are beyond the scope of the referendum power. The courts in that state have interpreted that state law broadly, including within its scope an ordinance approving long term tax abatement provided as an incentive to developers. In other instances, specific charter provisions may require hearings in the local zoning legislative process, and some courts have refused to authorize direct citizen actions that would bypass the specified hearings.

§ 2. The Role of Planning

Chief among the disputes incident to the land regulatory process is that concerning the role of planning. Some states view planning as the primary function and consider zoning as merely one of the tools of plan implementation. Indeed, in at least one major city, there continues to be no zoning. In the absence of local regulations, the planning function has been left to the forces of market realities and private covenants. In other states, planning is seen as simply a means of assisting zoning to improve upon its ancestors—fire codes and the cataloging of public nuisances. Some view zoning as the antithesis of land value protection and the free market, designed primarily to protect the residential home, responsive to special interests, not market oriented directions. Others view the planners as too remote, attempting to dictate results without regard to human needs or desires. It is no wonder, then, that consistency is not the hallmark of the relationship between planning and zoning.

In some jurisdictions, the planning function is merely tolerated and the results have value only in providing reasoned input and in predicting what action the city council might take. In other jurisdictions, the results of the planning function are given almost a determinative role in the outcome of zoning disputes.

Whatever the differences between planners and lawyers or government officials, the role of planning is undergoing a marked expansion. A number of recent developments have given renewed impetus to the role of planning in the land use process. Offerings of federal grants for housing, highways, sewage disposal systems, renewed city areas, and pollution controls now frequently attach conditions requiring local or state planning regulation. The periodic possibility of federal land use legislation has also had some impact. Similarly influential has been the growing insistence upon municipal recognition of the external and internal social consequences of land use policies. And finally, growing public dissatisfaction with municipal balkanization, and the complex policy problems of growth and no-growth, availability of housing, need for more effective transportation and energy use, and environmental degradation have had a role as well. Results have thus far included: broad based coalitions supporting serious, effective planning at local, regional, state, and interstate levels; state requirements of local, comprehensive, land use plans, some expressly prerequisite to local governments' authority to recoup development impact costs; increased state involvement in planning for environmentally sensitive areas, and requirement of local recognition of statewide interests; improved scientific data for planners; and increased grants of extraterritorial zoning authority for municipalities.

§ 3. "Plans" and "Maps"

The terms "plan" and "map" are used so frequently in any discussion of the process that it is necessary to make certain distinctions.

In most jurisdictions, zoning ordinances are required to conform to a comprehensive plan. "Comprehensive plan" may, but need not, refer to a master plan or collection of master plans. It may mean no more than a requirement that the zoning ordinance be reasonable, that it not create undesirable spot zoning, or that the city council have conformed to publicly understood municipal land use purposes.

The master plan (or aggregate of sectional master plans) is the published result of efforts by the planning commission or department, often in cooperation (if required) with affected municipalities, to guide the coordinated development of the area in question. Most plans traditionally have mapped land use locations. Recently, however, dissatisfaction with the inflexibility of the predetermined location of use districts has led to development of plans which verbalize municipal land use objectives, with mapping of illustrative location. The newer plans are designed to guide plan implementation in the mix of uses with only necessary fixed location advice, leaving most eventual locations to the interplay of other growth determinants. In either event, the master plan will give an overview of the mix of uses (and use districts, traditionally) and will provide for various kinds of agricultural, residential, commercial and industrial uses; open space, water, forest and soil conservation; transportation and roads; public building and school locations; hospitals; parks and recreation facilities; flood control; staggered development; and building and population density. In many instances, the master plan is advisory only and serves as a persuasive and predictive resource. In some jurisdictions, it plays a greater role, as we shall see.

The "official map" designation is customarily used to refer to the map of projected street extensions, proposed parks and recreational areas, and, perhaps, future public buildings. The importance of the map depends upon the land use limitations which derive from its adoption by the city council, as will be indicated infra. A cognate limitation derives from ordinances banning construction in flood plains.

The term "zoning map" usually refers to the actual results of the municipality's zoning ordinances, the geographic locations of approved use districts. Thus, the zoning map classifies all territory within the jurisdiction according to permitted uses. The graphic significance of such a zoning map will become apparent in our later discussion of floating zones.

§ 4. Techniques of Plan Implementation— Official Maps, Master Plans, Subdivision Control, and Other Devices

It would be inaccurate to say that even the most advisory of master plans is no more than that. Techniques of plan implementation accompany planning results in almost all jurisdictions and require adherence to some if not all of the plan.

Official Maps

Under appropriate enabling legislation, municipal councils have adopted official maps, often prepared by the planning commission, so as to identify and indicate future locations for such public uses as streets, street extensions, public buildings, and parks. Some form of enabling legislation exists in the majority of states. The laws may expressly include the power to reserve the specified privately owned land for streets (more than half of the states) and for parks (only one-third of authorizing states)

in order to prevent land development in the projected streets, extensions and parks which will increase
the future cost of street and park construction. The
result of the reservation is that for a statutorily
specified, brief time, the private owner will be denied permission to build in the bed of the proposed
street, or in the area to be devoted to the park or
playground. Since compensation to the owner will
not accompany the denial of requested permits, it is
necessary to provide a constitutional safety valve
whereby the landowner is entitled to participate in
a hearing to show that the entire property cannot
yield a reasonable return. To prevail, the landowner
must also establish that, in balancing the interests
of the city in keeping future acquisition costs low
against the owner's interests in developing property, justice and equity require the granting of the
requested permits. If the administrator or the board
of zoning appeals grants the permits, such grant
may be accompanied by reasonable restrictions in
the city's interest.

The courts have not favored official map ordinances when reviewing permit denials. Where street
extensions are involved, the courts generally are
constrained by precedent to uphold the system. But
several courts have refused to extend the concept to
parks, because the impact upon the landowner can
be significantly greater, and also, perhaps because
of the lesser importance attributed to parks than to
roads. These courts have concluded that the attempt to freeze the land value so as to reduce future
compensation costs constitutes a taking. In those

cases, the law as applied is unconstitutional and compensation must be paid for the time of the unlawful designation.

Some courts have tried to find a middle ground. One court has recommended that, during the years of the "freeze," compensation take the form of an option to purchase with the option price to include taxes accruing during that time. If the city takes up its option, full compensation is then to be paid. Other courts have ordered tax rebates during the "freeze" period.

Master Plans

As has been indicated, in many jurisdictions the master plan has only advisory, persuasive and predictive influence unless and until zoning ordinances are adopted to conform to it. In these localities, court challenge to the planning commission's plan is both premature (no damage until zoning) and unavailing.

But some jurisdictions have given greater sway to the plan by such means as denominating the master plan(s) the required "comprehensive plan," by forbidding the council to amend the zoning map in a manner inconsistent with the master plan, or by providing that any rezoning by the council inconsistent with the master plan must be approved by an extraordinary majority of councilors.

Subdivision and Development Control

One of the major techniques of plan implementation is authority to control the manner of development and subdivisions. For purposes of this discussion, we are assuming that appropriate zoning exists. The subdivision of one large tract of land into smaller lots for residential construction and sale has a substantial impact on the community. Even greater impact may attend multiple use development. Subdivisions' and developments' impacts include problems of traffic congestion, development ingress and egress, sanitary and storm sewers, water and utilities, safety items such as sidewalks and street lights, aesthetic and safety items such as curbs and street signs, and increased burden on roads, water systems, schools and recreation areas. Not surprisingly, local governments seek to recoup many of those costs from the developer.

Certain assumptions have become fairly settled. The subdivider is deemed to receive a benefit from government permission to subdivide because of the administrative convenience of platting, as opposed to cumbersome metes and bounds descriptions. The subdivider further benefits because the approval of street access, sewers, water, utilities, and attractive plat design makes the property more marketable and hence more valuable. Similarly, mixed uses and higher density increase the value of development projects. The point of plat or permit approval is a usable control point to require from the developer certain exactions to alleviate the impact upon the existing community.

Accordingly, under a variety of state legislative delegations, local units have been empowered to set conditions upon subdivision plat or development permit approval in accordance with those expressed in the state delegation or those set forth in the resulting municipal ordinance. The administrative function is normally carried out by the planning commission (or the zoning commission or town council if it "wears both hats") with which the developer files preliminary plans designed to meet the guiding standards. The commission may modify the plan. A few commissions are also empowered to pass upon both the necessity for and the size of any proposed subdivision. Final approval often awaits final plans or performance bonds. Some of the conditions such as street construction details, lights, and environmental controls are police power requirements analogous to building lines, setbacks, and minimum lot sizes. Others relate to reducing the impact upon the existing community, and it is in connection with these that much litigation occurs.

It must be remembered that the costs of all conditions will be passed on to the purchaser. Indeed, many could later be accomplished through special assessments. Certain ceilings may thus be operative. The city gains the double benefit of having the municipal improvements paid for by the developer and the ultimately higher value of the improved property, which in turn leads to higher property taxes. Market dynamics may create some stark choices, however. The city may have to choose between imposition of the exactions and the availability of low and medium cost housing. The developer may be faced with market realities in deciding to pass on the costs. At some point, increased cost exaction may be confiscatory. On the other hand, market realities may allow, even impel, the developer to enter into an agreement with the local government to share or bear even more costs so as to avoid delay resulting from efforts to slow growth. Opponents of developers' agreements will argue that the local government is improperly contracting away its authority.

As land set-aside conditions led to in-lieu fee requirements, judicial scrutiny intensified. Where the developers did not voluntarily accept the exactions and, instead, challenged them, the courts held that the conditions must find their authority in the delegations of power. Even if authorized, they could be confiscatory if not attributable to development impact. The litigated issue then involved such requirements as land set-asides or dedications for schools, parks and public uses in proportion to the population density of the project, or the contribution of fees in lieu of the dedications. The courts differed in their assessment of what was attributable to the impact. Some limit conditions to those "specifically and uniquely attributable" which would otherwise be borne by the public. Courts adopting this stricter and more searching review reject as confiscatory land set-asides and "in lieu" fees which involve speculation concerning future impact, combination of existing problems and project impact, or use of the exacted fees to provide city services elsewhere in the city. Other courts were more flexible in defining the impact to include future as well as present needs, and in upholding the dedications and "in lieu" fees if the evidence reasonably established that the city would be required to provide more land for schools, parks and playgrounds as a result of the plat approval. In short, these courts demanded a reasonable relationship or a rational nexus (majority) between the development and the exactions.

As set-asides, in-lieu fees, and other exactions evolved, it seemed a short step to charge developers a monetary fee in exchange for the provision of off-site improvements related to the developments. In turn, a growing number of municipalities have turned to impact fees, charges specifically calculated to defray the government's costs of such development-driven capital burdens of population growth as collector and arterial roads, sewer and water treatment facilities, and schools. Impact fees have been accompanied by data attempting to demonstrate the target project's proportionate share of increased burden caused off site. They typically involve fixed, per-unit charges that reflect that proportion. A few cities, willing to risk the disincentives to development that these fees create, have adopted linkage fees that condition some development permissions on the developer's construction of or contribution to the cost of low-and moderate-income housing. Courts that sustain the linkage fees find a rational relationship between the commercial development's creation of new employment opportunities with a resulting increased housing demand caused by the influx of those employees.

Sustaining courts have found the fees imposed in these circumstances to be valid regulatory fees, or user fees, or have found express or implicit statutory taxing authority ("fixed benefit assessments," "developer excises," e.g.). Most invalidating courts have found that the local government's statutory authority did not include the exactions. Others have held that, in the absence of evidence of particular impact and planned use of the money, no rational nexus existed to support regulatory exactions. They were, as a result, unauthorized exercises of taxing power. Yet others have ruled that, even if the taxation were authorized, the classification violated applicable state constitutional requirements of uniformity of taxation.

Reflecting the increasing importance of the U.S. Constitution's takings clause to the legitimacy of land use regulation, the Supreme Court issued two important opinions invalidating exactions imposed on landowners as conditions to development permission. The two cases, Nollan v. California Coastal Commission (S.Ct.1987) and Dolan v. City of Tigard (S.Ct.1994) set the federal constitutional standards for land use exactions. As a general matter, all exactions involve three important elements: the government goal being furthered; the condition imposed on the development (the exaction itself); and the impact on government services and infrastructure caused by the development proposal. The double nexus text established by the two Supreme

Court cases requires that the exaction have an "essential nexus" with the goal for which it is adopted, and that the development's impact be "roughly proportional" to the exaction imposed. At least three important questions remain unanswered. First, does the Court intend to limit the analysis to cases of required landowner dedication of property rights, or will the analysis apply more broadly to other exactions, such as impact fees? Second, is the test limited to costs imposed on landowners as a condition to government permit approval, or does it apply generally to other government-imposed costs and limitations on property's developability? Third, is the double nexus limited to judicial review of individualized "adjudicative" decisions or does it extend to evaluate the impact of broad, "legislatively" adopted exactions?

So long as the state court's test meets the Supreme Court's double nexus criteria, states may impose a heightened level of scrutiny to invalidate exactions that would pass muster under the Court's test. Though somewhat rare, the "specifically and uniquely attributable" test appears to provide greater landowner protection than the constitution requires.

Certain additional considerations deserve mention, although they are a matter of local procedure. Statutes define the minimum subdivision subject to control and it may be a division of land into as few as two or more parcels. Different conditions may apply to smaller and larger subdivisions. Both the promulgation of standards and conditions and the approval or denial of the subdivision plan may be preceded by required hearings. While the due process requirements of fundamental fairness and substantial justice must be met, the hearings on approval are administrative in nature and need not observe the strictures of judicial hearings. Appeals from the action of the planning commission may be made to the board of zoning appeals or to the municipal council. Where no such appeals are provided, or after they prove unavailing, judicial relief may be sought.

Other Devices

A major problem in plan implementation is the ability of government units to withstand the pressures of development and land speculation inconsistent with the master plan either in location or timing. This is especially true if support services are provided by independent special districts not required to conform to the plan. Municipal councils have responded in a number of ways. Many have simply yielded to market forces. Others have attempted to reduce the pressures by limiting times for submission of rezoning petitions, by rezoning to create more restrictive zones for largely undeveloped areas, by temporary moratoriums and the like. In addition, municipal councils have experimented with land banking plans, which involve government purchase of land to hold for later resale in order to influence development and control land values. Opponents of land banking decry the increase of government interference with the market, the heavy cost to public funds, and the loss of property tax revenues.

Some local governments have adopted a somewhat less expensive program that grants property tax exemptions to private owners of undeveloped land. In exchange for the immediate tax benefit, the owner must provide the government an option to purchase the land at a future time for the price prevailing at the time of the option. A similar concept was borrowed from density sharing with neighboring property and has also been used to offset the restrictions imposed on private landowners pursuant to landmark, historic district, or environmentally sensitive designation. It envisions the imposition of development restrictions coupled with landowner ability to sell transferable development rights ("TDRs") to buyers who can use them to increase development density in specific transfer or receiving zones.

Other devices have included ordinances (sometimes adopted by initiative) allowing measured development within specified annual limits, and timed growth ordinances that relate development to infrastructure and service availability.

Reduction of the market pressures caused by land speculation may also be accomplished by attaching "use-it-or-lose-it" deadlines to rezonings and by state taxation of the gains from the sale or exchange of land other than up to one acre used for principal residence, with the rate of taxation increasing in proportion to the size of the profit and decreasing in proportion to the length of time the land is held.

§ 5. Zoning

Zoning may be characterized as a tool of plan implementation. More traditionally, it is seen as the primary function in the land regulatory process. Irrespective of its perceived role, zoning is unquestionably the focal point of the political pressures associated with municipal land development and the legal point at which the plans become effective as adopted in the zoning ordinances. The historical impetus for zoning was multi-faceted. The documented inadequacy of its ancestors, such as fire codes and nuisance designations, in protecting the public health, safety, morality and welfare was a major factor. Zoning also arose as a means of protecting residential neighborhoods, ensuring maximum property values, and effectuating the many goals of planning. Some would end the process, some would radically reform it, and some would remove it from the province of local governments. Political realities suggest that some would agree with its relevance to the public choice theories of "exit" and "voice," and more would especially agree with judicial expressions of its primacy as a local government function to protect the quality of life and the judicial deference deemed necessary for effective zoning and land use control.

Perhaps as a reaction to the futile property-by-property or block-by-block efforts of nuisance and fire code control, one of the initial foundations of zoning schemes was the division of land into districts, where permitted uses are limited and specified. More recently, districts have served other community goals, such as the "storing" of land for "foreseeable" industrial or other uses, the reduction of acquisition costs for industry, and the avoidance of economic and social mixes. This expanded use may have served to enhance the permanence of zoning. As a consequence, though, more flexible techniques have necessitated additional state authorization and have been demanded by courts disturbed by the external consequences of traditional zoning.

Customary state zoning enabling legislation has conferred authority for the division of the municipality into districts of such number, shape and area as may be deemed best suited to promote the public health, safety and welfare. Resulting local laws typically regulate the structures to be permitted, the uses to which the property may be put, and the general trend and kind of building and property development to be allowed.

Ordinances enacted under customary state authority are, like police power exercises, subject to challenge under the Due Process and other clauses of the constitutions. Thus, they must be reasonable and will be judicially presumed so unless facially invalid or unless a challenger shows clear and satisfactory evidence of invalidity. Among the factors influencing a determination of reasonableness are the uses and zoning of nearby property, the extent property values are diminished by the proposed restrictions (although substantial diminution of the protester's property value is rarely determinative standing alone), the benefits sought to be obtained, the relative gain to the public as compared with the hardship to the landowner, and the property's suitability for the zoned uses. The ordinance will thus be tested as it relates to the particular property in question. As is the case with police power regulation in general, judicial view of appropriate zoning objectives has expanded to include aesthetic concepts. But when the ordinance exceeds the judicially determined bounds of reasonableness, it will be invalidated as confiscatory.

§ 6. Rezoning

Rezoning, as we have seen, is nothing more than the enactment of a law that amends the original zoning ordinance. The power to enact includes the power to amend. As such, rezoning will similarly be accorded a presumption of reasonableness and will usually be judged by the same standards as was the original legislative decision that imposed the zoning classification now sought to be changed. It should be recalled that local procedures may require adherence to the master plan or passage by an extraordinary majority of the council. It should also be noted that several jurisdictions add to the rezoning's test of reasonableness the requirement that the applicant show that the circumstances have changed substantially or that there was an original mistake.

The often used terms "spot zoning" and "strip zoning" describe two common fact patterns in rezoning litigation. Spot zoning refers to rezonings which seem to single out a small parcel of land for use or uses different from the surrounding area, seemingly on behalf of one owner. Strip zoning involves a rezoning for commercial purposes, one lot deep, along main roads. Both allegedly produce a harm to the detriment of the public health, safety, and welfare. The terms are really epithets, descriptive rather than legal. Neither type is ipso facto unreasonable although it may be more vulnerable. The fact that one property or one owner is benefitted is not in and of itself determinative. If the rezoning of a small parcel does constitute "invidious spot zoning," that is, if it is held to be unreasonable, it will not be solely the size of the spot that produces the result. Single parcel rezonings, however, have so resembled adjudication rather than legislation that, as was noted earlier, some courts have preferred to treat them as such. The result is the necessity of hearing protections and delegation standards, and the unavailability of customary legislative presumptions, and of initiative and referendum.

§ 7. Zoning   Devices—Euclidean,   Density, Floating, Conditional, Contract, Cluster and Planned Unit Development

In addition to the question of reasonableness, zoning and rezoning ordinance challenges often raise the questions of unauthorized or illegal action. This is particularly true where modern modifications of traditional zoning devices have been used.

Euclidean

The traditional, district-and-use form of zoning ordinance most clearly conforming to the enabling legislation summarized above and to that approved in the seminal U.S. Supreme Court case, Village of Euclid v. Ambler Realty (S.Ct.1926), is known as euclidean zoning. As an aside, it is worth noting that the term derives from the name of the village involved in the litigation and is not, as is sometimes supposed, a reference to the founder of the discipline of geometry. Basic euclidean zoning envisions the specification of determined geographic areas separated according to zoning districts with the uses permitted in each district set forth in the ordinances. Thus, the zoning map will specify every parcel's designated zone classification; reference to the zoning ordinance's text is required to determine the range of permitted uses and other applicable governmental restrictions, such as, perhaps, landscaping and parking requirements, density calculations, and height limitations.

Floating

Traditional enabling legislation tends to produce inflexibility. Spot zoning challenges further limit a municipality's power to modify its zoning regulations to respond to locale-specific concerns. The use of floating zones offers the possibility that a municipality could continue to rely on standard euclidean zoning classifications while introducing some parcel-specific flexibility in the implementation of its ordinance. This device envisions the creation of exceptional districts for such wide ranging uses as shopping centers, garden apartments, light industry, mixed use projects, planned unit developments, or marine recreational centers. At the time of ordinance approval of the use districts, the floating zone classifications are not attached to any specific parcel. Rather, it is incumbent upon the applicant (usually either the property owner or the government itself) to initiate a rezoning to attach the floating zone to a particular tract. The new classification must be reasonable in light of the realities of land development in the community. The rezoning that produces the floating zone classification will follow the same procedures as other rezonings. Thus, the floating ordinance provisions are potentially available for any suitable parcel irrespective of its original zoning classification. The potential breadth of the classification requires that they be carefully drawn to require minimum qualifying acreage and to insure, through specified restrictive conditions, minimal deleterious impact upon the surrounding area. Judicial reaction has been mixed. The persistent challenges to the validity of floating zones illustrate the staying power of euclidean zoning and the instinctive vision of zoning enabling authority as synonymous with euclidean methodology. Challenges to authority have been accompanied by assertions of improper delegation with vague standards as to location, of usurpation of the proper power to grant variances, and of invidious spot zoning denying equal protection.

Conditional and Contract

Municipalities may wish to reduce land speculation, to avoid blight resulting from delayed development, or to exact conditions upon rezoning which reduce the economic impact or other negative effects upon surrounding property, particularly if buffer properties bordering less restrictive zones are involved. Under standard euclidean zoning ordinances, uses are segregated and permitted or denied as a matter of right within each district. Conditional zoning describes a zoning change that permits a particular use of property subject to conditions not generally applicable to land similarly zoned. Contract zoning, which also involves a quid pro quo negotiated by the zoning authority, is the term used to designate unlawful contracting away of the government's police power. The real distinction between the two, however, may be less a matter of substance and more a question of a court's willingness to allow municipalities to engage in what some have appropriately described as dealmaking. That is, if the conditions exacted by the government in exchange for the rezoning strike the court as an impermissible interference with the market, unrelated to community health, safety, and welfare, or an unnecessary restriction on individual property rights, the court is more likely to attach the contract zoning label and invalidate the action. If, on the other hand, the court is convinced that the conditions rationally protect legitimate community interests and offset foreseeable negative impacts of the proposed use, the conditional zoning categorization, followed by judicial approval, is likely.

The conditions may be recommended by the planners, and may be imposed in the rezoning ordinance itself (limited time for completion, e.g.), or may be contained in a separate agreement. The agreement may be accompanied by a deed or option that will permit city enforcement of the covenants, although enforcement thus far has tended to take place under the zoning ordinance. The conditional ordinance may contain its own enforcement provision (for example, a "use it or lose it" provision, whereby failure to develop in accord with the conditions will cause the property to revert to its original zoning classification). Judicial reaction to these techniques has been mixed. They will be challenged, sometimes successfully, as unauthorized by enabling statutes. Provision for automatic resurrection of the original zoning upon breach of the conditions will be challenged, sometimes successfully, because legislative preliminaries or procedures will not have been observed in that "automatic" legislative decision. The agreement will be challenged, sometimes successfully, as an invalid bargaining away of government power. Many courts perceive a difference between a city's binding itself to act in a certain way (bilateral?) and a city's deciding to act conditioned upon receiving the enforceable agreement from the landowner (unilateral?). Courts frequently conclude that since the rezoning can be tested in its own right, the additional conditions merely amount to a benefit to the community.

Opponents of conditional and contract zoning contend that such devices will make it easier for councils to act favorably upon rezoning applications they would otherwise (and ought to) have rejected, thereby undermining the stability of zoning. Proponents point to the public advantages derived from municipal flexibility and discretion to adopt a finely tuned agreement about land use and offsetting its probable negative impacts.

Cluster, Density, and Planned Unit Development

Traditional zoning and land use density techniques had been designed to limit individual lot coverage, building height and structure, and number of units per tract, for the purpose of improving community aesthetics, health, safety, and property value. For similar reasons, classic zoning had moved from cumulative to non-cumulative (infra), stressing use homogeneity within districts. Modern techniques have used density as a tool for other purposes and have sought to mix uses for value, transportation, and ambience goals. Thus, much of the current wisdom among land use planners stresses the inadequacies of euclidean rigidity and seeks to implement land regulation that rejects notions of strict use segregation. Cluster zoning, density regulation, and planned unit developments reflect the view that mixed use development may better enhance property value, efficient transportation, and the conservation of environmental features.

Original density limits may be defended against due process and other challenges. Nevertheless, increased density permission may be a reasonable "trade-off" for developer commitment to achieve other land use or social goals of local governments. In urban areas, the concept may have originated in ordinances that permitted one property's unused floor area ratio to be allocated to the next door property provided the overall density of the two did not exceed the sum total of the two individual lots' permitted densities. Similarly, in suburban areas, cluster zoning permitted smaller lot sizes in return for developer provision of common open space, at least so long as the number of units did not exceed the non-clustered number contemplated by the ordinance.

Today, density "trade-offs" may be implemented to achieve such goals as: support for the arts; more public open space; mandatory and voluntary set-asides of low-and moderate-income housing units in otherwise upscale developments; linkage fees; value for TDRs accompanying landmark, historic, environmental, and agricultural-land preservation; and other results that also serve to relieve pressures on tax revenues. Developers benefit if the increased density's revenues exceed the cost of the public objectives. Indeed, if the sale and rental markets cooperate, the density trade-offs may result in more rational and profitable uses of expensive land.

Density flexibility may require state enabling legislation, although a persuasive argument can be made that it is impliedly within traditional zoning and police power authority. Great care is required in drafting the necessary ordinances and designing the inevitably large administrative role of planning commissions and departments to avoid improper delegations of legislative authority (giving planners the final decision on location of TDR transfer districts, e.g.).

In a planned unit development (PUD), uses and density requirements are mixed. In some urban areas, therefore, density ordinances and the single building agreements that have increased density in exchange for on-site public space may use the PUD term. In the more far-reaching PUD concept, though, the goal is a self-contained mini-community, built within a zoning district, under density and use rules controlling the relation of private dwellings to open space, of homes to commercial establishments and other uses, and of high income dwellings to low and moderate income housing. For example, a PUD ordinance might provide for single family attached or detached dwellings; apartments, accessory private garages; public or private parks and recreational areas including golf courses, swimming pools, and ski slopes so long as they do not result in noise, glare, odor, or air pollution detrimental to existing or prospective adjacent structures; public buildings; schools; churches; professional offices; certain types of signs; a theater; hotels and motels; and dining facilities.

The ordinance might, for example, specify that the PUD may have a maximum of eighty percent of its land devoted to residential uses; a maximum of twenty percent to commercial uses and enclosed recreational facilities; and a minimum of twenty percent to open spaces. Residential density provisions would limit the number of units per acre, height, proximity, and the number of units in permitted town house structures.

§ 8. Flexibility Devices—Exemptions, Accessory Uses, Special Exceptions, Variances, Nonconforming Uses, and Cumulative Zoning

Straightforward, unwavering application of a zoning ordinance may create a hardship for individual owners. To allow necessary support services to be located in appropriate areas, and to achieve some flexibility in zoning ordinance implementation necessary to avoid confiscatory results, cities may turn to a number of exceptional zoning devices which permit individual land uses in apparent conflict with the use classifications of the surrounding zone.

Exemptions

A number of zoning enabling statutes expressly exempt, or are interpreted to imply local power to exempt individual parcels from the operation of local zoning ordinances. Commonly exempted is the property of paramount government units (with the resulting intergovernmental power disputes as defined described in Chapter I) and property of the zoning government itself. These governmental exemptions are generally limited to property used in the performance of governmental rather than proprietary functions, whether the use be by the government directly or by private parties to whom the property is leased. Even if an exemption is not expressed in the zoning ordinances, a court will decree that a municipality is not subject to zoning restrictions in the performance of its governmental functions. Under exemptions, for example, municipalities have been permitted to construct fire houses and sewage disposal plants in single family residential districts.

Exceptions

There are a number of ways in which a landowner can obtain special permission to use property otherwise governed by the zoning ordinance. The applicant may seek a permit for an accessory use, a special or conditional use or exception, or a variance. Occasionally, legislation, local jurisdictions or the courts confuse or intentionally commingle the standards applicable to each status. Frequently, one jurisdiction will list as a permitted accessory use what another will only accept as a permitted special exception. Occasionally, generic standards governing administrative determinations in the accessory and special use areas, particularly where the contemplated uses are not listed, will result in judicial declaration of improper delegation. Our present discussion will present each as a discrete device for exceptional use, recognizing that the subject of the permit or the standards governing its grant will not always be classified with the same clarity.

Accessory Uses and Structures

Municipal zoning ordinances regularly permit the establishment of accessory uses on a lot. Some uses denominated accessory are incidental to the primary use and allowed as a matter of right, such as frequently is the case for detached garages and tool sheds. A "permission assumed" accessory use is variously defined as one secondary to the primary use, one auxiliary to the primary use, one so customarily incident and so necessary or commonly to be expected that it cannot be supposed that the ordinance was intended to prevent it. When the use is of such a nature or extent as to impair the character of the neighborhood, it will be assumed that the ordinance was intended to prevent it. Much litigation is involved, particularly with respect to residential zones. It may be illustrative to compare doghouses, ham radio antennae and private religious, educational, cultural and recreational activities with kennels, loudspeakers, satellite reception dishes, multiple person professional offices and spotlight systems for night recreation, although predicting the outcome of accessory use litigation is risky.

A second type of accessory use has the same label but may require a special permit to be established. Residential zoning will frequently permit customary home occupations (piano teaching, e.g.) and those of a recognized profession, often listing doctors, dentists, lawyers, accountants, engineers, veterinarians, etc. The provisions will often limit the number of participating professionals to those actually residing in the dwelling. Some will expressly forbid medical or dental clinics. What may distinguish this category of exception from the accessory uses above, may be the requirement of a permit. What distinguishes both from the exceptional categories that follow is that an accessory use must be subordinate in fact to the primary use of the property. When the accessory use, even though permissible in theory, becomes the paramount use of the property, termination will be ordered and appropriate penalties will follow failure to terminate the offending use.

Special Exceptions

Applicants may seek special exception status, i.e., may apply for conditional use, special use or special exception permits. Such permits are designed to meet the problem that arises when certain uses, although generally compatible with the basic use classification of a particular zone, should not be located as a matter of right in every area included within the zone because of hazards inherent in the use itself or special problems which its proposed location may present (traffic, noise, smell, etc.). Special use or conditional user permits afford the local government the flexibility to allow the use when its impact is minimal, allow the use and impose mitigation measures to address concerns, or deny the use if the concerns cannot be resolved. Standards should govern permit approval and the ordinances ordinarily list the possible exceptional uses. Examples are churches, schools, philanthropic homes and hospitals in residential zones; and gasoline stations and shopping centers in commercial zones. Exceptions may include structural conditions (height, density) as well as the type of activity. Special uses or exceptions differ from variances in that the former are compatible with, supportive of, and permitted in the zone where they will be most effective and least detrimental, while the latter are prohibited uses, and allowed only in cases of undue hardship.

Variances

The history of zoning is replete with charges of maladministration and favoritism, contributing to an image local government finds hard to change. One of the most frequently criticized aspects is the grant of variances. The variance device is easy to describe but extremely difficult to administer. In virtually all jurisdictions, deviations from the explicit text of the zoning ordinance may be permitted, with appropriate protective conditions, if enforcement of the ordinance upon the landowner's property in question would cause practical difficulty or unnecessary hardship. The standard has generally been upheld as providing sufficient guidance to prevent arbitrary implementation. The applicant is required to establish the factors governing the hardship determination. They generally include the following:

(i) The property could not yield a reasonable return if used only for the permitted purposes (although increase or decrease in value alone is not determinative); and

(ii) The problem of the owner's property reflects unique circumstances and not conditions common to the neighborhood which would reflect upon the reasonableness of the ordinance in general.

One seeking a bulk variance will show the practical difficulty and, like the seeker of the use variance, will have to show the absence of negative factors, namely that:

(i) The use or area change sought will not alter the nature of the local area;

(ii) The variance will be "in harmony" with the comprehensive zoning plan; and

(iii) The variance will not seriously impair the public health, safety, morality or welfare.

As a matter of land use planning principles, use variances have profoundly different consequences for the surrounding properties than the more common setback, bulk, or density variance. In fact, use variances are the functional equivalent of rezoning an individual parcel, yet they may not involve legislative action. That is, if a parcel is given a variance to engage in a use not permitted within its zoning classification, it has essentially acquired a new zoning designation. For that reason, many local laws and some judicial decisions prohibit the use of the variance to produce a use change. The other, more modest variances more clearly constitute minor adjustments, allowing the zoning authorities to adhere to the spirit of the underlying zoning classification while waiving some of the specific provisions to avoid undue hardship for the owner.

On that basis, for example, a variance from ordinance set-back requirements might be possible for a residential landowner of an odd-shaped lot who, to meet zoning requirements, would otherwise have to build a dwelling ninety feet long by ten feet wide. Allowance of more extensive lot coverage would not markedly distinguish this planned dwelling from houses built in the neighborhood prior to the ordinance. The court's decision (and that of the board of zoning appeals) might have been otherwise if the landowner had also owned an adjacent lot which could have been combined to permit a building in conformity with the zone. Likewise, the court would generally not approve of a variance if it found the hardship to have been self-created by the landowner.

Nonconforming Uses

The question of confiscation is most apparent in the case of a property use that pre-existed enactment of the zoning ordinance. Suppose the government proposes a residential zoning classification for a large residential area containing a few commercial uses. The effect of the zoning is to render the commercial uses nonconforming with the ordinance. The problem is in part avoided by the provision in virtually all zoning ordinances for the continuation of nonconforming uses that were operating lawfully at the time of the zoning. There are, however, three main areas of dispute: when does a use qualify for a nonconforming continuance status; what limitations may be imposed upon its continued existence; and how may it be terminated.

While there is much factual litigation, the first two legal standards are fairly well settled. The use must be in existence or there must have been substantial investment or construction prior to enactment of the ordinance that renders the use nonconforming. A race to begin construction and substantially complete may not qualify the property for nonconforming status. Though the nonconforming uses are generally lawful, the city may limit the owner's future modification of the property in many ways. For example, it may forbid expansion or material change, it may disallow resumption when the use is abandoned, and it may prohibit rebuilding after total destruction caused by fire or other disaster. Some courts distinguish between natural and unwarranted expansion, holding that an overly technical assessment of an existing nonconforming use cannot be utilized to stunt its natural development and growth. Several jurisdictions have enacted discontinuance laws designed to enable prompt judicial abandonment determinations. Nevertheless, courts will often import the more demanding, common law abandonment doctrine in making these decisions.

The original theory behind the doctrine of nonconforming uses was that these uses, because of their inconsistency with the overriding zoning classification, would eventually disappear on their own. History has demonstrated, however, that market forces operated in exactly the opposite direction. That is, the owner of a legally operating nonconforming use, say a grocery store in a residential neighborhood, has a lawfully sanctioned monopoly that may create strong economic incentives to remain at that location. As a result, municipalities have developed methods to encourage the conversion of nonconforming uses to new permitted uses. Clearly, those uses that are substantial nuisances, detrimental to the public health, safety, morality and welfare may be expeditiously terminated under the appropriate procedures. For other uses, a jurisdiction may require termination after a reasonable period of time during which the owner may have a fair opportunity to amortize investment and make future plans. The courts are generally favorable although they sometimes rigorously and sometimes inconsistently review the amortization period to avoid unconstitutionally confiscatory results. Among the factors of reasonableness are the amortized life of an existing structure, the balance between the social harm and the private injury, availability and cost of relocation, the nature of the neighborhood, and the possibility of a saving modification. Amortization has been used fairly widely as a tool to help municipalities decrease the visual clutter and asserted safety hazards caused by a large number of billboards on arterial streets. In at least one state, though, amortization of a lawful nonconforming use has been found to be impermissible under the state constitution's "inherent and indefeasible" right of its citizens to possess and protect property. The courts of that state have interpreted the provision as preventing municipal termination of a pre-existing adult business in an area rezoned to exclude such businesses. They have, however, allowed municipal discontinuation of an abandoned nonconforming use. Thus, in that state, the municipal power to terminate existing nonconforming uses is circumscribed.

Under appropriate state enabling legislation, some localities have been permitted to condemn nonconforming uses under the eminent domain power, to pay just compensation to the owner, and even to obtain revenues therefor by special assessment imposed upon the district benefitted by the condemnation. In other jurisdictions, courts have upheld as valid under the traditional zoning enabling and eminent domain authority municipal zoning with compensation whereby the zoning restrictions are imposed as well upon what would otherwise have to be nonconforming uses and compensation is paid for loss in value shown to have resulted from the restrictions.

Cumulative and Non-cumulative

Related to the matter of nonconforming uses is the question of cumulative zoning. As we have seen, zoning principles have long been premised upon the establishment of districts, for example, single family or agricultural ("highest" or "most restrictive"), multi-family, commercial or business, light industry, medium industry and heavy industry ("lowest" or "least restrictive"). In the early years of zoning, ordinances were cumulative. That is, more restrictive uses were permitted as a matter of right in less restrictive districts—a house next to the factory, or an apartment next to a commercial use. In the decades following World War II, the ascendancy of planning was accompanied by non-cumulative zoning ordinances which prohibited the more restrictive uses in less restrictive zones. This in turn aggravated the matter of nonconforming uses. Cumulative concepts are again in use. Planners have moved beyond pure, map-located districts to statements of use-relation. Industrial and environmental protection technology has resulted in some zoning which permits the location of industry to be determined not on the basis of what is manufactured, but rather in accordance with that industrial concern's ability to meet the "higher" district's aesthetic, health and safety standards. The growth of mixed use development and negotiated density standards has contributed to a rethinking of exclusive use district classifications.

§ 9. Enforcement

The zoning ordinances above described and the accompanying land use regulations may be enforced by injunctions obtained by the city or in many jurisdictions by neighboring landowners suffering damage. As with other police power ordinances, the city may also prosecute in quasi-criminal or criminal actions. In some localities, administrative cease and desist orders may be available.

§ 10. Accompanying Land Use Regulations

As a part of zoning ordinances and implementation of their generic police power authority, municipalities have enacted a host of regulations affecting uses of specific parcels of land.

Nuisances and Other Restrictions

As has been noted earlier, local ordinances prohibit a large number of uses of land that are deemed so detrimental to the public health, safety, morality or welfare as to be nuisances. These prohibitions raise the question of whether the nuisance declaration, which may totally prohibit an ongoing use of the land, constitutes an unconstitutional taking of property without just compensation. Because of the applicability of the federal takings clause to state and local government action, the standard is one of federal rather than state judicial decisionmaking. Recent Supreme Court case law makes clear that government regulation that prohibits a properly defined nuisance will not be invalidated as an unconstitutional taking, irrespective of its financial impact on the property. That standard is generally referred to as the nuisance exception to the takings clause. At the same time, though, the Court has made clear that state and local power to prohibit nuisances is strictly limited to those nuisances found to constitute a part of the "background principles" of property ownership. The nuisance limitation, the Court has stated, must "inhere in the title itself." Those statements are potentially quite circular in their reasoning, and have created much uncertainty for state and federal courts alike. At a minimum, though, state and local governments have interpreted the Court's opinion as imposing strict and narrow limits on the range of activities subject to prohibition as a nuisance.

The list of valid limitations on otherwise permitted uses is limitless, covering everything from chickens in residential yards to pigs in the parlors. The regulations govern structures, their construction, height, size and appearance; minimum floor spaces on sliding value scales; front, back and side yard requirements; signs and aesthetic considerations. Such restrictions are often justified as promoting or reducing light, air, view, accessibility to police and fire fighting personnel, traffic noise and dangers, fire safety, traffic view and pedestrian safety, and attractiveness.

The once insufficient general welfare interest in aesthetic preservation has acquired increasing judicial acceptance. While one person's aesthetic sensitivity may not be sufficient to support a finding of reasonableness, broad aesthetic considerations, frequently implemented by architectural advisory boards, have been deemed appropriate to protection of the public welfare. Judicial support for the human and economic value of aesthetic regulation in such areas as urban renewal, billboard and sign restrictions, residential zone uses, single family limitations, the locations of adult bookstores and theaters, and particularly the preservation of historic landmarks and period architecture has received much of its impetus from U.S. Supreme Court opinions. Again, state court constitutional adjudications have been stricter in all these areas. Some state courts uphold the legitimacy of aesthetic justifications for land use regulation only when the government can show that the aesthetic considerations were tied to more objective criteria, most commonly to concerns about the preservation of property value in the community.

Despite the deference judicially given to local land use regulation, and the difficult burden of challenge, there have been successful claims that restrictions were unreasonable. In one case, for example, a property owner was prohibited from building a house conforming to a particular architectural period with original materials collected with great difficulty for the purpose because the house would not comply with the district's minimum floor space requirements. Ruling for the owner, the court found that the requirements were not reasonably related to the public health because they were not tied to the number of dwelling inhabitants and were in fact more restrictive than those applicable to neighboring single family districts under the same ordinance. The court further found that the requirements could not be justified by either subtle differences in aesthetic concerns or preservation of economic value. Restrictions of this type may come under more rigorous judicial scrutiny and became more vulnerable to the reasonableness challenge under state constitutions as courts in some states demonstrate greater awareness of the external consequences of the exclusivity the restrictions support and sensitivity to pressing priorities of housing need for those of low and moderate incomes. We shall again explore challenges to zoning and accompanying police power restrictions in section 11, infra.

Housing and Building Codes

Housing and building codes are the focus of much dispute concerning their effectiveness and their impact on the production of needed housing. They are similar in that they both consist of municipal regulations establishing minimum health and safety standards for building facilities, equipment and construction material, and procedures. A housing code sets basic requisites for human use and occupancy of all buildings, but generally has few implications relating to the structure. It treats such matters as sanitation and trash facilities, heat and temperatures, exit safety requirements, and room and window sizes. There is some overlap with the building code, and what may appear in some jurisdictions' housing codes will be a part of others' building codes. The building code standards for new construction will include structural (earthquake resistance, e.g.), material and equipment requirements, everything from the distance between studding, to the number of required electrical outlets, to the types of pipe permissible for the transmission of water or sewage.

Two housing problems are intimately related to the codes: upgrading of existing housing and providing needed additional low and medium cost housing. With respect to the former, the major complaint has been inadequate municipal enforcement of the housing code. Efforts to protect complaining occupants from retaliatory eviction have met with some success. Additionally, the courts have been willing to treat the housing code as a minimum standard by which to judge the conduct of recalcitrant landlords under tort or contract theories of damage recovery and rent withholding. The impact of tenants' rights, rent controls, and the burdens of the property tax (Chapter V) combined to spur conversion of adequate rental units to condominiums and abandonment of inadequate units. Moratoriums on the conversion of rental units to condominiums were followed by conversion limitations and procedures designed to protect the interests of long term, and often needy and/or elderly tenants. The effectiveness of municipal regulation of the economics of income producing land is subject to continuing debate.

There are more than five thousand building codes operative throughout the country, with innumerable differences in standards. Many code enactments have adopted the proposed codes of the U.S. Department of Housing and Urban Development or of such organizations as the National Fire Insurance Underwriters. But many city councils have been unable or unwilling to keep pace with technological change. Political pressures brought to bear by the development community and local landlords is likely to be influential. The alternative of delegating to building inspectors under generic "public health" and "safety" standards authority to keep pace with technological change and to approve or disapprove construction techniques and quality and newly developed materials may, some would argue, be an improper delegation leaving too much discretion to the building inspectors. As the building industry has expanded beyond local boundaries, becoming regional or even national in scope, the variety in standards combined with the antiquated technological burdens of individual codes has allegedly contributed to substantially higher housing costs than are necessary. In addition, the police power regulations have focused more intensively on environmental protection in construction, prohibiting open burning and requiring such measures as underground utilities, drainage, dredging and bulkheading, safety rules, wetland protection, grading erosion and silt control, tree protection, storm sewers and water run-off promotion, together with the lot size and open space requirements mentioned earlier. Although some studies dispute the conclusion, the cost of conforming to the building codes and the environmental regulations is said to have combined with rising land, labor and material costs to price housing out of the low and medium markets. As a result, those who need low and medium cost housing are turning more and more to industrial housing and mobile homes, and municipalities have had to come to grips with their stereotypes of the traditional zoning pariah, the trailer park.

§ 11. Federal Constitutional Challenges to Land Use Restrictions

The federal constitution offers two primary challenges to the exercise of local zoning power. First, pursuant to the Due Process clause of the fourteenth amendment, which is explicitly applicable to the states, judicial review is available to determine whether the regulation's objective is within the goal of the police power and whether the means adopted by the regulation are rationally related to a legitimate objective. The Supreme Court long ago narrowed the potential breadth of the Due Process clause in zoning cases, when it determined that local zoning is entitled to a presumption of validity, that local governments may properly exercise widespread discretion in promoting the health, safety, and welfare of the community through the adoption of land use regulations, and that if the validity of the zoning classification is debatable, the legislative judgment will win out. Though some members of the current Supreme Court would perhaps favor increased judicial scrutiny under due process when applied to zoning challenges, the minimal review that accompanies the presumption of legislative validity continues to inform due process challenges to land use regulation.

In contrast to the narrow scope of judicial review under the due process clause, the takings clause has been broadly interpreted as providing extensive owner protection against land regulation that severely limits the developability of the profitability of the land. Here the basis is the fifth amendment's language (as applied to the states through the due process clause) that "nor shall private property be taken for public use, without just compensation." The local government, properly authorized, may take private property in a formal condemnation action in which the government plaintiff seeks to exercise its power of eminent domain. Challenges that fall under the rubric of inverse condemnation actions, however, derive their title from the fact that the plaintiff landowner asserts that a particular land use regulation has such a negative impact on her property as to constitute the constitutional equivalent of a condemnation without compensation. That is, the plaintiff argues, because the regulation has resulted in a taking of property, and because no compensation has been forthcoming, the regulation is either invalid or can only be sustained by payment of compensation. This line of argumentation, though recently the source of much litigation in federal courts, has its origin in a 1922 Supreme Court case involving a landowner challenge to state limitation on the right to mine coal. Pursuant to Pennsylvania's Kohler Act, coal companies owning subsurface mining rights were prohibited from extracting that coal in such a way as to cause subsidence of the surface. The Court noted that although "government hardly could go on if to some extent values incident to property could not be diminished without paying for every such change," when a regulation "goes too far it will be recognized as a taking." Pennsylvania Coal Co. v. Mahon (S.Ct. 1922). Key to the Court's conclusion were its observations that the law made the mining of coal "commercially impracticable," that the state of Pennsylvania recognized the mineral estate as a valuable property right, and that the Act had in essence taken a private right (the right to cause subsidence) and transferred it to a private individual (the surface owner). Although the Supreme Court did not return to the regulatory takings arena for approximately 50 years, recent surveys of judicial opinions show that regulatory takings opinions have assumed a position of great prominence and importance in all state and federal courts.

At least four groups of federal cases are relevant to a review of the law of regulatory takings. The Court has articulated two per se takings rules, it has announced a set of standards to apply to takings challenges to government exactions (requiring dedication of land in exchange for permission to build), and it has articulated a multi-factored inquiry that applies in the remaining situations. The goal of each of these tests is to effectuate the important policy underlying the takings clause, that individuals should not be singled out to bear a public burden that is more fairly borne by the public as a whole.

First, a permanent physical occupation accomplished by government regulation without exercise of the condemnation power will constitute a per se, automatic taking. On that basis, the Court ruled that a state law authorizing cable companies to install cable boxes and wires on privately owned apartment buildings was per se invalid. Even though the installations were tiny, almost unnoticeable, and were not alleged to interfere with the owner's use and enjoyment of the property, the Court concluded that this permanent deprivation of the landowner's ability to exclude constituted an unconstitutional taking. Loretto v. Teleprompter Manhattan CATV Corp. (S.Ct.1982).

The second important regulatory taking theory involves another per se takings rule. If a land use regulation deprives the owner of all economic value in the land it is a categorical and impermissible taking. Lucas v. South Carolina Coastal Council (S.Ct.1992). In that case, the owner challenged a state law that applied environmentally based setback requirements to coastal property so as to render his lots completely unbuildable. The Court did not decide whether the property's total value had been destroyed in this case, but rather sent the case back to state court for further proceedings applying the total takings rule. The majority opinion, however, made quite clear that the Court was not impressed with the argument that the land retained some residual value, because the owner could walk, camp, or otherwise use the lot. As subsequent cases have stressed, the total takings test is fairly narrow and applies only in those rare situations where the landowner has established that the regulation has left the property with no economic value at all.

Third, the Court has developed standards that apply to evaluate takings challenged brought by a landowner against a government action that has conditioned the owner's right to build on her agreement to transfer property rights to the public, for public use and benefit. Those "exactions" cases, and the applicable Supreme Court rules, were described in our earlier discussion of subdivision regulations in section 4 of this chapter.

Finally, the test to be applied to all remaining takings challenges to land use regulations operates against the two pronged backdrop announced by the Supreme Court. In Agins v. City of Tiburon (S.Ct. 1980) the Court stated that a regulation will be deemed a taking if it either fails to advance a legitimate state interest or if it denies the owner of economically viable use of the land. That standard seems to subsume due process concerns (legitimacy of the government's objective) into the analysis of the impact of a regulation on a parcel of land. From the owner's perspective, of course, the importance of the government's goal matters little. Deprivation of property rights has the same impact irrespective of the importance of the regulatory purpose being furthered. Nevertheless, this statement perhaps reflects an unstated judicial understanding that as the importance of the government's objective increases, the greater individual burden the court will accept for the protection of the public welfare.

To guide the regulatory takings analysis, the Supreme Court has articulated a multi-factored, ad hoc balancing test. The cases seek to give meaning to the thought that "if a regulation goes too far," it constitutes an impermissible taking. Originally announced in 1978 in a case involving the historic preservation of Grand Central Terminal in New

York City, the test was recently reaffirmed. Tahoe–Sierra Preservation Council v. Tahoe Regional Planning Agency (S.Ct.2002). According to these cases, several factors are relevant. The court must inquire whether the regulation leaves the owner with a reasonable economic use of the property; whether the restriction's economic impact destroys distinct investment-backed expectations; and whether, despite restrictions on some segments of the parcel, the parcel as a whole has retained valuable use. As is inevitable with the application of tests requiring multi-factored, case by case analysis, this test has spawned a huge volume of litigation.

Two related principles are relevant to takings challenges. One involves the timing of the lawsuit, and the other delineates the remedies available to a successful plaintiff. First, with regard to timing, the owner must first seek alternative government development permissions or variances, the granting of which could reduce economic impact. A takings challenge brought before doing so is premature unless the effort would be demonstrably futile. The Court's holdings on ripeness have limited judicial access for many landowners whose development plans have been thwarted but for whom development under a constitutionally permissible framework is still possible. For there to be a violation of the Takings Clause, the challenger must seek and be denied compensation at the state level. Note that these requirements relate to the violation, not to any mandate to exhaust administrative remedies. Distinguish also the requirements of maturity from the requisites for an assertion that the regulation is unconstitutional on its face. If there is room for administrative discretion or any other fact sensitivity, facial takings challenges will be rejected.

With regard to remedies, if a regulation has been invalidated as a taking, the government has three choices. It may abandon its plans, modify them to avoid unconstitutionality in the future, or go forward in the original form and pay compensation. It should be noted that actions under the civil rights laws, specifically 42 U.S.C.A. § 1983, involve that statute's independent remedies, both injunctive and damages, whether the claim be due process or takings. Even if the government decides to rescind the unconstitutional ordinance, however, the landowner retains the right to damages to compensate for the time during which the property was unconstitutionally "taken." The case law involving judicial calculation of damages for this so-called "temporary taking" has produced confusing and contradictory formulas and measures of damages. Most common and straightforward, perhaps, is the calculation of the rental value of the property for the time period during which its development was impermissibly prohibited.

Similar efforts have been undertaken to expand the takings and taking-and-damaging interpretations of state constitutions. Congress and state legislatures have joined in the effort to define the dimensions of a regulatory taking and insist upon compensation therefor, in part, perhaps, because property ownership and expectations so intimately

relate to a person's sense of individuality and freedom, and in part, perhaps, because the ensuing
chilling effect on "overregulation" is seen as a
useful restraint.

§ 12. Exclusionary Zoning

The issue in land use regulation may not simply
be whether the individual property owner or the
regulating community should bear the cost of a
social objective. Some federal and state courts have
identified the external consequences of local land
use laws and the broader societal objectives thereby
implicated. As a result, they have been persuaded to
impose upon the regulator as well as the regulated
the obligation and the cost of giving greater priority
to regional considerations than to local objectives.
These courts, though limited to a handful of states,
have been willing to examine the extraterritorial
impacts of local land use regulation. Multi-acre lot
minimums for construction of a single family home,
for example, were traditionally viewed as legitimate
means for a community to preserve its rural, bucolic
character. More recently, though, plaintiffs have
had some success in refocusing the judicial inquiry
to include consideration of the way in which the
minimum lot size requirements contribute to regional shortages of affordable housing. The courts
that have been receptive to these so-called exclusionary zoning challenges base their analyses on the
starting point that affluent communities, as a part
of the region in which they are located, cannot build

a moat around their borders to wall themselves off from regional problems.

All zoning ordinances are in some senses exclusionary; their purpose, after all, is to limit the development of land that would otherwise occur if market forces were left unchecked. The term has acquired a more specific meaning, though, as it characterizes ordinances challenged as unreasonable and invalid in that they fail to protect the broader public health, safety, and welfare. Courts sitting in states with heavily congested areas and strong traditions of local authority, autonomy, and involvement in land use regulation, and also generally possessing active views of the role of the state constitutions, have sought to expand local governments' consideration of regional social and economic factors in their regulatory decisions. The possible legal doctrinal bases for this greater level of judicial review are at least twofold. First, since zoning powers, like all municipal powers, are delegated from the state to the local government, some courts have held that municipal zoning laws that ignore the broader health, safety, and welfare of the state constitute a violation of the scope of the delegated powers. Second, if the right to housing is seen as something akin to a fundamental right for purposes of a state constitution, the court will be justified in applying heightened review to municipal ordinances that have a negative impact on the regional housing supply.

While they have for the most part limited their role to ordinance invalidation, some of the courts

that have engaged in exclusionary zoning review
have urged the state legislatures to exercise stronger involvement to resolve the tensions between local
power and the broader state interest. Some legislative action has sought to require local sensitivity to
regional or statewide housing supply for low and
moderate income residents. In New Jersey, the Supreme Court's *Mount Laurel* rulings interpreted the
state constitution as requiring local efforts to assure
that each locality bear its fair share of the need for
low and moderate income housing in such detail
that popular reaction produced, with court acquiescence, a legislatively created state agency. It was
designed to achieve court-mandated goals, to remove the courts from primary roles, and to use
processes ostensibly better designed to reflect such
economic factors as the pressing need for housing
renewal in existing urban areas. With these rulings,
the New Jersey courts moved beyond the invalidation of impermissibly exclusionary zoning ordinances; their rulings imposed the requirement that
the exclusionary municipality adopt regulations
that would affirmatively include housing for the
excluded class. Their somewhat unusual approach
to affordable housing led to the coining of the term
"inclusionary zoning," because it rests on the principle that municipalities in growth areas have an
affirmative obligation to meet their fair share of the
regional demand for affordable housing.

Courts in many states have not shared the enthusiasm for exclusionary zoning challenges; rather,
they have continued to uphold ordinances with doc-

umented exclusionary impacts, deferring instead to considerations of local control over the shape of local development. Nevertheless, it is undoubtedly the case that the trendsetter courts have affected the debates, the scope of reasonableness, and local government willingness to impose draconian growth controls.

The issues play out differently in different types of communities. Some municipalities have experienced sizeable recent population growth and are grappling with the problem of increased demand on support services. Others see increased growth on the horizon and wish to assimilate the growth and meet the resulting service demands of expansion in coordinated phases. Yet others desire to retain their existing character and resist change. Many of the desires are neither whimsical nor improperly selfish. Some are, and are masked in terms of customary police power objectives. All, if implemented, may contribute to the present unavailability of low and medium cost housing and consequent homelessness, and deny owners' wishes to use their property. An absence of effective regional planning and land use control can serve to aggravate the balkanized existing social and economic land use patterns.

The no-growth strategy has been preferred by many affluent communities. It has also been adopted by some less affluent, but rapidly growing locales whose schools are overcrowded, whose sewers are at capacity, and whose tax revenues are simply insufficient to provide the infrastructure demand created by the growth. The municipal ordinances, adopted by both city councils and through citizen-adopted initiatives alike are varied. Some have decreed rezoning moratoriums and have engaged in downzoning of presently undeveloped land to defuse development pressures (sometimes with sale of transferable development rights for use elsewhere in the community). Others have enacted numerical annual limitations on the city's population increase or on development permits. Still others have retained or imposed restrictive minimum requirements for lot size, floor space, number of bedrooms, open space, parking, and landscaping, and have adopted stringent definitions of family for purposes of single family zones. Some state legislatures have, however, created appeal mechanisms for developers of low and moderate income housing whose efforts might be obstructed in customary land use decisional processes. As we shall see later, some courts have applied state and local discrimination laws or the federal Fair Housing Act and its Amendments Act to make the local laws more responsive to group homes.

The challengers frequently have been the landowners or prospective buyers who wished to develop the land profitably but whose developments were prohibited by the ordinances. Less frequently, where rules of standing allowed, challenges came from nonprofit organizations developing property for the benefit of minorities or low income persons and from the potential beneficiaries themselves. The exclusionary ordinances were said to be unreasonable in that there are other solutions available for the problems they sought to resolve without depriving those who would be affected by the zoning of housing opportunities, the right to travel, freedom of association, equal protection, and privacy.

Judicial invalidation of existing land use regulation, without more, did not necessarily lead to the challengers' desired uses of the land in question. As a result, some courts and legislatures have created the builder's remedy. On that basis, for instance, the New Jersey Supreme Court ordered that, if the challenging builder's proposal met specified regional housing objectives, invalidation of the exclusionary ordinance was to be accompanied by the court ordered approval of the plaintiff's development project. Other courts have, on a case by case basis, ordered a builder's remedy without specifying a general rule. In yet other jurisdictions, especially as funds to support non-profit challengers have lessened, interested persons have turned to administrative and legislative forums.

In responding to these challenges, it would not be unexpected for courts to invalidate moratoriums which freeze a landowner's ability to seek a profitable property use without some municipal commitment to the completion of necessary planning and decisionmaking within a reasonable period of time. Nor is it at all surprising that courts which discerned unconstitutionally discriminatory motivation and effect would invalidate zoning or denials of public housing permits and would allow the housing to be located not only in predominantly minority citizen areas, but also in dominant majority areas as well. While federal constitutional violation requires proof of intent as well as impact, state constitutional reasonableness may be held to include awareness of external impact. Deference to municipal legislation may be seen as abdication of judicial responsibility when the exclusionary zoning restrictions create a protective wall that "denies, rather than plans for the future." Property values, increased tax burdens, water and sewage demands, and the customary aesthetic arguments have not overcome judicial insistence that the wall not be built.

The burgeoning population and development do present real problems, however. Whatever planning and foresight were lacking in the past, more and more communities are facing development pressures likely to overwhelm existing support services, both in terms of capacity and in terms of the revenues needed to continue to provide the services. To resist the growth solely because of increased tax burdens is probably impossible. To forestall it through moratorium and downzoning techniques without more will probably not long be tolerated. Courts have, however, allowed municipalities to control the rate at which growth occurs. Thus, some communities have adopted ordinances that tie permitted growth to the completion of necessary capital facilities and other support services, in turn the result of government, private, or mixed efforts and contributions. Land in the meantime is zoned more restrictively. Judicial approvals suggest that such ordinances will be upheld where they do not cloak

no-growth intent. Examples of local growth regulation that has been upheld by state courts include:
plans requiring construction of some low and medium cost housing; ordinances regulating the provision of services and construction of infrastructure
according to a specified time schedule which reveals
a reasonable attempt to accommodate growth; provisions allowing landowners to accelerate the provision of services by assuming to underwrite their
costs and thus build on their land at an earlier date;
and the reduction of property tax assessments to
reflect present use restrictions. In all of these examples, the courts' decisions to uphold the local
growth initiative were based on the assumption that
the local governments were committed to allowing
growth within a reasonable time and that the property owners whose plans had been delayed would
ultimately experience appreciation in value.

Exclusion may be more limited; it may involve
only certain, non-nuisance uses in particular zones.
Illustrative, as noted earlier, are group homes. They
may aid in placement and treatment of the mentally
retarded, of alcoholics, of drug addicts, or of prison-
ers. They envision a limited number of residents
with counselors, in homes located in single family
residential zones. They may trigger restrictive private covenants limiting uses to single family and
the like. (Judicial enforcement is mixed.) They may
also involve denials of permits based on single-
family definitions and occupancy restrictions in the
applicable zoning ordinances. Many of those who
would live in the homes are protected by law

against discrimination (disabled, the Fair Housing Amendments Act of 1988, e.g.), and are thus distinguishable from groups of students wishing to room together whose exclusion has been upheld in federal courts. The federal laws prohibit discrimination against persons on the basis of a disability, and require municipalities to make reasonable accommodations in rules, policies, practices, or services when they may be necessary to afford disabled persons equal opportunity to use and enjoy a dwelling. A local government's refusal to make such reasonable accommodation may amount to disability discrimination. The U.S. Supreme Court has ruled that the exemption for legitimate occupancy restrictions in the Fair Housing Act does not cover ordinance provisions defining single family as persons related by blood, marriage or adoption, or up to five unrelated persons.

CHAPTER IV

ACQUISITION, LIMITATIONS ON USE, AND DISPOSITION OF GOODS, SERVICES AND PROPERTY

As with the other local governing powers, the powers to acquire, use and dispose of goods, services and property must find their source either expressly or by implication in state authorization through constitutional home rule clauses and specific or general state statutory provisions. Exercise of the powers will also be subject to state and federal constitutional protections and to the limitations in the local governing entity's charter.

Our discussion of acquisition will focus primarily on purchase and on taking under eminent domain, both of which must serve a public purpose or permit a public use. Central to purchasing are municipal contracts. Our discussion thereof will nevertheless recognize that the contract has many municipal uses in addition to purchasing such as leases; agreements whereby private contractors undertake to provide municipal services to the public or to perform functions traditionally performed by the municipality ("privatization," see Chapter II); contracts in connection with zoning;

and intergovernmental agreements. We shall additionally see some aspects of acquisition by gift, dedication, adverse possession and prescription and user.

To illustrate the number of limitations which may be imposed upon municipal use of property by constitutions, statutes, charters and the common law, we shall focus upon nuisance uses, limitations incident to the manner of acquisition, and civil and constitutional rights.

The discussion of disposition of goods and property (again often a matter of municipal contracts) will include actions affecting uses of property (franchises, e.g.) and transfers or loss of title (sale, e.g.).

It bears repeating, as noted in Chapter I, that the exemption from federal antitrust laws for state actions which are anticompetitive in nature does not, without more, apply to municipal activity which is alleged to be anticompetitive in violation of those laws. To be exempt, the municipal action must be designed so as to implement a clearly articulated, affirmatively expressed state policy. It must be authorized by something more than the often customary generic authorizations or the implications of home rule, although several longstanding statutory arrangements have passed muster. In an anti-trust challenge to municipal actions, the Court concluded that, if the anti-competitive municipal behavior was the foreseeable result of the local activity authorized by the state, the state authorization requirement had been met.

Judicial recognition of possible municipal antitrust liability for its activities or those in which it joins with private parties, whether labeled governmental or proprietary, resulted in such a rapid escalation of claims that Congress removed the damages remedy under federal antitrust law. Illustrative of the potential reach are occupational licensing and regulation, operation of sports and convention facilities, zoning and rezoning, urban development, award of franchises, operation of garbage collection services, transportation services (including taxicab monopolies, transit systems, airports, and parking lots), and the provision of utility services. While courts have found appropriate authorization for much municipal activity alleged to be anticompetitive, and have found other instances where the exemption could not be extended to the challenged activity, the issue of the municipality's exemption is, of course, not synonymous with the question of its ultimate liability under the antitrust laws, a much more difficult matter for the plaintiffs. The state exemption, and where merited, the local exemption are not always applicable. For example, the Robinson–Patman Act does not exempt from its proscriptions the sale of pharmaceutical products to state and local government hospitals for resale in competition with private pharmacies.

A. ACQUISITION BY CONTRACT

§ 1. Introduction

General principles of the law of contracts govern determination of the existence, interpretation, and enforcement of municipal contracts. Additionally, customary principles of implied contracts and of quasi-contractual relief and restitution may govern municipal relationships with others. While a municipality may not irresponsibly repudiate its obligations, there are many restrictions peculiarly pertinent to municipal contracting having their source in common law, constitution, statutes, charters, and ordinances, violation of which may render a contract void, voidable or unenforceable in some manner. The issue may arise because an attempted municipal contract is challenged as invalid by a municipal citizen with proper standing (see Chapter VI), because the city resists payment, or because, while the contract is invalid, either the municipality or the other party may nevertheless be seeking quasi-contractual relief or restitution. Breach of contract processes will likely be deemed adequate to protect a contractor's property interests for due process purposes.

In these situations, courts may invalidate the attempted contract on several grounds: as being ultra vires; "specifically prohibited by law;" against public policy or illegal; or infra vires but entered into in a defective manner. The significance of such classifications may be seen in the relief that is afforded. If the original contract will not be enforced, can it have been ratified? Has the city waived the limitations? Will the municipality be estopped to deny the agreement's validity? Is quasi-contractual relief available? May the municipality or the private party recover what it has transferred pursuant to the invalid contract? Apparently inconsistent use of these classifications or labels and answers to such questions as the availability of quasi-contractual relief may stem from the underlying judicial objectives in the particular cases. Some courts are merely imitative in the unquestioning application of debatable precedent. Other courts attempt to give substance to the protections that were ignored during contract formation, sometimes to the point of penalizing the participants while guarding the interests of the taxpayers in general. Of the latter courts, while some will feel the necessity to label the attempted contract ultra vires or the like in order to achieve this goal, others may deny requested relief without regard to the label. An increasing number of courts have enforced the taxpayer protections by invalidating the purported contract but have not deprived the parties of at least quasi-contractual relief.

For example, let us suppose that the city of Allgood had signed a contract for construction of the superstructure of the domed stadium without first advertising for bids as required by its state's law. Assume that at the prescribed times for compensation of the contractor under the agreement, the city refused to pay. At some point, work would be terminated and the construction firm would sue. Its goals would be enforcement of the contract, either as initially executed or as ratified, or declaration that the city had waived the restrictions or was estopped to deny the contract's validity, or failing that, payment of such sums as would reflect the unjust enrichment of the city which gained advantage from the firm's labor and materials.

The court has a number of choices. It cannot declare the original contract valid, find a waiver, or allow ratification of it because the citizens would not then have received the protection of the bid requirements. If the contract had been virtually fully executed and if the flaws had rendered it voidable rather than void, the city's failure to declare it void would result in judicial enforcement of the contract. If work had proceeded to an advanced stage and there were other acts by the city which misled the contractor, the court might hold that the doctrine of estoppel prevented the city from denying the validity of the contract, by finding that the construction firm justifiably relied to its detriment. The court could declare the contract invalid but could order the city to compensate the construction firm for its labor and materials in an amount reflecting the benefit by which the city was unjustly enriched or the costs to the construction firm. If the court were troubled by the labels, it could choose to find that although the city was empowered to enter into such contracts, contract formation had been accomplished in a defective or illegal manner.

On the other hand, the court might be concerned with municipal illegality and extravagance. It could conclude that to give any relief to the private party would be to undermine the safeguards designed to protect the taxpayer. This might be especially likely if there were evidence of bad faith. In this case, the court would be likely to declare that those who contract with the city are charged with knowledge of the limits of the city's authority and that those who fail to observe those limits must suffer the consequences. If the court felt it necessary to underscore denial of relief with the appropriate label, it could decide, for instance, that a contract let without adherence to state bidding requirements was against public policy, or was specifically prohibited, or that the city only had the power to enter into such contracts when they were preceded by bids and had thus acted ultra vires.

For those who desire predictability in this area, precedent is, of course, a significant factor. Evidence of fraud or bad faith is also a significant factor. While many commentators argue that there are other remedies and that the courts should not intermix principles of quasi-contractual relief and individual penalties, the degree of egregiousness surrounding the soiling of the parties' hands in failing to observe municipal limitations will continue to play a determinative role in the outcome.

§ 2. Authority to Contract

Accordingly, the basic question is whether the municipality was empowered to enter into the contract. General authority to contract is uniformly available, and specific statutory authorizations abound. As in other power contexts, the courts will be interpreting express powers and those to be necessarily or fairly implied, and the outcome will often turn on the court's liberality of interpretation. Illustratively, one court upheld a municipality's purchase of a senior citizens' recreation and residence property in a resort city in another state, finding authority in both state constitutional and statutory provisions. State constitutional clauses authorized the municipality to undertake "all works which involve the public health or safety" and public works "within or without its corporate limits." In addition, a state statute authorized municipal borrowing for housing facilities and for the construction of public improvements within or without the city's corporate limits. Though none of these sources specifically addressed the legitimacy of the city's extraterritorial purchase, the court found the totality of the clauses sufficient to uphold the municipal action.

A contract which is declared ultra vires, because there is no authority therefor in any sense, or because the contract is specifically prohibited, or because the ignored manner of contracting is deemed central to the existence of the power to contract, will be void. Since there is no authority to contract, there is no authority to adopt or ratify the agreement; nor can a contract in fact be implied. The ultra vires determination may result as well in judicial refusal to apply estoppel or to grant quasi-contractual relief lest the result be to enable the municipality to do indirectly what it cannot do directly. On the other hand, some jurisdictions follow a general rule that one who makes a contract with a municipality is estopped to assert that it was ultra vires when it is sought to be enforced *against* him or her. Again, modern decisions are more likely to accord quasi-contractual relief except where there is fraud or bad faith.

§ 3. Conflict of Interest

Our earlier discussion of provisions designed to assure the integrity and undivided loyalty of municipal officials alluded to the invalidation of municipal contracts attended by the appearance of conflict of interest. It also described possible criminal penalties for officials and employees who, while associated with the municipality or (sometimes) during a specified period thereafter, contract with, or acquire financial interests in contracts with, their local government. Such contracts are considered at common law to be against public policy and in addition are specifically prohibited by statute or charter in many jurisdictions. Prohibited are contracts in which a member of the government or an officer of the municipality has a conflict of interest. The ban is categorical and has no regard to the fairness of the contract to the municipality, to the level of involvement of the member or officer, or to whether improper influence was actually exercised. In some jurisdictions, a conflict of interest of a municipal employee will suffice to invalidate a contract if the employee could have possibly influenced the award of the contract.

The contracts will be deemed either void, or voidable at the option of the city. The judicial application spectrum ranges from a few decisions validating contracts where the affected person's vote was not controlling, to several decisions extending the debilitating interest to ones remote and indirect, and not necessarily financial in nature.

Here, as in connection with other restrictions on the power to contract, there arises the problem of an emergency. Conceivably, a municipal official might be in a unique position to render services or provide products needed to assist the government in meeting a sudden emergency for which, through no fault of its own, it was unprepared. Some courts have upheld municipal contracts in such circumstances. Equally conceivable are attempts by a local government to bypass contract protections by responding to debatable emergencies or to undoubted emergencies which arise because the government has negligently failed to deal with the problem until it was too late. Accordingly, to avoid multiplication of exceptions devouring the rule, other courts have ruled contracts invalid even if there was a real emergency. Courts which recognize the exception insist that the fact of emergency is subject to judicial review.

Because conflict-of-interest contracts are specifically prohibited by many jurisdictions' statutes, or will be deemed contrary to public policy, the doctrines of ratification, waiver, and estoppel will not help to save them. Again, quasi-contractual relief may not be given, although there are cases permitting it, especially where, under the applicable law, the contract is voidable rather than void. Here particularly, the nature of the circumstances will play a determinative role.

§ 4. Other Contracts Against Public Policy

A number of local government contracts run a sizeable risk of invalidation as contrary to public policy by reason of their duration, the nature of the delegation or of the government's promise, invidious discrimination, or improper purpose. The challenges may be brought by the municipality in defending its refusal to honor the contract, or by challengers seeking to enjoin the contract's implementation or to recover value given by the city pursuant to the allegedly invalid contract. Arguments raised by the challengers may be extremely wide-ranging: that the contract will extend for an unreasonable length of time; that it will extend beyond the term of the present governing body; that it has unfairly or unwisely tied the hands of the local council's successors; that the government has agreed to exercise governmental powers in predetermined ways, or to refrain from exercising them; that the agreement amounts to an invalid delegation of legislative power to others; that there was a conflict of interest; or that the agreement is intended to achieve some purpose, such as influencing state legislation, which under that particular jurisdiction's law is contrary to public policy. Successful characterization of the contract as being thus against public policy will result in its invalidation, will bar ratification, will prevent use of theories of estoppel even if the other party has completely performed, and, as we have seen, will have inconsistent but increasingly less "penalizing" results on the matter of quasi-contractual relief.

The question of the contract's duration may involve a statutory limit (e.g., "no contract shall extend beyond ... years unless approved by the electorate at a special election called for that purpose"). It may also involve judicial analysis of what, under the circumstances, is a reasonable duration. For example, in an interlocal contract of long or unlimited duration, the city's cost of performance may have become grossly disproportionate to the benefits to the other entity, with substantial consequential detriment to the city and little to the other party. While perpetual agreements without specific state legislative authority have been invalidated, some rather long durations have been declared reasonable.

The governmental-proprietary dichotomy, and its difficult and unpredictable delineation, pervades this area. Courts are much more likely to sustain "proprietary" contracts which are alleged to contravene the above listed public policies than they are to uphold "governmental" ones. For example, a municipal contract contained two provisions pertinent to our discussion. Under one, the city granted to the other party the exclusive privilege of buying from the city all wet garbage collected by the city, to be processed by the other party into commercial products for personal profit. The private party in turn agreed to construct an adequate disposal or processing plant. By the second provision, the city agreed "through passage and enforcement of appropriate ordinances and the discharge of the police power of the city" to provide for the collection of wet garbage in separate containers from trash and other dry refuse at the source of accumulation.

The garbage processor built the expensive processing plant. A new city council was elected and repudiated the contract. The garbage processor's trustee in bankruptcy sued for damages which included the difference between the cost of construction of the plant and its salvage value, but not including anticipated profits.

The court upheld the first provision but not the second, concluding that the latter provision was not central to the enforcement of the garbage disposal contract. The two provisions offer an interesting contrast. Garbage disposal can be seen as clearly related to the public health. As such, it can be characterized as a governmental power. If it were so characterized, the court might have been disturbed that the contract was to last for fifteen years and that it was exclusive, thus extending for an unreasonable period of time, beyond the time of the contracting council, and unfairly tying the hands of the successor council.

On the other hand, there is authority for the proposition that garbage disposal is a proprietary matter, a service provided to the corporate members not in the exercise of sovereignty but in lieu of private commercial arrangements. As a proprietary matter, it was an appropriate commercial understanding and did not disable the present or successor councils in their governmental role.

The second provision, however, was clearly an agreement intended to bind the present council and its successors to exercise the police power, the governmental power to regulate citizen conduct (separate trash containers) in a predetermined way. As such, it disabled the governmental function in a manner contrary to public policy.

Challenges to contracts as extending beyond the government's term, tying the hands of successors, agreeing to predetermined manner of governmental power exercise and agreeing to refrain from power exercise are to a large extent different focuses on the same underlying problem. Their outcome is rarely predictable for a number of reasons. First, they may be specifically authorized by state legislation and thus valid. Second, there is the unclear distinction between governmental and proprietary matters. Thus, judicial recognition of practicalities has resulted in approval of teacher and other employment contracts, arbitration provisions, annexation and subdivision agreements, etc., which could only in the most attenuated sense be classified as proprietary. Third, there are decisions which are premised upon the continuing nature of the local government entity (especially where councilors have staggered terms) thereby obviating the problem of tying hands or extending beyond the term.

Nevertheless, successful public policy challenges, as noted above, may occasionally preclude even quasi-contractual relief.

§ 5. Bidding Requirements

While the requirement that municipal contracts be preceded by bids and selection of the lowest ("highest" where payment is from the other party) responsible bidder is a pervasive one, it does not apply to all municipal contracts. The requirement does not exist at common law and must be imposed by constitution, statute or charter. It is, however, a very common feature of state and local law, designed to guard against extravagance, favoritism or fraud. Nevertheless, specific provisions or judicial interpretations may exempt certain contracts from adherence to bidding requirements. Illustratively, in many jurisdictions award through the bidding process is not required for contracts for some professional services, for services provided by a legal monopoly, and for particular real estate (sanitary land fills, e.g.) or other items or services where the courts agree that it is impossible or impracticable to draft specifications which will satisfactorily and realistically permit competitive bidding.

Two significant exceptions divide the courts. One is the existence of an emergency. As noted in our earlier discussion, while the courts insist upon the right to decide whether there was an emergency in fact, many will uphold municipal response to a real emergency taken without adherence to the prescribed bidding process. In other jurisdictions, to ensure that the exception will not devour the rule, courts will not accept emergencies, real or imagined, as justification for municipal failure to follow the bid requirements. Even where the usual bidding requirements are lawfully bypassed because of an existing emergency, a city may be allowed to review or modify the resulting contract.

The courts also divide on the question of the power of the contracting government to bypass the bidding process when it arranges for the original contractor to do additional work required by unforeseen construction problems, or when it needs to make minor alterations after awarding the contract, sometimes in emergency circumstances. The statutory provision may itself speak to the matter, and its dictates must be followed.

Municipal efforts to evade the bid requirement are not uncommon. In addition to specious emergency declarations, municipalities have attempted to subdivide a large undertaking into smaller individual contracts none of which was large enough to fall within the statutory amount which triggered the bid requirement. Others have attempted arrangements whereby private parties lent funds to the city to accomplish the result desired by both, with later repayment by the city. Such evasive efforts have been rejected by the courts.

As noted earlier, the bid requirement may be strictly enforced by the courts, and the labels chosen may predict the result of any dispute. The contract may be seen as generically authorized but specifically entered into in an improper manner. Or the generic authority itself may be held to be circumscribed by the bid requirement, and any contract in violation may be deemed ultra vires. Since there are many steps to the bidding process, determination whether the contract is invalid may turn not only on whether the requirement was observed at all, but also on the manner of compliance with each of the required steps. Here again, many courts will deem the procedures mandatory and require strict compliance, while others will hold them to be directory with substantial compliance satisfactory. The end result of the labeling will be the invalidation of any contract found deficient, and, of course, refusal to recognize attempted ratification. In many cases, courts have refused to apply estoppel against a city's eleventh hour challenge to its contract. Here as elsewhere, quasi-contractual relief is dealt with inconsistently in the courts. Absent egregious circumstances, courts may be more likely to award it than they would be in cases of ultra vires contracts, those against public policy or specifically prohibited, or those resulting from or accompanying conflicts of interest.

Steps in the bidding process provide several check points at which the bona fides of the municipality and the competitive compliance by bidders may be evaluated. The process begins with the advertisement for bids. Public announcement must give accurate notice to prospective bidders of the item or service to be contracted, the specifications to be met, the working conditions to be observed, prequalification of bidders, and subcontract specifications. The specifications must be sufficiently definite to produce a competitive bidding process, without being so restrictive as to make compliance possible only by a predetermined, favored bidder. Where the latter event occurs, it is possible, although difficult, to convince the court that the municipal end can only be served by an item or service meeting the restrictive specification. Whether such restrictions as patented items, union manufacture, local business, or favorable preference to taxpaying bidders may be included is a matter for which the local laws or cases must be consulted. It is also a matter that may involve the federal fourteenth amendment's prohibition of discrimination (racial or alienage grounds, e.g.), impact on the constitutional right to travel, questions of infringement upon areas of exclusive federal control such as immigration and foreign trade, the possibility of impact on interstate commerce, and statutory requirements preventing use of subcontractors which invidiously discriminate. An attempt, for example, to specify U.S. or locally manufactured products as authorized by statute might raise such questions as: whether the city's purchase of materials (if for a governmental purpose, earlier exempted from a predecessor General Agreement on Tariffs and Trade made between the United States and foreign signatories) would now violate binding treaty obligations as a restraint on trade under the presently adopted Uruguay Round G.A.T.T.; whether the specification constitutes an impermissible intrusion into the foreign affairs powers of the national sovereign; or whether the requirement unduly burdens foreign commerce in violation of the federal Commerce Clause. Cases have given conflicting answers.

Also illustrative are efforts to exclude from the pool of potential bidders those persons or firms that have violated the National Labor Relations Act with specified frequency (not preempted by the federal labor law or denied to market participant governments by the dormant Commerce Clause), and efforts to dictate that the composition of the private contractors' and subcontractors' labor force must meet local residency requirements. Resident preferences will raise equal protection questions involving the reasonableness of the classification. Although the government's contract role as market participant will avoid judicial scrutiny under the Commerce Clause, the preference may implicate the Privileges and Immunities Clause if it is seen to frustrate private employment of citizens of other states. The private employment opportunity has been held to be "fundamental" to the promotion of interstate harmony; the ordinance must then be justified by substantial reasons. That the ordinance seeks to prevent qualified local workers from remaining unemployed while nonresidents work on a project funded by local government has been held to meet the test.

Contractors' attempts to extend federal, patronage-limiting, first amendment principles to local government contracts have received conflicting results in the federal courts, with some judicial receptivity to first amendment assertions by contractors whose voiced complaints led to denial of substantial amounts of government business.

Mandatory set-asides designed to involve minority businesses and to remedy past discrimination involve suspect racial classifications and, whether imposed by federal, state, or local government, will be strictly scrutinized. To be valid, the set-aside must serve a compelling governmental interest, and must be narrowly tailored to further that interest. In addition, the city must provide direct evidence of discrimination or an inference drawn from a disparity between the qualified minority business pool (not the whole minority population) in the city and minority business contracts. It is not enough to show general societal discrimination, but the city may justify a program by proving "passive participation" in discriminatory practices. So, for example, it is insufficient to prove an entrenched pattern of discrimination in trade unions making it difficult for contractors to procure city contracts, but it is sufficient to show that the city required membership in a union as prerequisite to bidding, while knowing that unions erected racial membership barriers. Then, it must design a remedy narrowly tailored to alleviate the effects of prior discrimination that cannot be remedied by race-neutral means. The question then remains whether a justified program nevertheless violates state requirements that the municipality award the contract to the lowest responsible bidder. On that issue, one state court has ruled that, given the number of exceptions traditionally accompanying a charter-imposed bid requirement, a minority business outreach program was well within the customary objectives of such a provision.

The bids themselves and the resulting contract must conform to the advertised specifications. The bidders may be required to post bonds or submit deposits and may have to prequalify in accordance with standards governing their financial capacity and prior experience. These requirements have frustrated some municipal attempts to erase past discrimination by expanding their business with minority contractors and subcontractors.

Specified procedures will govern the opening and reading of bids. The municipality will customarily reserve the right in its advertisement to reject all bids, lest all bids exceed the city's contemplated expenditure ceiling. If the municipality does not have automatic legislative authority to reject, if it fails to reserve this right, or if it does not exercise it, it will be required to select the lowest (or highest if a sale of municipal property is involved) responsible bidder, if any is responsible. So long as the municipality chooses the bidder at the lowest submitted cost, likely in regard to skill, ability and integrity to meet the contract's objectives faithfully, conscientiously and promptly, according to its specifications, the courts will not interfere with the city's discretion. Difficulties arise when cities attempt to enhance cost savings and timely completion by engaging a construction management firm at the time of architectural drawings and specification preparation with the understanding that the firm will do the project (need authority if bypassing bids), or when the city passes over a qualified lowest bidder in favor of a higher bidder deemed more qualified. Judicial reviews of "relative superiority" selections are mixed.

The bidder who submits the lowest price thus may not be selected if its ability to meet specifications is surpassed by a higher priced bidder. This low bidder may seek to challenge the award to the other as defective. In several jurisdictions, administrative procedures exist and must be followed. Absent administrative procedures, especially where the city has reserved the right to reject all bids, the low bidder may be unable to challenge in court unless it is a taxpayer in the jurisdiction. In many jurisdictions, only taxpayers have standing to challenge such contracts because the protections are designed to benefit them, not the competing bidder. Some jurisdictions accord standing to the low bidder who is not a taxpayer in order to increase vigilance over municipal contracting. At least one has held the rights under the bidding system to constitute property interests whose denial without due process is challengeable under 42 U.S.C.A. § 1983.

A bidder may suddenly find that its bid is mistakenly low. In the absence of a statutory provision governing mistaken bids, or provision in the advertisement excusing such mistakes, the inevitable acceptance of the bid will impose upon the bidder the obligation of performance, or, failing that, will result in forfeiture of deposits and surety bonds. Customary contract principles apply: a competitive bid is an option based upon the valuable consideration of the privilege of bidding and legally binding assurance to the successful bidder of an award as against all competitors. As such, it is both an offer and a unilateral contract. When accepted, it becomes a mutually binding contract. Some courts will not rescind for such reasons as antecedent arithmetical mistake. Others will do so only if it is shown that the unilateral mistake of fact is so great that to enforce the acceptance would be unconscionable, that the mistake is material, that it happened notwithstanding reasonable care by the bidder, that notice of mistake was prompt, and that rescission would not seriously prejudice the municipality other than by loss of its expected bargain.

In an effort to reduce the differences in state and local laws and procedures in this area, the American Bar Association has approved a Model Procurement Code for states and a Model Procurement Ordinance for cities. Many codes and ordinances based on these models were adopted. In 2000, the ABA adopted a revised version of the Code, now entitled the "Procurement of Infrastructure Facilities and Services." Among the Code's goals were reducing transaction costs for government entities as well as private suppliers, increasing flexibility to chose among different procurement methods, encouraging new forms of project delivery, and facilitating intergovernmental cooperative procurement.

§ 6.   Limitations to Assure Citizen Vigilance

Many limitations of local government contract powers are designed to augment citizen vigilance against municipal extravagance. Illustrative are requirements that a municipal contract (often defined to be one in excess of a certain sum) be in writing; that it be approved by ordinance or resolution; that it be voted upon by the electorate; that it be preceded by appropriations; that it not exceed the cost estimates drawn up by municipal engineers or other officials; and that it be recorded and published. With occasional variations in situations evoking the suspicion of bad faith, the courts are likely to permit quasi-contractual relief, although ratification is impossible when the defect involved conditions precedent. Deficiencies in these matters are usually deemed to be defects in entering upon an otherwise authorized contract although the protections themselves are likely to be mandatory. There is some authority permitting municipalities to bypass the protections in responding to a real emergency.

§ 7. Agency

In many municipal contract disputes, the courts have indicated that the private contractor acts at its peril and must know the limits of the municipality's contracting power. This is particularly the case when the question is the extent of the authority of municipal personnel who enter into the agreement. Persons dealing with agents of the municipality must be aware of the authority of such agents, and if the agents' actions are beyond the limits of their authority, the municipality will not be bound. The contracts may, of course, be ratified by the council or other government officer or entity vested by law with the appropriate contracting authority. Courts are not unwilling to find ratification, and evidence thereof may include express resolution or circumstances (such as knowledgeable acceptance of benefits) from which the inference of ratification may be drawn. Under customary principles of apparent authority, municipalities have not been allowed to deny the authority of their agents when the municipalities have dealt before with the private contractor and others in such a way as to justify the contractor's assumption that the agents possessed the necessary authority. Where municipal agents have exceeded their authority and there has been no ratification, courts are increasingly inclined to permit quasi-contractual recovery, although there remain a number of cases reaching the opposite result.

§ 8. A Note on Some Common Municipal Contract Clauses

Municipal contracts will usually be required to contain a number of clauses in addition to those already mentioned. Illustrative are clauses exacting penalties for late performance; setting forth labor protections, anti-discrimination provisions, applicable price controls, and contract dispute settlement and arbitration procedures; protecting the municipality against liability for personal injury; reserving such rights to the municipality as the right to pay subcontractors; requiring performance bonds and industrial compensation contributions; providing for payment by municipal warrants or coupon bonds; and limiting municipal contract cost liability to funds derived from special assessments. Legal disputes about such clauses typically involve the questions whether the municipality is authorized (for example, in the exercise of its police power) to impose and enforce them, and whether it may waive nonperformance.

Arbitration deserves further comment. The general rule is that, in the absence of statutory prohibition, a municipal corporation has the power to submit both present and future disputes to arbitration. The power is implied from its general capacity to make contracts and settlements and its authority to sue and be sued. When the contract involves interstate commerce, it falls within the meaning of the Federal Arbitration Act, 9 U.S.C.A. § 1 et seq., under which courts must resolve any doubts in favor of arbitration. They must ask two questions: whether an express agreement to arbitrate exists between the parties; if so, whether it has been breached. In short, is the issue arbitrable? If it is, the courts may not delve further into the dispute.

§ 9. Relief and Restitution

It is important to note that classic principles of sovereign immunity required the sovereign's waiver before suit could be brought to impose contract liability. While much of that immunity no longer exists at the state or local levels, there are occasional statutes that serve to immunize states and even local governments for some of their contracts or in some circumstances.

Where, under applicable contract principles, a municipal contract is not to be enforced, where an agreement is not to be implied in fact, where estoppel will not be applied, and where ratification will not be allowed, there remain several questions to be resolved. Will quasi-contractual relief be allowed on behalf of the private party? If so, what is the measure of relief? May the municipality and the private party regain what either or both have given up under the alleged contract?

Of course, there are many situations not involving the legality of attempted express contracts where customary quasi-contractual principles would impose a duty upon the municipality to compensate a person at whose expense the municipality has been unjustly enriched. Such situations include the wrongful taking of private property or withholding of funds and municipal benefit from another's services or from another's performance of duties imposed upon the municipality. Proof of unjust municipal enrichment is the crux.

Where the question involves the invalidity of an attempted contract, we have seen that the results may turn on the nature of the invalidity, on precedent, and on the courts' inclination to penalize egregious conduct. As a general matter, it is safe to say that relief is more widely available today than it has previously been, but some risk of unpredictability remains.

Where relief is to be granted, the traditional measure has been the value of the benefit to the municipality, however much the costs to the private party may have exceeded that value. Occasionally, the injustice of this measure or the impracticability of its determination has compelled courts to allow the contractor to recover costs and expenditures incurred (the contract price less profits), or to award the reasonable value of the improvement supplied or the cost that would have resulted from municipal observance of the legal requirements, whichever is less.

The apparent inconsistency that has accompanied other decisions in this area pervades the matter of the city's recovery of what it has paid under the attempted contract and of the private contractor's regaining what it has given, in circumstances where the contract will not be enforced. At the extremes, results are somewhat predictable. Where an attempted contract is ultra vires, the doctrine's purpose to protect the taxpayer logically commands the return to the city of value given by it pursuant to the attempted contract. Courts seeking to "penalize" those who fail to observe contract protections, particularly in ultra vires transactions, will refuse to order the municipality to return value given it by the private contractor. In cases where both parties are attempting to reclaim what they have given (where the city has not consumed what it has been given, e.g.), courts tend to conclude that it is unjust to permit the municipality to retain the benefits it has received under the contract and at the same time to recover what it has given to the private contractor.

B. OTHER METHODS OF PROPERTY AC-
    QUISITION—GIFT, DEDICATION, AD-
    VERSE POSSESSION, PRESCRIPTION
    AND USER

§ 1. Public Purpose and Methods of Acquisition

As we have seen, the municipal corporation may acquire goods, services and property by contract of purchase. Such purchases are limited to those that serve a public purpose. This limitation, applicable to all municipal expenditures, does not lend itself to precise articulation. Public purpose generally includes all purposes or uses specifically indicated in statutory grants of authority (although some may later be disapproved by the courts) and all those necessary to the proper achievement of the objectives for which the municipal corporation was organized.

One of the most extensive efforts that has been found to meet the public purpose requirement involves direct government expenditures to compete for economic development. The purposes clearly include increased jobs and ancillary tax revenues. In the absence of national policy, competition persists among states and localities, both domestically and internationally, to attract or retain businesses, especially during downturns in the economy. There are varied opinions on what works, if anything, and on how to ensure the public purposes. Techniques range from tax expenditures to sharing employee-paid revenues with employers.

The public purpose requirement may also govern future municipal use of property obtained by prescriptive acquisition. While acquisition of property by adverse possession or prescription and user necessarily involves use by the public for the statutory period, future municipal uses may not be relevant to these title disputes. Hence, whether the property will be put to a public use is rarely litigated in the disputes concerning such acquisitions.

The public purpose limitation also applies to municipal acquisition by lease or by exchange of properties. We shall see that a cognate (if not synonymous) limitation applies to acquisition by eminent domain. It is possible that property, goods or services may be given or willed to the municipality even if the municipality would not have been able to purchase the same property. Acceptance of such gifts has been sustained by the courts.

The dedication device is an appropriation of land to some public use, intended and made by the owner of the fee, and accepted for such use by the municipality. By definition, then, acquisition by this method meets a public use or purpose requirement. Recall what public purpose must be met where the city seeks to require dedication, as in the case of a subdivider, discussed above in Chapter III.

Customarily, and frequently by generic delegations, municipal corporations, especially the traditional local governments, are authorized to acquire by gift, dedication, adverse possession, prescription and user. Property obtained by gift or dedication may be accompanied by donor conditions and reservations of rights so long as they are constitutional, reasonable and do not thwart the municipal purposes for which the property is given.

§ 2. Illustration

Let us return to the city of Allgood. Assume that the city is exploring contingency plans in the event of failure of its extraterritorial domed stadium plan. Assume further that within its boundaries is a large open area presently used for public recreation and playing fields, adjoined by a strip of land presently used by the public as an alley way. May the field and adjoining strip of land be used for construction of the domed stadium? The answer to this question will turn, inter alia, on whether the city has any title to the areas, how title was obtained, what title it has, and what flexibility it has in determining the uses of municipal property.

§ 3. Estate Obtained—The Fee Simple Absolute (Directly or by Implication); Acquisition With Conditions

First, the city may hold both properties in fee simple absolute. Under appropriate authority, title could have been obtained outright through purchase, eminent domain, dedication, gift or adverse possession. If the purchase contract satisfied all limitations or if the taking or acceptance of the full fee had been authorized or was legally unobjectionable, and if no appropriate conditions or reservations accompanied the acquisition, the plan's success would depend upon a court's view of the city's ability to change or expand the use. Whether the stadium constitutes a change in use and whether the city will be held to its original use remain to be determined.

Second, the city may have obtained one or both properties by transfer accompanied by conditions, the effect of which may bar the plan.

Third, the city may conclude that its title to the property was impliedly obtained. Difficulties lie in acquisition of title by implication. Is there sufficient evidence to warrant proper municipal title to the property at all, and particularly title in fee simple? The courts will incline to the private owner's property rights. Accordingly, the burden of establishing title by implication is a heavy one, often expressed as requiring clear and satisfactory evidence, whether acquisition of the fee be alleged to be by adverse possession or implied dedication.

In order to establish title by adverse possession, the city must show actual use by the public for the jurisdiction's prescribed number of years under a claim of right. Such use must be open and notorious. The city must show possession, peaceful control, exclusive, continuous and uninterrupted dominion, without acquiescence by the owner. Where the owner has acquiesced in the use for the prescriptive period, it would be more correct to speak of acquisition by implied dedication.

Implied dedication need not always involve public use for the prescriptive period, however. It requires clear and satisfactory circumstantial evidence of the required elements of any dedication, viz., the owner's intent to dedicate the property to public use and the city's acceptance thereof. Use by the public alone will not satisfy the evidentiary burden, and merely sporadic city care of the property may not be enough. Of course, the owner's payment of property taxes or special assessments and the like will be detrimental to the city's case.

§ 4. Estate Obtained—Easement

Finally, by whatever method of acquisition, the city may have obtained only an easement. For example, it is difficult to imply acquisition of the full fee if the public use to which the property has been put during the period in question could have been accomplished by a lesser estate. In appropriate cases, even though the city may seek to establish ownership through adverse possession, a court may turn instead to the theory of prescriptive easements. In those instances, while the municipality is deemed to have established an easement and is thus entitled to use the property, the original landowner retains ownership of the underlying fee, which has been deemed the servient estate subject to the easement.

The same result may follow a dedication. At common law, dedications which did not say otherwise were deemed to have transferred only an easement. The express dedication may have specified the full fee simple absolute. Or the dedication may have been accomplished by the filing of plats and maps as required by the city's appropriate subdivision control laws. If Allgood's state statutes called for, or were interpreted to permit, dedication of parks and recreational areas or streets in fee simple (rather than the common law easement) acceptance of the dedication could have resulted in transfer of the full fee. This might occur automatically under the statutes, formally through resolution of acceptance or approval of the subdivision plat, or informally by exercising control over the land (repair and maintenance, e.g.). In the absence of clear expression in the dedication or authorizing statutes, the fee simple absolute may not have been transferred.

§ 5.   Effect of Estate Obtained and Method of Acquisition Upon Municipal Flexibility

What limitations accompany whatever estates the city has acquired? If Allgood had obtained the full fees by any of the means of acquisition, or by dedication to it by the state of state lands, and had devoted the properties to the playing fields and passageway uses, it is nevertheless possible that some courts would invalidate those actions as an impermissible change of the original use. To accomplish this, the court would rule that the property had been dedicated to those initial uses, or that the property was held in trust on behalf of the public for the particular public uses (particularly if the passageway be deemed a public street). The more likely result, however, at least in the absence of any additional factors, would be judicial approval of city flexibility.

The stadium plans would face more challenging obstacles if the city's title had been obtained in a manner signifying the imposition of a trust with conditions. If the trust is constitutional and reasonable, if the conditions allow the intended public use, and if the city's proposal will not be within the cy pres contemplation of the trust, the trust will be enforced and the city will not be allowed to change the use. If the contemplated use can no longer be made, the property will revert to the settlor,

Allgood's title may have resulted from the transfer of a defeasible fee, or one accompanied by covenants. The courts do not favor forfeitures and will strive to construe use limitations as precatory words, or, if binding, covenants. In those circumstances, changes in use might not be enjoined. If the language compels the conclusion that the municipality owns a defeasible fee, the courts are likely to favor conditions subsequent, which require affirmative exercise of the reserved power of termination, over fee simple determinable followed by automatic reverter. In addition, they may be less rigid in their interpretation of restrictions on government ownership than in private transfers with similar specified conditions or limitations on use.

If Allgood had obtained only an easement by dedication (or by any of the other means of acquisition), different rules would apply. In that case, the court would ask whether the stadium plan constituted a new public use not within the terms of the original dedication, the scope of the prescriptive easement, or the reasonable contemplation of the non-prescriptive easement. If the answer is yes, the change would be held to create an impermissible additional burden upon the servient estate, imposition of which would need a formal taking of private property requiring compensation to the private owner or successors.

Much, then, depends upon how the city's plan is viewed. If the use to which the property is now put is proper in light of the method of its acquisition, and if the stadium is deemed to be commensurate with that use, absent other restrictive but proper conditions imposed by the grantor, it will not make much difference how the property was acquired by the city. But if the planned changes are viewed as new uses, the city's title and the court's view of municipal flexibility given the property interest acquired will be determinative. If the alley way be deemed a public street, the court's view will likely be strict. We shall see more of the limitations on municipal property use, infra.

C. ACQUISITION UNDER EMINENT DOMAIN

§ 1. Authority

Municipalities do not possess inherent authority to take private property by eminent domain. Such authority must be expressly delegated by the state. Delegations are commonly made to the traditional municipal corporation, less commonly to special districts, and occasionally to private actors. Without express indication to the contrary, the delegation will customarily not be interpreted to permit the power's extraterritorial exercise. When eminent domain power is exercised, the taking must be only of the property and interest necessary for the public use or purpose unless the statute authorizes taking the fee simple absolute. In addition, the taking must be necessary and for a public use or purpose, and just compensation must be paid to the condemnee, or else the taking will violate provisions of the federal and state constitutions.

§ 2.   Some Interests Subject to Eminent Domain

Limitation to the property interest needed in the absence of statutory fee authorization suggests correctly that any property right necessary to a public use or purpose may be condemned under proper authorization. Such rights may include, in addition to the full fee, rights of access, easements including those limiting the landowner's use of the land, contracts, rights to enforce restrictive covenants, and leasehold interests. Some deserve additional comment.

Streets and Abutters

As we have seen, the municipality may obtain property devoted to street uses in fee or by easement. While city possession of the fee simple absolute may determine the rights to underground mineral deposits and the like, city ability to open the street, to change or expand the use or to permit private encroachments upon the street seems to be unaffected by the property interest it holds.

Irrespective of whether the fee is owned by the landowner whose property abuts the street or by the city, the abutter has and may enforce a property right of access. While the right may not be exercised to compel opening of the street, it is defined to include ingress, egress, light, air, view, having the street kept open and continued as a public street, and whatever else adds to the value of the street to the abutter.

The abutter's right is commonly raised in challenges to such municipal activities as street closings, the creation of cul-de-sacs, changes of street grade, and limitations of street access. Similarly, the abutter's right may be implicated by municipal actions such as increased traffic routing, subway construction, street repair and parking regulation. The abutter's right is not absolute. It has frequently been held unimpeded by partial limitations, parking rules and temporary obstructions for repair or construction. Nevertheless, when the city's action is deemed to be unauthorized or so inconsistent with reasonable exercise of the abutter's right when considered in light of the municipal objective that it constitutes a taking (or under appropriate state constitutional clauses a damaging) of the abutter's property right, constitutional due process and takings protections will apply. Compensation for the value of the right taken will be required under traditional eminent domain principles. Additional statutory provisions may call for compensation for specific city street actions such as changes in grade.

Scenic and Development Easements

Many cities are authorized to condemn easements which limit the landowner's use of the property. Illustrative are scenic easements that protect historic or aesthetic interests from encroachment. Often, as in the case of billboards, cities will attempt to achieve such results by exercise of the zoning and other police powers. If the action is upheld as a police power exercise, compensation to affected individuals will not be required.

Because under defined circumstances overflights may constitute takings, airport authorities with eminent domain power will acquire navigational easements to fulfill airport use plans.

We noted earlier that government's land use tools may include easements restricting development. Objectives include preservation of agricultural land and deceleration of population and commercial growth. We shall return to accompanying value "trade offs" like TDRs.

Restrictive Covenants

Occasionally, a municipality may condemn property for a public use in violation of what would otherwise be a binding restrictive covenant on the parcel. The covenantees may contend that their right to enforce the covenant with respect to the taken property has itself been "taken." Some of the cases considering the matter have held that the right to enforce a restrictive covenant is a property right which must be condemned with compensation when the restricted land has been taken for a public purpose. More recent decisions tend to disagree because the covenant agreements necessarily imply the government's important police power (and thus public purpose) objectives and because, as a practical matter, the older majority position imposes too expensive a burden on the city's exercise of the power of eminent domain.

Contracts

In a number of situations ranging from the taking of property subject to a lease to the unilateral termination with compensation of its own contract in order to expand the original public purpose, the municipality may use its delegated eminent domain power to condemn a contract. Such action involves compensation and hence has been held not to impair contractual rights within the meaning of the U.S. Constitution's clause barring such impairment.

Public Uses

May a municipality exercise its delegated power of eminent domain to condemn property already devoted to a public use? The courts have held that it may not unless the power to do so is conferred in express terms, or by necessary implication, and have further held that the rule of strict construction will be followed in making this determination. There have been a few decisions favoring the "more necessary public use."

§ 3. Necessity and Public Use or Purpose Requirements

We have assumed, for purposes of the foregoing, that the takings in question were necessary and for a public use or purpose. These are, of course, fundamental prerequisites to a proper exercise of the eminent domain power, even if specifically authorized by state legislation.

Necessity

The wisdom of the municipal plan and the necessity for its implementation are questions that the courts leave largely to the reasonable discretion of the local legislature. In a small number of states, no local legislative finding of necessity is required. In a few other states, the question of reasonable necessity is reserved to the judicial forum by state constitutional provision. Absent such a provision, resistance by the condemnee on the ground that the taking was unnecessary will likely be unavailing. This aspect of the necessity of the taking should not be confused with such other aspects as when the property is needed, what property interest is needed, or how much property is needed. The courts will readily involve themselves in those determinations but tend to be deferential to municipal judgments.

Public Use or Purpose

It is essential that the taking be for a public use. The courts may frequently use the terms "public purpose" and "public use" interchangeably in this connection, although some insist that use imports more than benefit. Under the federal constitution, the U.S. Supreme Court has held, the public use requirement is coterminous with the range of the state's police power, and the courts will not substitute their judgment unless the legislature's determination of public use is demonstrably without a reasonable foundation. Some commentators believe that the fluidity of "public purpose" for eminent domain purposes can exceed the scope of government's regulatory powers, so long as compensation is paid. As noted earlier, the terms defy concrete definition. By whatever name, the concept will evolve with the changing circumstances and conditions of society. Public use or purpose is determined on a case-by-case basis, and most courts give it liberal construction. As we said at the outset of this text, the question is largely one of the court's view of the appropriateness of the activity for government. What may at one time have been thought to be a more appropriate activity for private enterprise may today withstand public use or public purpose scrutiny.

Of course, takings that clearly promote the public safety or general welfare satisfy the criterion, and takings that solely benefit private interests do not. But between those two poles are takings of property with a range of purposes: to serve purposes that benefit the public although the property will not be used by the public; to be used by a portion of the public; to benefit the public because of public controls over later private owners; and to accomplish objectives traditionally within the purview of private enterprise. These may be illustrated respectively by: condemnation of non-conforming uses; condemnation for local parks; condemnations of property later sold to private developers in the implementation of urban renewal programs; and condemnations to build industrial plants for rental to private industry or to retain industry that is threatening to leave.

While a few courts and commentators may insist that property condemned for public use must actually be used by the public and retained in public ownership, the vast majority upholds indirect benefit to the public as satisfying the public use requirement. In determining whether there is such benefit, courts give great, though not controlling, weight to the state and local legislative judgment. Thus, while in their particular factual setting each of the takings examples in the previous paragraph may be disapproved by some courts, the greater number of courts would fairly easily find all but the last to serve a public use or purpose. In appropriate circumstances today, recognition of the importance of economic development might mean that even the last would survive challenge.

Private Actors

In one area, the courts very strictly enforce necessity and public purpose requirements. Where, by state statute, private persons are authorized to seek judicial assistance in accomplishing a taking to serve the public health, safety, or welfare, there must be strict legislative standards governing the actions of these agents and they must be meticulously observed. Such statutes, for example, may permit the condemnation of an easement so that a landowner may connect to a sewer across the intervening land. They may even serve economic development objectives.

§ 4. Excess Condemnation

The necessity and public purpose requirements are most graphically illustrated by the problem of excess condemnation. The term is used to describe municipal taking of property not strictly needed or the taking of more property than is needed for a public use or purpose. To be distinguished is the requirement that, absent statutory authority, eminent domain should result in the taking of only such property interest or estate (normally liberally construed) as is needed to accomplish the public objective. It should also be recognized that property taken in excess of that needed for a particular public use or purpose may nevertheless be justified as necessary to another one. Finally, the city may validly consider that future expansion may be necessary and may thus wish to take additional land. Thus, for example, a city may condemn the property necessary for an eventual four lane road, even though immediate construction plans are limited to two lanes of traffic. Generally, the future purpose has to be realized within a reasonable time, however.

There remain three theories under which the city may hope to justify taking more property than is needed: the remnant theory, where takings leave remaining property remnants having little if any value to the owner, or where severance damages or damage litigation would involve costs greater than the taking costs; the protective theory, where additional takings would afford aesthetic benefits protecting appearance, view and air; and the recoupment theory where additional takings could be then sold to recoup sums to defray the cost of the planned public improvement or of compensation.

While the owner of a remnant may prefer the taking, mandamus will not lie, courts may not readily accept the damage comparison rationale, and vigilant taxpayers may challenge the expenditure as illegal. Generally, in the absence of constitutional authorization or a separate public purpose, courts will disapprove of excess condemnation in response to the recoupment theory. Some courts strictly interpret the constitutional authorizations that do exist in some states.

§ 5.   Quick Condemnation

We shall see that the just compensation requirement of eminent domain actions usually results in a measurement of the taken property's value as of the time of the taking. Occasionally, state statutes will specify a different time for valuation. Where the condemnee wishes to challenge the taking, however, actual possession by the municipality may be significantly delayed. The delay increases municipal costs (construction, e.g.) and impedes realization of the public objective. The delay also is a detriment to the condemnee who cannot realize income from the property at the levels that preceded the announcement of a future condemnation. Moreover, in some jurisdictions, even after the delay has caused severe detriments for the condemnee, the city may abandon the condemnation.

Accordingly, an increasing number of jurisdictions are by constitutional amendment and enabling legislation authorizing the procedure of "quick condemnation," whereby upon payment in escrow of its estimate of just compensation, the condemnor immediately takes title, leaving the actual compensation amount for later determination. Quick condemnation is usually authorized for objectives whose status as a public use have long been approved and are relatively invulnerable to challenge.

§ 6. De Facto Taking and Inverse Condemnation

Earlier, the concept of a regulatory taking was discussed. While the principles of just compensation would play a role in the determination of damages for a temporary taking, unless suit is brought asserting the independent damages remedy of 42 U.S.C.A. § 1983 the ultimate outcome would be invalidation of a regulation that denied an owner economically viable use of the land or did not substantially advance legitimate state interests. Some regulatory takings might even be accompanied by an exaction of property interests on behalf of the public, as in grant of a public easement as a condition of building permit approval. While it remains possible for the legislature subsequently to use its taking power and compensation to achieve its regulatory objectives, invalidation of the original regulatory ordinance serves to distinguish regulatory takings from those resulting from the exercise of other government powers.

Even though a government may not have eminent domain power or may not be deemed to have caused property damage that rises to the level of a taking, it may nonetheless damage property in a non-regulatory exercise. As a result of this damage, it may be liable to the owner under tort principles of nuisance and trespass. The damages may well be related to diminution of the property's value.

Regulation may be challenged as a de facto taking. That is, an owner may claim, not that a regulatory ordinance is invalid, not that the city is liable in nuisance or trespass, but that the city has in fact taken property and that compensation is owed. The assertion of a de facto taking may be made by a plaintiff owner in the classic "inverse condemnation" case. For example, an owner may seek compensation when overflights to a public airport result in substantial damage to property owners below the flight paths and no navigational easement has been formally acquired. The assertion may also be made by the owner as defendant in a condemnation action arguing, for example, that a de facto taking actually occurred earlier than the formal date of condemnation and that damages should be measured as of that earlier time.

In an inverse condemnation case, to determine whether a de facto taking has occurred, the court must determine whether the defendant was clothed with the eminent domain power, and whether the defendant's actions directly and necessarily caused substantial deprivation of the use and enjoyment of the property. In these cases, the burden of proof will be on the complaining property owner.

The use of the de facto taking concept in formal condemnations is problematical. The courts do not wish to impose costly burdens on government decisions to exercise eminent domain. Thus, it will be difficult, but not impossible, for an owner to demonstrate that a city's eventual decision not to go through with its planned condemnation was preceded by many damaging city actions that amounted to a de facto taking for which compensation is now required. Equally difficult will be the condemnee's demonstration of affirmative actions by the condemnor city warranting the conclusion that valuation should be measured as of the time of a de facto taking. The fact that damages might thus be higher and interest would run from an earlier time led one court to hold that value would be measured as of the time of formal taking, but that expert testimony could be offered to establish the decrease in value caused by the city's actions.

§ 7. Some Aspects of Just Compensation— Fair Market Value, Methods of Appraisal, Apportionment, Highest–and– Best–Use Factors, and Substitution

The procedures for determining just compensation and the other procedures for the exercise of eminent domain and judicial review thereof are heavily statutory, and the statutes must be strictly followed. There are, however, some common aspects of just compensation which deserve limited discussion in this text.

Appraisal

The basic standard for determining just compensation is fair market value: what a willing buyer would pay a willing seller in an unencumbered market transaction. Fair market value will be ascertained as of the date of the taking pursuant to one of three recognized methods of appraisal:

(i) The most common is the market data approach utilizing recent sales of comparable property. Obviously, other condemnation compensation awards are not relevant. The courts do allow evidence of comparable sales and rentals even if reported as hearsay evidence as substantive proof and as bases for expert opinion on the subject. This method is virtually always used for land and property rights, and frequently for single family, residential structures. Difficulties include property for which there is no recognizable market, selection of comparable time periods, differences in dollar purchasing power, zoning, different construction materials, and gaps between value and assessed value for tax purposes.

(ii) Where the subject property is specialty property for which there is no market and the value as a specialty outweighs its value for other purposes, courts frequently allow appraisals based upon the costs of reproducing less depreciation as evidence of value to be considered, adding the resulting value determination to the value of the land. The difficulties of determining construction and labor costs and estimating depreciation are obvious.

(iii) Income producing property is frequently valued by capitalizing the net income the property would have produced during its remaining useful life to determine the price a buyer would pay for an investment with such a level of risk and productivity. Difficulties include projecting rent schedules of relevant comparison properties, vacancies, taxes and debt service, insurance, and estimating the useful life of the building and the probable duration and certainty of its income.

Leaseholds

Where there are several interests in the property to be compensated, procedures will call for the apportionment of the award according to the measure of the value of the interest. The leasehold interest may serve to illustrate. The value of the leasehold interest is the present value of the difference, if any, between the lease rent and higher fair market rent (market data approach) for the term of the lease. Questions include whether the terms of the lease bar compensation to the tenant, whether the term of the lease should include its option period, and whether the rules of evidence bar long term, speculative income assumptions.

Highest and Best Use

In determining the fair market value of property taken under eminent domain, the property's highest and best use (whether it is actually put to that use presently) is a valid measure. The phrase "highest and best use," taken at face value, can be misleading. It does not mean the imaginative conclusions of unsupported speculation. If damages are sought on the premise that property has a more valuable use than its present one, the condemnee must establish by competent proof not only the property's physical adaptability to the suggested use but also the need and the demand in the market at the time of condemnation for such use in the area.

Zoning in the area, of course, plays a substantial role in affecting what can be posited as the property's highest and best use. While the condemning government may not place property within a street bed on an official map, condemn it and pay only compensation for its depressed value as so limited, it may validly raise existing zoning as a limitation upon projected uses of the property. But rezoning in the area may be probable and this fact would be likely to influence the price a willing buyer would pay. Thus, the condemnee may show, and the jury may consider, not value of the property as rezoned, but value to a buyer of property subject to a relatively probable rezoning.

So too, in measuring the value of property with mineral deposits, it would be inappropriate to measure the value of the property and add to it the full estimated value of the mineral deposits (which when mined and sold will bring their own price). Rather, the "willing buyer" should appropriately be put in possession of information which would influence the price offered. What would the buyer offer to pay for land with mineral deposits of specified estimated quantity?

Substitute Compensation

Where under appropriate authorization one government entity exercises its power of eminent domain in taking property from another government entity that is already devoted to a public use, some circumstances may justify the conclusion that just compensation requires that the government condemnee receive costs of substitution. By law many government properties (such as water and sewage facilities, schools and roads) are required to be replaced. Because of the difficulty of ascertaining the market value of a public use, customary valuation methods may not work. The U.S. Supreme Court has held that the federal constitution does not mandate a substitute facilities measure of compensation where the market measure of compensation is both possible and fair, even if the local government condemnee has a duty to replace the condemned facility. Other courts reach similar results applying state constitutional provisions. If no fair measure is possible, or if some state constitutions are interpreted to require a different result, substitute compensation will be constitutionally permissible. Since substitute acquisition (perhaps by condemnation) will then occur, the just compensation amount for the original condemnation is allowed to include a sum permitting duplication of the facilities taken. Indeed, there is authority permitting the original condemnor to take additional property necessary to replace the disrupted public use, or to take such property interests as are necessary to make whole even a private condemnee (whose right of access had to be replaced, e.g.).

TDRs

Preceding sections of the text have noted that municipalities have coupled land use regulation with fiscal arrangements to offset the financial burden suffered by the landowner. Examples include zoning with compensation and restriction of development capability of specific property with purchase of the development rights or permission to use them elsewhere (transferable development rights in landmark preservations, e.g.). In the context of regulatory ordinances not considered takings, such arrangements may, but need not, be germane to judicial assessment of noncompensable regulatory reasonableness and constitutionality. As possible compensation for takings, however, such arrangements may be of insufficient value or may be so incapable of valuation as to be deemed unsatisfactory.

As we have seen earlier, transferable development rights (TDRs) are a case in point. When, in order to require preservation of a landmark, for example, the municipality severely restricts development of that property, it may allow the owner to transfer or sell the development potential that has been eliminated by the land use restriction. Once the rights are transferred to properly designated parcels, these receiving lots are authorized to undergo more intensive development than would otherwise be permitted under the zoning laws applicable to that district. But the value of these "floating TDRs" is difficult to determine. Until the use of TDRs has become so extensive as to provide sufficient evidence of market value, valuation of TDRs will be considered speculative and their worth as just compensation difficult to assess. Accordingly, some local governments purchase the restricted property's development rights, thus attempting to compensate the owner if the regulatory effort were deemed a taking. The purchased rights are then "banked" and later sold to developers who own potential receiving lots in the designated transfer-repository districts. As a result, a market-like transaction recoups in whole or in part the cost of compensating the original owners of those rights.

§ 8. Consequential and Severance Damages, Offsetting Benefits

In addition to just compensation for the property taken, payment may have to be made for special damage to nearby property or to the portion of property remaining in the hands of the owner from whom part was taken.

We have already seen the possibility that the taking may have to be accompanied by compensation to other signatories of restrictive covenants whose rights to enforce them against the taken property are deemed expropriated. Similarly, the courts have been willing to award consequential damages to owners of nearby properties whose properties are specially injured in a manner peculiar to them and not suffered by the public as a whole. Compensation may be ordered if the damages rise to the level of a taking under the applicable constitutional provision, or if a state provision requires compensation for damaging as well as for taking. The courts will distinguish damages held to be required by the constitutions (value of taken property interest or right) from those that may be required by statutes designed to compensate more completely (good will, moving costs, other economic consequences, e.g.).

When there is a partial taking, the landowner is to be compensated for the part taken in an amount reflecting the difference, if any, between the fair market value of the entire property before the taking and the fair market value of what remains after the taking. However, the condemnee may be able to show to a reasonable certainty that by virtue of the taking and its public purpose, damages have also resulted to the remainder. To be compensable, the damages may not be remote or speculative, yet they need not be peculiar to that property to the same degree required in the case of consequential damages to a nearby owner's property. Severance damages to the remainder must result from the taking. More importantly, the owner must establish injury to the remaining lot that will be caused by the use to which the appropriated parcel is to be devoted. If there are damages that can only be determined if the remainder is separately valued, or if benefit offset is involved, the measure of damage may be the fair market value of the part not taken before and after the taking. Some elements not to be valued in and of themselves may nonetheless be relevant to calculating the diminution in value of the remainder. An illustrative example involves an award that compensates the condemnee for the loss of seclusion suffered by the remainder and produced by the government's taking and use of the rest of the property. Under a "unity of use" theory, courts have awarded such severance damages where two separate properties are treated as one because they are so inseparably connected in the use to which they are put that injury to one will necessarily and permanently injure the other.

Where the severance damages to the remainder are measured by the remainder's before-and-after valuation, the courts frequently allow them to be offset by benefits to the remainder if the condemnor can offer convincing proof of benefit. Some courts allow a set-off for any benefits and some allow a set-off against the total award. There are many variations, but the most frequent result is to allow the condemnor to prove special benefits to the remainder, the value of which will be set off against the diminution in value of the remainder only. Here the benefits must be special, that is, while not necessarily unique to the residue property, substantially greater in degree than those accruing to the other properties in the community. Since just compensation is a judicial question (court or jury), determination of special benefits is a matter for case by case determination.

D. SOME LIMITATIONS ON MUNICIPAL USE OF ACQUIRED PROPERTY

Briefly, the municipality's use of its property may be limited by common law, legitimate private restrictions, trusts, the constitutions, or judicial or statutory policy.

§ 1. Nuisances

A municipality will not be allowed to use its property in ways that will be deemed nuisances. At the behest of persons injured by municipal nuisances more than speculative in nature, judicial relief will be available. Many courts will apply this restriction even to property held in the city's governmental capacity.

§ 2. Inconsistent Private Uses

The municipality has no power to permit private uses of property held by it in trust on behalf of the public (streets, e.g.), if the private use would be inconsistent with the public objectives. Such private uses are frequently termed "purprestures," a form of common law nuisance constituting an encroachment upon lands or rights and easements incident thereto, belonging to the public or to which the public has a right of access or enjoyment. Thus, while the city may permit temporary private activities or structures on, above or beneath the streets, it cannot allow permanent uses which are not deemed customary street uses.

§ 3. Constitutional Limitations

While the city has reasonable discretion in the management of its properties, it cannot use them, permit them to be used, or lease them to others who will use them, in violation of the federal and state constitutions or of constitutionally protected rights. It may not restrict use of its property in a manner violative of first amendment rights, which have been relevant to judicial challenges to vague discretionary restrictions on the dissemination of religious information in airports, or restrictive parade permit requirements. Its limitation of use to its own residents may be valid if it does not impact upon others' constitutional right to travel. It cannot in the use of its property violate the federal first amendment's Establishment Clause (some Christmas and other religious displays, e.g.), or ignore the notice and hearing requirements of due process in the face of a legitimate claim of entitlement (eviction of public housing tenants; termination of utility services, e.g.). While it may classify reasonably in the availability of city services, it may not intentionally provide those services in a racially discriminatory manner in violation of equal protection commands. A local government that uses its regulatory or tax powers to charge less for disposal in the local landfill of waste generated within its bounds and nearby than for waste generated outside the area or to deny landfill disposition of out-of-state waste, may be deemed to have discriminated against interstate commerce in violation of the dormant Commerce Clause.

The constitutional restrictions are applicable even where the violative use comports with the expressed intent of one granting the property to the city in trust. The classic equitable doctrine of cy pres provides for interpreting trusts as nearly as possible in conformity with the testator's intent, where literal interpretation would be illegal, impractical or impossible. Nonetheless, while reasonable construction will be given to the conditions and the cy pres rule is still available in some jurisdictions, the failure of such efforts after a determination of unconstitutionality will lead to reversion to heirs or residual devisees.

§ 4. Holding City to Present Use

If the municipality has acquired property subject to legitimate and reasonable private reservations and conditions, we have seen that it must abide by them. Our earlier discussion of the city of Allgood's stadium plan and the city's estate in lands possibly to be used for that purpose indicated that the stadium plan might be thwarted if the court were to hold it a change in use for the properties presently used as playing fields and as an alley way. Such result could follow a court ruling that the property had been "dedicated" to that current use (although the city held the fee) or that the city held the property "in trust" on behalf of the public, or that the city had received the property in trust or by transfer of a defeasible fee. Such result might also follow a decision that the city's estate was no more than an easement. If the city were to use its eminent domain power to acquire the necessary interest to go forward with its plan, or if persons were to challenge the city's change of use, it is important to know who may enforce the above limitations upon the property.

It is possible that any taxpayer with appropriate standing might enforce the limitations especially if they resulted from the "city dedication" or "in trust" interpretations. The taxpayer may also attempt to hold the city to the use contemplated by defeasible fees lest failure trigger the possibility of reverter or permit assertion of a power of termination. The actual trust may be enforced by the grantor or successors and the covenant by the promisee or successors. The easement limitation will be enforced by the owner of the servient estate. It is thus possible that one who abuts the street where a city holds only an easement may be attempting to assert servient-estate rights and the conceptually independent right of access of an abutter.

In many instances, a number of persons will purchase property from a plat showing land reserved for streets, parks and public squares. On a theory of accepted dedication or estoppel, purchasers from the plat may hold the city to the limited use, and even where the city has not accepted the plat, may nonetheless hold the developer to the reservation under such theories as easement or restrictive covenant.

Those of the above challengers who claim return of title because the city has failed to honor their restrictions may be estopped if they have sat by while the city made large expenditures in accomplishing the change of use. In addition, courts will decline to order reversion so long as there is a reasonable possibility of restoration of the original use.

§ 5. Change of Use of Property Held in Fee

As noted earlier, courts may hold that property held in fee simple absolute, however acquired, may nonetheless be held in trust for the public. This is particularly true of streets. In such cases, changes of use will customarily be barred. Of course, all streets need not be open to all street uses; conversion of a street to a pedestrian use is not a prohibited change of use. It should be noted that statutes occasionally bar a change of some uses (schools, e.g.) even where the full fee is held. Similarly, some courts have have expressed resistance to changes by concluding that the land had been "dedicated" to a particular use which the fee-owning city was not now free to change. Absent these statutes or judicial restrictions when the full fee has been obtained by eminent domain or by purchase, or when the property is otherwise free of trust, or when a fee-dedication's use has been fully complied with, the municipality may change the use in its discretion.

E. DISPOSITION AND LOSS OF
MUNICIPAL PROPERTY

In discussing restrictions which attend, and results which follow a municipality's disposition of its property, it may help to consider, first, municipal actions affecting the property's use and, then, municipal actions involving a transfer or loss of the title to the property. The two overlap since, as we have seen, some municipal actions affecting the use will work a title transfer or reversion. Those actions which affect the use are abandonment, leases, franchises and vacation. Those which raise the question of title transfer or loss include gifts, sales, mortgages, adverse possession, estoppel to claim title, forfeiture, eminent domain and compulsory transfer. The entire area is heavily affected by statutes.

§ 1. Abandonment

The municipality, absent statutory direction to the contrary, may abandon the use to which property is put, including street uses, with little interference by the courts in this area of municipal discretion. Abandonment is especially unremarkable where the city owns the fee simple absolute. However, when the city's estate in the property is less than the full fee, or is subject to forfeiture or loss, and a claimant is asserting an ownership interest therein, difficulties may arise in determining whether abandonment has occurred and, if so, what results will follow.

Abandonment needs no formal action by the city. Its elements, including intent to abandon, may be shown circumstantially. The burden of proof is upon the claimant to show that the use has entirely failed. Courts have not been persuaded by evidence of non-use or misuse, or of city acceptance of tax payments from the claimant. If the grant to the city was accompanied by clauses intended and interpreted to work a reverter or permit assertion of a right of entry upon total failure of the use, abandonment may achieve that result. But the courts do not favor forfeitures and will not divest the city if the intended result of its failure to use the property is unclear or if there is the possibility of resumption of the determinative use.

§ 2. Lease

Authority must be found in order for the municipality to lease its governmental properties or those held "in trust" for the public. There are many enabling statutes, including, for instance, laws that authorize abutting owners to lease air rights over city streets for specified building purposes. Any doubts concerning city authority are resolved against the city, and the courts take a very broad view of what properties are governmental in this connection.

There is case law inferring authorization to lease from the power to acquire, own and control property. This inferred power is generally limited to upholding leases of governmental properties for private, temporary uses not inconsistent with the public rights. Some uses, such as concessions in public buildings, will be deemed licenses, not leases, and thus will be approved. There is authority permitting leases of governmental property no longer needed for the governmental purposes. No specific authorization is needed for the leasing of proprietary properties although the courts take a restrictive view of what properties fall within this class. Some state statutes require the government lessor to issue a request for bids from prospective lessees. Other contract protections, such as those discussed earlier in this chapter, will frequently be applicable as well.

§ 3. Franchises

Some state constitutions commit the granting of franchises to local, politically accountable bodies. Even without such clauses, local involvement is frequent. Cities award franchises to utilities and others for use of public streets (transit, power, water and sewage, cable television, e.g.) below, above and at ground level. A franchise is a right or privilege, essential to the performance of the primary purpose of the grantee, which can only be granted by the government. It is a contract conferring upon the grantee a property right, analogous to an easement between private parties. As a result grantees can be protected against such incursions as municipal impairment although they may accept their rights subject to an implied obligation to relocate the facilities at their own expense when necessary to a proper government use of the streets. A city must have both the authority to require the grantee to seek the franchise and the power to award it. The constitutional or statutory sources of this authority may circumscribe it by limitations prohibiting exclusivity, perpetual franchises, irrevocable grants, and unreasonable time periods and requiring voter approval. Because many municipal franchises are sought competitively, in the award to one or more grantees and in the subsequent city actions in relation to the franchise, the awarding municipality must be careful of such local matters as the bid specification considerations mentioned earlier, the impact of open meeting or "sunshine" requirements in its proceedings, the possibility of antitrust liability under federal and state law (state law may follow federal law, may exempt local governments in some manner, and may permit indirect challenge), and constitutional rights and equal protection and due process requirements.

Where constitutions are not interpreted to require exclusive local control, state involvement varies, some requiring approval by state commissions, some retaining sole power in the state, and others refraining from any involvement.

In the sound discretion of the city, municipal grants may be accompanied by such conditions as city ability to prescribe or regulate rates and fees, to require a public utility to pay to the city a percentage of its dividends, to require the grantee to collect city service charges, and to mandate other reasonable benefits. Terms of the franchise, particularly those relating to exclusivity, will be strictly construed against the grantee. The contract will terminate in accordance with its terms, or if not specified therein, then in the reasonable discretion of the city.

What were viewed as exorbitant conditions imposed by cities on cable franchises (reserved channels, numbers of channels, fee sharing, programming, e.g.) and the demonstrable economic risk to the industry of competition driven promises to municipalities led Congress to enact a statute designed to encourage the growth of cable systems. While the city franchise role was not totally displaced by this 1984 law, city (and state) efforts to set certain costs, to dictate cable fees, and to regulate the content of programming and advertising were preempted. There was some regulation by the Federal Communications Commission, but escalation of the then deregulated rates charged to cable subscribers, inter alia, resulted in congressional legislation in 1992. That law subjected the industry to rate regulation by the F.C.C. and by local government franchising authorities, prohibited the latter from awarding exclusive franchises, imposed various restrictions including the controversial and litigated provisions requiring cable operators to carry a specified number of local stations, and directed the F.C.C. to impose technical standards. Additional telecommunications legislation passed in 1996 focused on reducing local monopolies, ironically, by relaxing the rules regarding the number of services that single telecommunications companies could provide. It was thought that by allowing providers to deliver an entire package of services, such as cable, internet and telephone service delivery through a single line, competing systems could break local monopolies. Under the 1996 legislation, municipalities can enter into direct competition with private telecommunications providers, sometimes raising cries of unfair advantage and anti-competition because local governments do not have to bear the expense of franchise fees and other costs.

§ 4. Vacation of Streets

In virtually all states, either pursuant to state statutes or local charter provision, the vacation of streets (and occasionally of other municipal properties) is authorized. The laws typically detail the specific procedures that must be followed. While the courts give deference to municipal discretion, they insist that the power to vacate streets be expressed or necessarily implied; that vacations serve the public interest; and that, if there are benefits to private interests such as the abutters who petitioned for vacation, those interests be incidental to predominant public interests. The municipality will be allowed to impose conditions upon uses of the property after it is vacated.

Abutters upon streets which are vacated may seek damages for special injuries (to rights of access, e.g.) different from those suffered by the general public. Non-abutters who can demonstrate special injuries may also recover damages. Special injury to a non-abutter is a difficult matter to prove although street closings can be shown peculiarly to affect rights of access.

When streets are vacated and the city possesses only the easement, title to the property will then likely be held by the abutters, and not (if not an abutter) the original grantor, unless the grant provided for reversion and statutes permit. When the city holds title in fee, upon vacation it should be free to use the property as it sees fit, although there are statutes and authority which nevertheless pass title to the abutters.

§ 5. Gift, Pledge, Mortgage

Turning now to transfer of title, property held "in trust" and governmental property may not be given away by the city. In addition many state constitutions contain clauses prohibiting gifts or the lending of municipal credit to private interests and in those states gifts may not be made. There have been decisions approving gifts even of governmental property when made to another public body for the governmental use. Absent statutory authority, which some courts find in the power to sell, the city may not pledge or mortgage its property. Some courts have found implied authority to pledge income from city business ventures and proprietary assets.

§ 6. Sale

Sale of municipal property, like other methods of disposition, requires statutory authorization. Statutes, charters and ordinances set forth procedures which must be honored, including notice and bid requirements, electoral approval, council approval,

and other procedures discussed above in our exploration of municipal contracts. Commonly, the city
may impose reasonable conditions on the subsequent use of the property to assure beneficial tax
revenues; to maintain existing characteristics, income of citizens, and the availability of additional
housing; and to ameliorate the effect of the proposed use upon other municipally owned lands.
Imposition of conditions of this sort has enabled
urban redevelopment resale of property to private
owners in the face of challenges alleging improper
landing of credit and violation of public purpose
restrictions.

There are additional difficulties. Cities cannot sell
property obtained through dedication to public uses
or held in trust. A city may not sell its governmental properties, and particularly its streets, without
specific statutory authority. The power to sell proprietary properties, however, is readily implied.
Some courts have approved sales of governmental
properties no longer needed for governmental purposes, and sales where changed conditions do not
permit accomplishment of restrictions.

When the city does have the power to sell, courts
will not interfere with municipal discretion except
in cases of fraud, illegality, or clear abuse even if a
better price could arguably have been obtained.

§ 7.   Adverse Possession, Estoppel to Claim Title

A city cannot lose title to its governmental property by adverse possession. Such property as is

deemed proprietary may be acquired from the city by adverse possession but "proprietary" in this connection is probably limited to vacant or "private" lands. Many states have also adopted statutes that bar the acquisition of title to municipal property through adverse possession.

May the city be estopped to claim title to what was once municipal property and is now alleged to be owned by a private individual? The courts have applied estoppel in connection with clearly vacant or "private" municipal land. With the exception of a few decisions, they have refused to do so in cases involving governmental property. To be successful the private claimant must show abandonment , which includes proof of intent to abandon, prescriptive private use, inequitable conduct by the city approaching fraud, and reliance upon the conduct to the detriment of the private claimant. If those elements are established, and if there is clear evidence that the city has in the past treated the land as private property, courts may estop the city to claim title.

§ 8. Forfeiture

As we have seen in connection with acquisitions of and limitations upon the use of municipal property, municipalities may lose properties held in fee simple determinable or fee simple subject to condition subsequent for failure to satisfy restrictions or by changing the use specified in a dedication. The courts will be liberal in allowing the city the opportunity to establish compliance with the restrictions and thus restore the dedicated use. They may further refuse to set aside a dedication accompanied by private reservations and conditions unless failure is specified as a condition of forfeiture or reconveyance.

§ 9. Eminent Domain, Compulsory Transfer

Municipal property may be taken by higher government entities in the exercise of their power of eminent domain. There is authority suggesting that compensation must be paid for proprietary property. In addition, some state statutes require compensation whenever the state takes municipal property. The state may compel municipal transfer of governmental property to another public body unless limited by restrictions surrounding the city's acquisition of the property or constitutional provisions.

CHAPTER V

REVENUES

The various local governing powers explored in preceding sections of this text depend, of course, not only on authority to act, but also on being able to obtain the revenues necessary to support the power exercise. The considerations incident to the several methods of local government revenue raising, whether by licensing, taxation, user fees, utility revenues, assessment or borrowing, include questions of authority, procedures, purposes, and state and federal constitutional implications. This chapter is intended to illustrate a number of sources of financing and to explore some of the limitations and considerations incident to those methods. Our discussion will also highlight some salient issues concerning expenditure of local revenues additional to those which have been mentioned in earlier chapters.

A discussion of local government revenues cannot be divorced from prevailing political and economic realities and the consequent tensions. The states' revenue picture varies between, on the one hand, projected surpluses motivating elected officials to promote tax decreases and/or enhanced services; and, on the other, periods of intense revenue pressures producing retrenchment and tax increases.

For instance, as this edition went to press in 2003, state officials across the country were announcing their worst fiscal crises since World War II. Just several years earlier, the high tech boom and stock market delirium had generated sufficient tax revenues for program stability and flush state budgets.

In addition to the pressures imposed by external market forces, the federal influence on state government's financial situation is pervasive. Its sources are varied, including, for instance, reductions or reconstitution of intergovernmental transfers of funds; unfunded mandates for state and local governments; efforts to transfer government responsibilities (welfare and Medicaid, e.g.); and pressures on state taxation that would result from a new federal taxation method (a federal value-added tax and its effect on state and local sales taxes, e.g.), or from federal response to foreign trade objections to the World Trade Organization under the General Agreement On Tariffs and Trade, Uruguay Round, asserting the perceived restraining impact of state taxation of multinational businesses. Also predictably constant may be job losses related to government downsizing and corporate restructuring.

The impact of federal taxing and spending on local governments' fiscal position is stark. In 1997, local government units reported having raised a total of $887 billion in revenues. Nearly $47 billion of that amount came from the federal government, $267 billion from the states, and $41 billion from interlocal transfers, which primarily involve general purpose local government transfers to school districts. Thus, the total amounts raised directly by local governments themselves (referred to as "own source revenue") was approximately $535 billion. Although federal aid to local governments has continued to increase in terms of absolute dollar amounts, it has steadily decreased when expressed as a percentage of total local government general revenue. In 1976, federal grants comprised nearly 10% of local government income; by 1997, that percentage had decreased to approximately 4%. According to one study, in 1960 the federal government paid for 1/2 of the total national investment in core infrastructure, defined as including highways, transportation, water, and sewer systems. By the end of the 1980s, its share had decreased to 1/6. Coupled with this declining federal support, over those same decades local governments saw a tremendous increase in the number and scope of externally imposed legal mandates, many of which imposed obligations on them without providing a source of funding. For example, federal environmental mandates have applied to require enormous local expenditures in infrastructure for improved sewage disposal. As a result, local governments enter the 21st century with less financial support and greater regulatory burdens from the federal government; thus, they must turn to state and local sources to make up the difference.

State responses have involved retrenchments including its own intergovernmental transfers, increases in the marginal taxes and fees, enhanced licensing of gambling operations and the increased tax revenue they generate, and intensified regional, national, and international economic development efforts. The last often involve tax expenditures and other incentives designed to compete for new locations of businesses and jobs, to retain existing businesses, to encourage the development of job-creating small businesses, and to contribute to the citizens' psychological sense of activity and momentum. The wisdom, initial efficacy, fairness, and long term success of these tax expenditures and incentives are heavily debated.

The fiscal burdens on local governments are directly sensitive to the economic pressures on the states, because one of the primary targets of state financial reductions is its intergovernmental transfer to local governments, whether for education or other purposes. Because they too face revenue gaps, the major cities, especially, adopt the enhancement efforts of their parent states, including regional, national, and international economic development efforts. These measures, of course, rely on the use of tax expenditures, increased borrowing, and government funded incentives for business activity.

Risky investments of public funds have captured the headlines, but other fiscal problems are almost endemic to the modern urban existence. Among them are the labor intensive nature and high costs of municipal service delivery; increased citizen expectations derived from better economic times; the financial outlays required for educational improvement, and for fighting crime, drugs and epidemic disease; the enormous increase in the number of homeless persons and families; rising employment expenses in pensions and such remedial programs as comparable worth; federal and state mandates unaccompanied by funding and loss or restructuring of some federal programs; dramatically higher insurance or self-insurance costs; the imminent demands of long postponed maintenance of expensive capital infrastructure; the consequences of inadequate, unsophisticated management; the increased cost of over-extended borrowing; and broadened municipal exposure to liability for damages under state tort doctrines and federal civil rights laws.

At the same time, government revenues are not keeping pace with the higher costs. Intergovernmental revenues are moving from aid to governments to direct aid to people. The federal deficit will continue to restrict congressional largesse. Indeed, federal exploration of new tax revenues also threatens traditional local government sources. Federal tax reform has had mixed repercussions for state and local revenue raising, including the non-deductibility of sales taxes and limitations on local governments' tax-free borrowing powers. Local governments tend to rely too heavily on inadequately structured property taxes, the primary (though not the only) target of very successful taxpayer revolts and consequent limits. Tensions mount as the perceived goals of renewed economic development conflict with desires for increased tax collections. The results have included near bankruptcy of major and small municipalities, and the creative development of new and expanded sources of revenue (lotteries, user fees, increased licensing for revenue, increased use of borrowing, e.g.). Cities have attempted new management techniques ("reinventing government"), and expanded privatization. Accompanying these efforts have been major policy debates concerning the intrusion into local governing affairs by other government levels, the economic effects of vastly increased municipal debt, the social effects of gambling and of greater use of regressive taxation, the risks of private provision of services, and the wisdom of political limits on the major tax sources.

Of course, local governments come in various shapes and sizes, with a variety of roles. The urban problems that one associates with our largest cities are only infrequently experienced in the small villages. Governments charged with local administration of a wide range of services will feel a revenue gap more intensively than those whose service role is small. While some cities face outmigration of their middle class or of businesses, others are rewarded when newcomers take up residence, as Chapter I's allusions to the "exit" and "voice" public choice theories of local government may have suggested. Nevertheless, many of the problems intensifying revenue pressures cannot be localized, must be addressed regionally and statewide, and will have direct or indirect bearing on the revenue picture of all local governments.

Various state constitutional clauses have particular applicability in this area. Some have been discussed in earlier chapters, and others will be examined here. The relevant provisions include: clauses allocating home rule to municipalities; provisions deemed to commit to the state legislature exclusive authority to impose certain taxes; those prohibiting the state from levying taxes for municipal or corporate purposes; clauses commanding state equal protection and uniformity of taxation; clauses prohibiting municipal lending of credit to private enterprises; provisions imposing the public purpose or municipal purpose standard; and those imposing limits upon municipal debt.

A.　LOCAL REVENUE RAISING

There is a long history of state financial support for its political subdivisions. State transfers occur in a variety of initiatives: in direct revenue sharing programs; in state education budgets, with their frequent provision of funds for local school aid, resource equalization across the state, and money for capital construction; and in a host of appropriations for state social, health, and other services that are partially or largely provided at the local level. The history of state oversight is a mixed one, but as state transfers and local government fiscal problems have increased, state oversight of local fiscal powers, borrowing, and program implementation has grown. Thus, in emergency circumstances, under appropriate state laws, municipal fiscal administration has been taken over by state agencies, and school district fiscal and overall administrative authority has been seized by the state to avoid financial collapse or substantive program failure. Indeed, receivers have been appointed to take over all municipal functions. (Readers will note that how the state views the respective broad receiver roles is important. Recent experience suggests that there may be a difference across the country: some may preserve, even if under moratorium, pre-existing local government structures and powers, while others may recreate the local government at the end of receivership.)

The sun has set on federal revenue sharing, thus eliminating one major source of federal funds for local governments. The long shadow cast by the federal deficit, the impact of the 1986 federal tax law, especially on state and local borrowing, the number of federal and state unfunded mandates to local governments, and the challenges to use of the local property tax to fund public education, have led to efforts to increase state transfers to local governments. Basic policies are at issue as the state legislatures decide whether to respond. If direct revenue sharing is increased, will there be pressures to reallocate tax dollars to the more affluent political subdivisions? Should more oversight conditions be attached to state funding? Would it be wiser to increase local taxing authority? If so, is not such authority in competition with state revenue resources? Would state enactment of local option taxes be preferable? If local option taxes are enacted, or if new authority is granted, should the local governments or the local voters decide? Should state programs efficiently direct their aid to the people who are the beneficiaries rather than support local government providers even if state government is thereby expanded at the expense of the localities?

Congressional efforts to ameliorate the problem of unfunded mandates may trickle down to the benefit of localities. In addition, transfers of government functions to states with state discretion supported by federal block grants have been much discussed in Congress and federal agencies. Again, the trickle down impact on local governments is difficult to predict. At the state level, there have been substantial efforts ranging from legislation to constitutional amendments to protect local governments from state unfunded mandates. What the revenue results might have been are blurred by the states' habit of reducing intergovernmental transfers to local governments as a prime response to statewide or national economic downturns.

Proponents of balanced taxation argue that state tax systems should rely rather equally on income, ad valorem, and sales and other excise taxes because each reacts differently to economic cycles. Considering state and local taxes as a total system, one may find more balance than expected in most states. But some states do not rely on income taxes, and state governments often make little or no statewide use of the property tax as such. Local governments rarely are able to achieve the goals of balanced taxation. Many local governments are authorized to impose a number of types of taxation, but rely heavily on property taxes which, while declining somewhat as a source of local overall funds, remain by far the dominant force in local tax revenues. In declining order, local sales, gross receipts and other excise taxes and, in some states, local income taxes, are also relied upon to produce impressive results.

Classification

Because state constitutional clauses and statutes may grant or deny local government authority to impose certain taxes, because express taxing authority is required, and because due process, equal protection and uniformity play a role, it is important to know how a challenged tax is classified, what incident (subject) is taxed, what the tax's rate and measure are, and who bears the incidence of the taxation. Taxes are generally classified as ad valorem (property, e.g.), capitation (or "head" tax), income (some consider it an excise tax), or excise (imposed on an activity or event or the exercise of one or more of the bundle of property rights or on the privilege granted). For example, a city that had no authority to impose an income tax might successfully show that a broad based, occupational privilege license requirement was instead an authorized excise tax, imposed upon the privilege of holding occupations calling upon municipal services and protections, measured by the annual gross receipts (income) of the taxpayer, multiplied by a fixed rate, and paid (borne) by the occupation holder.

Due Process

As noted, due process, equal protection, and uniformity play a role. Important first amendment and related state constitutional issues may be involved. The pervasiveness of interstate commerce implicates the federal Commerce Clause as well. Whatever the demands of the other clauses, due process will require the existence of a minimal connection or nexus between the taxable incident and the local government, as well as a rational relationship between the tax and the local police power objective, as for example, the availability of municipal services and protections to one who earns income in the city. Federal due process challenges asserting that arguably excessive taxes threatening the taxpayer's existence are attempts to exercise a forbidden power (taking, e.g.) under the guise of taxation will be unsuccessful unless accompanied by another threatened fundamental right (first amendment, e.g.). While the state courts have hardly been uniform on the subject, there are a number of decisions invalidating prohibitive, confiscatory, arbitrary, capricious, or unreasonable local taxes under state concepts of due process. The burden of establishing the due process violation, however, is a heavy one.

The courts have applied to the required due process nexus for taxation the evolving minimum contacts doctrines of judicial jurisdiction. Some states, in an attempt to capture some sales tax revenue from mail order sales, have required the sellers to collect state taxes on state-resident purchasers. Such a tax will be found to satisfy due process when the out-of-state corporation purposely avails itself of the benefits of the state's economic market, even if it has no physical presence within the state. Although those efforts have been held not to violate due process nexus demands, the substantial nexus requirements of the Commerce Clause may be implicated. Similarly, the presence of a corporate taxpayer's intangible property (licensed use in the taxing state of its trademarks) was sufficient to establish the due process nexus; the taxpayer had "targeted" the state (in the due process sense) and had the ability to control its contact by prohibiting the use of its intangibles in the state.

Internet sales present another challenge for governments trying to prevent shrinking sales tax revenues. Some states have formed multi-state compacts to collect and remit use tax on electronic commerce, along with various other measures designed to encourage Congress to allow states to capture sales tax revenue from Internet commerce. The Internet Tax Freedom Act of 1998 did not address these compacts, however it placed a moratorium, set to end November 1, 2003, on new taxes on Internet access as well as "multiple or discriminatory taxes on electronic commerce." The Act aside, it is yet unclear what standard applies to existing sales and use taxes on Internet sales.

Equal Protection

Again, in the absence of suspect classifications, fundamental rights, and strict scrutiny, or other factors leading to heightened scrutiny, the federal equal protection analysis will turn on the reasonableness of the classification. The clause invalidates only taxation which fails to attain a rough equality among persons or property of the same class. California's Proposition 13, adopted by voter initiative, imposed an acquisition method of property valuation. As we shall see, the measure survived equal protection evaluation before the Supreme Court, even though it created enormously different tax bills for identical property. For the Court's majority, the purposes of neighborhood stability and tax predictability carried the day. State equal protection concepts have occasionally weighed more heavily on local property taxation. It should be noted that, while fewer than half the state constitutions have equal protection clauses, their uniformity clauses provide similar protections and serve as the basis of the analysis of local tax classifications.

Commerce

The role of the Commerce Clause is important in local taxation. For example, localities permitted to tax individual income are often also permitted to tax businesses' income. Property, sales, license, and other excise taxes apply to businesses, as do user fees. Many of these business taxpayers are assuredly engaged in interstate commerce. Congress has exercised its delegated commerce power, although not as frequently as proponents would wish. It has acted, inter alia, both to exempt (in the case of the insurance industry) and to preempt (to disallow enplaning taxes on passengers boarding planes, e.g.). It has: established the minimal, "doing business" nexus for states and local governments to impose business income taxes on interstate businesses; prohibited discriminatory taxation of railroads and other carriers; limited stock transfer taxes; and excluded the net value of federal securities from state and local corporate taxes based on valuation. Nevertheless, the dominant role has been judicial assertion of the dormant Commerce Clause.

Whereas the central concern of due process is the fundamental fairness of tax for the individual, the dormant Commerce Clause is concerned with structural effects of state regulation on the national economy. The U.S. Supreme Court has devised a four prong test that combines due process and commerce protective elements, although it is possible to satisfy the nexus requirements of due process without at the same time satisfying the more substantial nexus requirements of the dormant or negative Commerce Clause. The Court evaluates the practical effect of the challenged tax irrespective of any legislative efforts to classify it or to define the taxable incident so as to avoid directly taxing interstate commerce. The test balances the proscription against economic protectionism with the need to make interstate commerce pay its way. A state or local tax will be sustained against a Commerce Clause challenge when the tax is applied to an activity with a substantial nexus with the taxing entity, is fairly apportioned, does not discriminate against interstate commerce, and is fairly related to the services provided by the taxing entity. The Court has applied its test to state and local business franchise and income taxes, property taxes, and sales, gross receipts and other excise taxes.

Full exploration of the myriad issues arising under the Commerce Clause is beyond the scope of this text. Nevertheless, the significance of the evolving commerce jurisprudence to local taxation makes it important to explore the test more fully. In one case, the Supreme Court invalidated state efforts to compel out-of-state mail order houses to collect the use tax on sales made to their residents for in-state use, consumption, or storage. Without a substantial nexus, which in this case the Supreme Court defined as requiring a physical presence of the taxpayer in the state, the tax was found to be impermissibly burdensome on interstate commerce.

One appellate court extended the "physical presence" substantial nexus analysis to interstate Internet sales. In that case the court identified the issue as whether on-site service performed by independent contractors on behalf of a company with no other physical presence in the state was significantly associated with the company's ability to establish and maintain a market in that state. Federal legislation has been proposed to solve the commerce dilemma for states and local governments. Courts may try to limit the linkage between "substantial nexus" and "physical presence" to sales and use taxes, finding nexus requirements met, for example, by licensing the in-state use of trademarks.

The requirement of fair apportionment affects all types of taxation. For example, for real property taxes, the property's situs (domicile, business, or commercial) may be important. It may also be important to apportion movable property that is regularly located in the local government's territory. Business income and franchise taxes inevitably involve apportionment of the income of taxpayers whose income is derived from interstate sources. Interstate and multinational businesses frequently combine many corporate affiliates, subsidiaries and divisions. The courts and collectors will treat such a structure as a "unitary business" if they find functional integration, centralization of management, and economies of scale. The taxing jurisdiction may only tax income earned therein. For taxable situs reasons, it may distinguish between operational and investment income, using where possible the unitary business categorization, so as to divide business income from non-business income.

The difficulty and manipulability of separate accounting may tempt the taxpayer to allocate income to jurisdictions with lower tax burdens. Thus, government tax collectors have turned to apportionment formulas that compare in-state data to worldwide data on one or more of the "driving engines" in the production of income: the taxpayer's property, sales, and payroll. Usually, all three of these factors are used, but they need not be weighted equally. The courts have accepted these formulae unless the taxpayer can establish that the challenged formula does not compute the tax in a consistent manner. Consistency concerns apply to require the state to show that application of a similar formula by every state would result in taxation of no more than 100% of the taxpayer's income, and that the taxing jurisdiction has taxed only that portion of the interstate revenues which reasonably reflect the in-jurisdiction component of the activity being taxed.

Foreign commerce presents some problems whether the tax be on income, on property owned by foreign investors, or on a sale or lease of instruments of international transportation. Formulary use of foreign income has spawned great protest, federal jawboning, and retrenchment by the states. Taxation of unitary businesses with foreign subsidiaries or parents, or of the instruments of foreign commerce, has motivated the U.S. Supreme Court to add two considerations to its four prongs. The chosen tax method may violate the foreign commerce (dormant) concepts if: (1) it inevitably results in multiple taxation that would not be the result of another method; or (2) the United States needs to speak with one voice in the matter (for which the courts should look to congressional expression or silence in determining whether such need exists).

Many cases have examined the discrimination prong and have held that a tax may violate the Commerce Clause if it is facially discriminatory, if it has a discriminatory intent, or if it has the effect of unduly burdening interstate commerce. The U.S. Supreme Court has looked not only at the tax itself, but also at the effect of any credit provision or the use of the tax's proceeds to offer incentives only to in-state taxpayers, finding the credits and incentives to turn what appeared to be a fair tax into a discriminatory one. The Court has said that discriminatory taxes are "virtually per se" invalid, and it appears to apply a balancing test to determine whether nondiscriminatory regulations' incidental effects on interstate commerce are outweighed by the putative local benefits of the challenged tax practice.

The Commerce Clause is not limited to protecting out of state competitors; it also invalidates efforts to impose a disadvantage on out of state consumers. In any case, the Commerce Clause is designed to protect markets and market participants, not individual taxpayers. Accordingly, one who challenges a tax as facially discriminatory must establish that the allegedly competing entities are substantially similar, because a difference in products may indicate a difference in markets. Absent direct competition, there can be no discrimination disfavoring non-local entities. General Motors v. Tracy (S.Ct.1997).

Just because the tax must be fairly related to the services provided by the taxing government does not mean that the amount the jurisdiction receives in taxes may not exceed the value of the services it provides. Rather, when there is the required substantial nexus, the measure of the tax must be reasonably related to the extent of the contact. Like the Due Process Clause, the Commerce Clause is satisfied when the taxpayer is shouldering its fair share of the costs of the advantages of an organized and civilized society, established and safeguarded by the devotion of taxes to public purposes.

First Amendment

The interplay between taxes and the federal first amendment freedoms and similar provisions of the state constitutions has received judicial attention. The area will need more clarification. The U.S. Supreme Court has sustained property tax exemptions applied to religious institutions against the contention that they violate the Establishment Clause. Its language seemed to raise the question whether a law abolishing the exemption would itself be unconstitutional. More recently, the Court has struck down a state sales tax exemption for religious periodicals under various views of the Establishment Clause and upheld imposition of sales taxes on religious materials challenged as violating the Free Exercise Clause. Use taxes imposed on the sale of paper and printing-ink products used in publishing have been invalidated as infringing upon freedom of the press. State income tax deductions for educational expenses, available to public, private and parochial school parents alike, were upheld.

B. LOCAL TAXES

§ 1. Uniformity

Of the many state and federal limits on local taxation powers, the nearly universal state law requirement of uniformity of taxation is perhaps the most important. Uniformity requirements may be articulated in a separate constitutional provision or incorporated within the state judiciary's interpretation of another constitutional clause, such as the equal protection or special legislation clauses. In both cases, the uniformity principle establishes the fundamental norms that classifications of taxpayers must be reasonable and that treatment of taxpayers within classes must be equal. In some states, the constitutional uniformity clause explicitly allows reasonable classifications; perhaps the most common local tax classification is to set property tax levies at different rates depending on whether the property is devoted to residential, commercial, or industrial use. In other states, the power to classify is derived from general taxation powers. In a small number of jurisdictions, however, the uniformity clause explicitly prohibits classifications, thus requiring equal tax rates for all property or transactions subject to the local tax.

The uniformity principle does not guarantee that taxpayers will pay the same number or total amount of taxes. Rather, it focuses on the relationships among the parties to be taxed and the distinctions between those taxed and those not taxed. Uniformity principles limit the government's flexibility in establishing the *source* of the tax revenue, but they have no bearing on the government's ultimate *use* of the tax dollars. As a result, an important corollary of the uniformity provision is the legal irrelevancy of the taxpayer's assertion that he or she will receive no benefit from the service being funded by taxes. On that basis, no adequate claim for relief is raised by the challenge, for instance, that having no children in school entitles the taxpayer to an exemption from school taxes. Thus, uniformity guarantees that taxpayers will be treated reasonably when asked to make a financial contribution to the enhancement of the general welfare, not that taxpayers will receive individual benefits from general tax levies.

§ 2. Property Taxes (Real and Personal)

A property tax is imposed on real estate virtually everywhere in the nation. Indeed, it is very likely that an individual or business property owner's real property taxes will include a portion for the local general government, portions for special authorities and districts—school, library, water, fire, parks— serving the property, and portions for its county and state. In nearly all states there is also authority to impose property taxes on at least some specified types of personal property. Typically, the aggregate of state and local rates is applied to the assessed value of the property as of a certain tax day. Assessed value may be based on the cost of the property; its market value at the time of assessment; or its income value, which involves the computation of income capitalization for commercial property. The property tax is the product of two variables: the assessed valuation of the property and the tax rate. Thus, as the value of property within the taxing jurisdiction's borders increases, the tax rate necessary to generate any particular amount of money correspondingly decreases. In fact, in many wealthy jurisdictions, property tax rates are substantially lower than those imposed in poorer communities, yet the total revenues of the wealthy jurisdictions will be significantly higher. This connection between wealth and local revenues has led to many calls for reform of the local property tax system.

Personal

Personal property may be valued by the taxpayer or by assessors. Personal property taxes may be imposed on all tangible personal property, on inventory at a certain date, on intangible personal property, or on some types of personal property such as motor vehicles. Saddled with exemptions (freeport exemptions, e.g.), classification problems (fixtures, e.g.), constitutional questions (situs, apportionment, e.g.), avoidance techniques, and evasion, personal property taxes are generally less productive than those on realty.

The difficulty of collection inherent in property taxation of individually possessed personal property should not mask the possible productivity of the tax's use in business contexts. In contrast to realty, the situs of personal property is not fixed. Thus, the government must establish that the tangible property it seeks to tax is located within the borders of its taxing territory. The government may also attempt to levy a tax on some identifiable or formula-established percentage of the tangible property. The jurisdiction may be allowed, and may choose, to tax intangibles (rents, royalties, debts, shares, dividend rights, patents, copyrights, trademarks) despite the double taxation implications that have motivated other jurisdictions to prohibit or refrain from such taxation. If so, it will determine what intangible property has its situs in the taxing jurisdiction by applying the classic owner-location rule (mobilia sequuntur personam), whether domicile or commercial situs, or by finding that the property has acquired a business situs of its own because of its integration into local business transactions (licensed trademark uses, e.g.).

Realty

The real property tax applies a legislated rate to a full or fractional assessment of the value of the taxed property. Value may be determined in a number of ways: it may be the result of periodic assessment by local officials or by estimates of its fair market value. In one particularly well-known example, California voters adopted an acquisition value for real property. On that basis, taxpayers who remained in their residences or in their current business locations had their property assessment frozen. Only new purchasers found their assessments brought up to current market value as of the date of acquisition. Though this method may produce wildly different tax burdens for similar, indeed identical, properties, the Supreme Court upheld its legitimacy against equal protection challenges.

However it is calculated, the assessment will be made and revised periodically by the local appointed or elected assessor, or by a county, regional, or statewide assessment mechanism. The periodic revisions may be made for all or a portion of the properties in the jurisdiction, and may result in fully implemented or staged increases in assessments. State law may limit the rates, the size of individual assessment increases (for all properties or for those owned by persons of limited income), and the size of the overall result of the levy, and may specify the base from which the limitations are computed.

Fractional assessment is the practice of assessing property at a percentage or fraction of its fair market value. In theory, and so long as the fraction is constant across the jurisdiction, the use of fractional assessment should have no impact on any individual's ultimate tax bill. That is, if all property is assessed at a rate that corresponds to 50% of its fair market value, the tax levy will be higher than it would be if the property were assessed at 100% of its value. But the burden of the higher tax rate will be, in theory, equally distributed. Thus, to use a simplistic example, a 1/4% tax rate levied on property assessed at its full fair market value of $50,000 will generate the same amount of tax revenue as a 1/2% tax rate levied on property assessed at 50% of its fair market value, or $25,000. In both instances, the tax will generate $1250. Many states require assessment at full fair market value, but many courts have refused to order reassessment in the absence of inequality. Jurisdictions that permit fractional assessments, or that fail to compel compliance with full-value requirements, may actually discourage claims of unconstitutional over-valuation and remit challengers to the more difficult showing of comparative inequality. Other methods of discouraging claims also raise problems. The U.S. Supreme Court has said that a taxpayer may not be remitted by the state to the remedy of seeking to have the assessments of undervalued properties raised.

If the taxpayer wishes to challenge the assessment, specified administrative procedures may require protests to be filed within a short time after notification. If the administrative protest proves unavailing, the taxpayer's burden in court is a heavy one and in some, de novo procedures may be accompanied by the risk of increased assessment. Judicial inquiry into the propriety of property assessments made by the assessor and confirmed on administrative review will be restricted to whether the assessor performed the assessor's legal duty, i.e., whether the evidence viewed in a light most favorable to the taxpayer, amply discloses that the assessed value was so out of line with the level of value required by law, with other similar or comparable property values, or with actual cost or value, as to give rise to an inference that the assessor failed properly to discharge the duty. A taxpayer who seeks to moderate future increases, or who seeks to reduce the disproportionately high tax burden borne by recent buyers by forcing reassessments, or who seeks to moderate or decrease the commercial property tax load by increasing residential assessments, may challenge assessments at less than full value as violating state full value requirements. The majority of jurisdictions require property to be assessed at one hundred percent of its true value. Other jurisdictions may by state law use acquisition value computations, or may permit assessments at less than one hundred percent. In yet others, the assessors may be able to take into account an "inflation factor" with the result that the percentage of present market value is less than full.

In the usual case where plain, adequate, and complete state remedies are available, federal law (the Tax Injunction Act, 28 U.S.C.A. § 1341) and policy (comity) will not permit constitutional challenges to state and local taxation under the civil rights laws to be heard by federal or state courts. Federal law does contemplate federal court action in some cases, however, as railroad challenges to discriminatory property taxes illustrate.

Effectiveness of the Tax

Since World War II, the share of local revenues resulting from the property tax has decreased by almost twenty percent. Nevertheless, it remains an important source of substantial revenue, and it continues to be the major source of local own-source tax revenue. In actuality, however, full realization of its revenue potential has been hampered by (i) the "taxpayer revolt" and by such inefficiencies as (ii) poor administration, (iii) questionable operational premises, and (iv) historical or modern exemption choices.

(i) In many states and localities, taxpayers perceived that state and local government budgets combined, as a share of personal income, had risen dramatically in the years following World War II. Efforts to mobilize an anti-tax sentiment were effective in many states, with the result being the adoption of a fairly large number of provisions designed to limit tax burdens and to reduce government expenditures. These included a number of reductions of and inflexible limits on the growth of property taxes. Among the most popular are a shift from assessed value taxation to acquisition value taxation, rolling back taxes to reflect a base acquisition date; tax and expenditure limits keyed to inflation, population growth, or a percentage of personal income (with legislative safety valves for emergencies); "sunset laws" leading to automatic termination of programs unless reexamined and renewed under specified conditions; and specific relief for certain groups of property taxpayers (circuit breakers, homestead exemptions, e.g.). In some states these voter initiatives were added to the longstanding rate and rate-of-increase limits that may have already appeared in the state's laws. Other more limited taxpayer revolts have been less draconian, avoiding rollbacks but tightening future use of revenue sources, for example.

Taken together, tax limits have encouraged local governments to turn increasingly to user fees, special assessments, and whatever other revenue sources were unrestrained by the limits. These alternative revenue raising techniques will be discussed later in this chapter. Tax limits have also threatened or actually reduced expenditures for basic services, with some attendant reductions in the number of government employees. At present, the results of the taxpayer revolt, the availability of initiative, the recall of legislators who vote for tax increases, the psychological pressure of the potential of taxpayer reaction, and responsive election results are playing a very large role in local tax planning.

(ii) At the operative level, loss of potential revenues may occur as a result of inadequate or infrequent assessments, inefficient or understaffed assessor offices, and unwritten accommodation of wealthy residential and commercial interests.

(iii) Some operational premises may also be counterproductive. Many debate the effectiveness of the acquisition method. Similar problems attend the assessed value method. For example, it is common to assess real property by according one third of the value to the land and two thirds to the improvements thereon. The frequent criticism is that such division undercuts the desire to improve property, particularly in areas of urban density, and provides incentives for landowners to allow property blight, especially among those landlords in urban areas who are labeled with the "slumlord" epithet. In some cases, these criticisms have led to exploration of graded or site-value taxation. Conversely, the fear that assessments will contribute to development pressures has led several jurisdictions to use "use value" assessments where present uses serve the public interest in a manner that may not be reflected by the market (agricultural land, e.g.).

(iv) Substantial amounts of property are exempted in whole or in part from property taxation by state law or by state-authorized local ordinances. Some of the exemptions are designed to attract and retain industry and commerce in order to achieve other municipal purposes. Similar, more modern devices promoted heavily at state and local levels include "empowerment zones" and "enterprise zones," which may mix property and other tax relief measures with regulatory incentives (waiver of land use restrictions and building code, e.g.). The goal of these techniques is to attract otherwise unavailable corporate investment and expansion to specially targeted, depressed rural and urban areas with resultant economic and employment rejuvenation.

Tax incentive financing, designed to fund urban redevelopment, freezes local units' revenues from property taxes at pre-issuance levels, and uses the increased tax revenues that result from post-redevelopment assessments to pay off the bonds issued to borrow the funds for redevelopment. Tax incentive financing has been continued but constrained by strict definitional and overall volume cap provisions of the 1986 federal tax act. Economic cycles that slow down or stop property appreciation also constrain investment because the envisioned improvement in assessments may not happen according to plan.

In several states "circuit breaker" provisions provide tax protections to senior and low income citizens to shield them from the regressive impact of property taxes. These laws typically authorize a tax credit or rebate when the covered persons' property taxes exceed a specified percentage of their income. Several jurisdictions provide "homestead exemptions," which proportionately reduce property taxes for durational residence owners. The term may also be used to describe legislative limits in the annual percentage increase of any owner's property taxes. In all localities there are exemptions for non-profit, charitable, (sometimes on the theory that they are performing the public's business) and religious institutions. In toto, the exemptions represent a substantial reduction in available, taxable property.

On the other hand, the system is slowly undergoing some reform, and the politically difficult task of making the tax more effective has not been abandoned. Some state governments have reduced reliance on property taxes. Others may be motivated to retain the tax because of the way in which the federal income tax deduction in essence exports part of the tax burden to a much broader tax-paying population. They may also be persuaded by the proponents of balanced taxation who seek to mix income, sales, and property taxes to insulate revenues against the vagaries of economic cycles. Millage rates would then be permitted to be raised. (A mill is one-tenth of a cent.) Reforms have included administrative improvements requiring more equitable and standardized assessment procedures. Administrative reform has been spurred by court decisions reviewing fractional value and partial area reassessments.

Communities are rethinking the value of commercial exemptions and the especially difficult task of forcing beneficiaries to remain long enough for the community to realize its intended benefits. More confining "use" exemption laws are leading authorities to use more care in determining whether property owned by a tax-exempt institution is used for the purposes that underlie the exemption. The Pennsylvania courts' efforts to confine exemptions to property and entities serving strictly interpreted purposes are illustrative. Exemptions have been denied or their termination threatened where the property owners discriminate against women or on racial grounds in their use of the property. Some tax exempt entities have entered into P.I.L.O.T. programs, making payments in lieu of taxation to support the communities in which they are located.

Reform of operational theories is also politically difficult, but not impossible. One proposal is to alter the division of value between land and its improvements so as to reflect more accurately the potential of the land and to motivate further improvement, as was noted earlier. "Use value" assessment strategies will have to be abandoned as well. Measures are also being developed to increase the accuracy of the assessments of presently undervalued apartment properties and to share property tax deductions with renters. Metropolitan areas such as Minneapolis–St. Paul in Minnesota and Dayton in Ohio have adopted formulas to produce regional sharing of the commercial tax base.

Constitutional Challenges

Like other taxes, the property tax raises federal and state constitutional questions, and the answers are similar to those we have already seen. Thus, to be valid under the Commerce Clause, a property tax must meet the Supreme Court's four prong test. A legitimate property tax is not a customs duty and is not thereby constitutionally invalidated. It will not be invalidated under principles governing foreign commerce if its imposition will not enhance the risk of multiple taxation and if there is not a need for federal uniformity. Under varying state uniformity clauses, classifications may be prohibited or very strictly limited, or reasonable classification may be permitted. There may be other constitutional clauses allowing classifications and exemptions.

Equal protection clauses will permit reasonable classifications. For example, exemptions for widows (and not widowers) and for veterans, and favorable treatment for farmland have been upheld, while limitation of veterans' exemptions to those who resided in the state before the specified onset of war (and exclusion of those who moved in later) has failed. Substantial deference is accorded to the local legislature in applying the federal clause. Thus, transitional imbalance in assessment results may be tolerated, but over time the imbalance must be remedied. State clauses may be more stringently applied. Under both, a scheme of selective reassessments motivated by administrative convenience, and accompanied by disparate treatment of new property owners without rather prompt equalization, might be invalidated. California's acquisition value system has been upheld by the U.S. Supreme Court as rationally related to legitimate government objectives such as neighborhood stability and tax predictability.

For equal protection purposes, compare the following: making justifiable and permitted classification of properties and applying taxes differently to the different classes (valid); uniformly applying the taxes to all properties but, to do so, using different methods (income stream or comparable sales, e.g.) to assess their value (valid); applying to some classes of property full or partial exemptions on legitimate policy grounds (valid if not improperly truncated); and overvaluing or undervaluing property similarly situated to other property (invalid). The U.S. Supreme Court has said that the remedy of the overvalued taxpayer may not be limited to increasing the assessed value of the underassessed properties.

School Finance Litigation

The comparative inadequacies of the property tax bases of local governments for a number of years prompted equal protection challenges seeking to overturn the customary method of supporting local public education largely through property tax revenues of the particular locality or school district. Some districts have and spend more than others. The school support challenge began with an attempt to seek a requirement of equal per-pupil expenditures. Attention then turned to overturning the local property tax as the primary source of school funding by showing discriminatory disparities among school systems. After initial success in some state and lower federal courts, the attempt failed in the U.S. Supreme Court. The Court ruled that education was not a fundamental right and there appeared to be no definable suspect class giving rise to strict scrutiny requiring compelling state justification. The Court then upheld the reasons supporting local control and local property tax support to as a rational justification for the present system under the federal fourteenth amendment.

Using state clauses requiring equal protection, a complete and uniform system of public instruction, or a thorough and efficient system of public education, several state courts have overturned the traditional system, even where state legislative equalization efforts had occurred. Courts in other states have declined to do so although some spurred subsequent legislative activity. The issue has arisen in the vast majority of states. Where courts have required legislative activity, or where the legislatures have chosen to act, state legislatures have been involved in strenuous and contentious debates to identify the source of funding to replace the property tax. Among the possible substitutes are income taxes, sales taxes, statewide property taxes, interjurisdictional revenue sharing, and formulas for state subvention. There also remain the difficult problems of relating capital and operating expenditures to urban density or rural areas of higher need, to the desire to retain veteran faculty, to areas of higher cost of living and to a host of other legitimate factors affecting the costs of education. Indeed, the debates involve such basic issues as the objectives of public education, the value of local control, and the usefulness of the property tax in this connection. Some legislatures have restructured financing in expected or creative ways. Others have improved both financing and administration. Still others have rebuilt the public education system substantively (teacher and parental involvement, e.g.) and fiscally. State laws may provide for state assumption of school district responsibilities and authority in the event of substantive or fiscal failure.

The state problems of financing public education should be distinguished from state responses to judicial findings of de jure segregation in state school systems violating the federal Equal Protection Clause. Not surprisingly, given the problems and tensions involved, judicial remedies have become more detailed. The U.S. Supreme Court has held, for example, that the district court may not impose a property tax increase to fund a remedial desegregation plan, although it may require the local government to increase taxes and may enjoin impeding state limitations, but only to fulfill a remedy limited to the scope of the problem. Other issues include the standards for judicial termination of remedial desegregation orders.

§ 3. Sales and Use Taxes

Forty-five states impose sales taxes. To satisfy otherwise disadvantaged local businesses, they also impose use taxes designed to compensate for the fact that what might have been sold locally and taxed was brought into the jurisdiction for use, storage or consumption without paying the sales tax here. Credit for taxes paid elsewhere may be given. At least thirty three states authorize some or many of their local governments to impose sales and use taxes. In the alternative, a state may impose state-wide use taxes to compensate for local sales taxes.

Like other taxes, the sales tax is imposed upon the transaction, is measured by the price, and is multiplied by a specified rate. The tax's legal incidence is imposed upon either the seller or, more likely, the buyer. The obligation to collect and account is imposed upon the seller even if the obligation to pay is on the buyer. Related to these are other excise taxes like those levied on theater admissions, hotel and motel rooms, cigarettes and liquor, and gross receipts, all of which are collected by the seller or provider.

Sales taxes raise their own set of problems. Some of these are definitional, as for example disputes over whether and/or when the sale occurred, or whether discounts are available. Others are administrative, involving collection disputes, for instance. Still other problems are of a local economic nature, a when local officials must assess the competitive effects of local rate differentials. Although they are no longer deductible for federal income tax purposes, sales taxes still are the focus of intergovernmental competition, and their burden may still be exported in interstate transactions. Indeed, questions like whether there has been a sale also accompany the use of sales in income tax apportionment formulas. To the local effects of divergent rates may be added new state revenue needs, and federal consideration of a national sales tax or a value-added tax, all tapping a tax resource that needs careful structuring to moderate the results of its regressivity and that inevitably has both an economic and political tolerability ceiling. Apparently because the lowered tax brackets have softened the impact of the loss of federal deductibility, states and some local governments have accordingly raised rates and attempted to broaden the scope to some services. While theoreticians argue that recognition of the enlarging service component of taxpayer purchases makes the tax more effective, there, especially, effective resistance has imposed political ceilings.

Sales, use, and similar excise taxes are subject to the constitutional challenges illustrated earlier in this chapter. They have been scrutinized with varying results for first amendment implications where means of communication or religious publications have been involved. If the taxes are accompanied by credits or subsequent dispersal of the funds that serve to adjust the tax burdens in favor of domestic taxpayers, both equal protection and the dormant Commerce Clause may be implicated. Foreign commerce challenges to imposition on domestic transactions have been rejected by the U.S. Supreme Court. The Court has applied its dormant interstate and foreign commerce clause tests to uphold sales taxes on transactions whose taxable incidents occurred within the taxing state. On that basis, it has rejected challenges to taxes on the lease of instruments of international commerce, the transmission of interstate telephone calls, and bus tickets purchased in-state for multistate trips. State use taxes set at the average percentage of local sales taxes for which the state taxes were to compensate were invalidated because in the below average localities, the tax for interstate commerce exceeded the local sales tax, thereby unconstitutionally discriminating. Disparate waste disposal fees, alleged to be compensatory for domestic entities' tax burdens, were struck down as discriminatory by the Court because they did not relate to domestic tax burdens with the equivalence and specificity that the concept of a "compensatory tax" would require.

Three items deserve further comment: (i) the exponentially expanding role of mail-order, internet, and other out-of-state sales; (ii) collection of taxes by Indian retailers; and (iii) the possibility at the federal, state or local level of value added taxation.

(i) The first problem has been passed to Congress by the Supreme Court's continued adherence to the necessity, for dormant Commerce Clause purposes, of physical presence as the substantial nexus required to collect, and to require vendors to collect, the taxes resulting from mail-order and internet sales and other transactions outside the jurisdiction. For many years, Congress has considered legislation. The federal solution has been stalled, however, not only by industry opposition but also by the difficulties caused by the divergent local and state rates. In 1998, the Internet Tax Freedom Act imposed a moratorium, expected to expire on November 1, 2003, on "multiple or discriminatory taxes on electronic commerce." In the meantime, states have entered into border and regional collection agreements. Asserting challenging nexus interpretations, several states have merged their efforts regionally to audit, and to collect business and sales and use taxes from, businesses located in out-of-the-region areas in sufficient proximity to one another to make the effort worthwhile.

(ii) State and local governments may not tax sales to Indian purchasers by Indian retailers located in "Indian Country" (Congress' term). As was noted earlier in this text, relations between states and local governments on the one hand, and the Indian Tribes on the other, are based upon the customary principles of federal supremacy as informed by recognition of the dependent tribal sovereignty of recognized and registered Indian Tribes. While states may not tax Indians directly, and that will depend upon the legal incidence of the tax, they may insist that tribal retailers collect taxes on transactions with non-Indian purchasers (cigarette taxes, e.g.). But they may not sue the Tribe in order to enforce collection. One method of collection, prompted by suggestions from the Supreme Court, authorized pre-sale determination at the wholesale level of the likely percentages of a shipment to an Indian retailer that would be subject to the tax. With collection taken from the wholesaler, rather than from the Tribe, with later adjustment if necessary, the Court upheld the practice against commerce and Indian Trader Act challenges.

(iii) While the value added tax (VAT) is much more common overseas, its potential productivity has prompted periodic legislative consideration at the federal and state and local levels. Only one jurisdiction, Michigan, has adopted it so far, for its single business tax, upheld by the U.S. Supreme Court against a commerce challenge. The organizing principle of the consumption VAT, the most commonly considered type in these suggestions, is that at each stage of the producing process from beginning to retail sale, a tax is imposed on the value added at that stage. The value added is determined by using computation methods that credit earlier tax payments, that subtract purchase costs at the stage from sales revenues, or that add to the purchase cost at the particular stage that value producer's wages, rent, interest, and profits. Legislatively attached exemptions and provisions designed to increase savings, or to favor domestic industry or labor would inevitably somewhat skew the productivity. The VAT also raises the customary classic tax questions about regressivity, neutrality, collectibility, international acceptability, apportionability, and constitutionality.

§ 4. Local Income Taxes

Individual

Many local governments, including municipalities, counties, and school districts, impose individual income taxes. While on a nationwide basis the use of the local income tax is not as widespread as the use of property and sales taxes, where used it is very productive. Usually, the local income tax is treated as a distinct classification. In some instances, though, it may be more creatively structured, particularly in jurisdictions where there is no local authority to levy income taxes. In those cases, it may be levied as an excise tax, imposed on earnings in the taxing entity for the privilege of enjoying its services and protections, or even, perhaps, as a property tax, by treating income as property. A local income tax is likely to be distinguished from other local levies like gross receipts taxes because it is measured by net, not gross, value. The measure or tax base in many jurisdictions excludes property income but does not permit personal exemptions or deductions. Others measure income directly or indirectly as computed for federal income tax purposes and allow exemptions and deductions in full or in part.

Local income taxes are generally set at a low rate, and they are most commonly imposed at a flat rate as well, assessed across the board at a fixed percentage irrespective of income level. Some municipalities achieve graduated progressivity directly or indirectly, by their rate structure, by the exemptions and deductions they recognize, or by imposing a state authorized surtax on state income taxes that are in turn the result of applying a slightly graduated rate to the modified federal tax base.

The tax may be levied against residents' income even if not earned within the taxing jurisdiction. It may also be levied against nonresidents' income earned in the taxing entity even if their jurisdiction of residence also taxed it, did not allow a credit for other taxes paid, and was located out of state. Thus, for example, professional athletes may face local taxes as nonresidents in cities where their games are played. One common formula to measure their taxable income divides the athlete's income by the total number of "duty days," and multiplies the latter figure by the number of "duty days" spent in the taxing city. Cities may be particularly interested in levying income taxes on nonresidents who work within their borders. From the city's perspective, these nonresident commuters use the municipality and its services on a daily basis without contributing to the tax revenues needed to fund the services. In some cases, commuter taxes have been invalidated. The municipality may not, for instance, impose income taxes on nonresidents without taxing residents as well, nor may it discriminate against the nonresident income. On that basis, courts have invalidated several municipal attempts to levy income taxes on nonresidents. In one of these cases, the court rejected the municipality's attempt to characterize the tax as an "occupational privilege" excise compensatory for the nonresidents' alleged proportional receipt of municipal benefits. When municipal income taxes are upheld, the courts have left to regional solutions and the legislatures resolution of the policy disputes underlying claims of "double taxation" burdens and the alleged unfair rates of assessment. For that reason, a state court may reject a challenge to the higher tax that results when the local government measures income as if all had been earned in the locality and multiplying the resulting tax by the percentage actually earned there, rather than allowing the lower rates that would apply if the locally taxable earnings were deemed the full measure.

Because a resident may be taxed on all income, while a nonresident may only be taxed on income earned in the jurisdiction, states use combinations of domicile, place of abode and duration of residence to define a broad pool of individuals as taxable residents. These definitions may also serve to enhance the local tax base. Residence and source taxation of apportionable income of investors in pass-through entities like partnerships, limited liability corporations, and S corporations (where income may be taxed only once, in the hands of the shareholders) may illustrate not only the complexity of this deceptively simple tax type, but also the difficulties associated with collection. Collection difficulties have in turn prompted jurisdictions to offer amnesty periods for payment of back taxes, and to impose withholding requirements upon pass-through entities.

Like other local taxes, income taxation may be challenged as not authorized or as preempted by the state. Courts may find it is prohibited by the taxing entity's home rule charter or by constitutional provisions that so exclusively commit income taxes to the state legislature as to make alleged authorization an improper delegation of legislative authority. Like state taxes, local income taxation may be challenged on the federal and state constitutional grounds discussed earlier in this chapter. The interrelationships among local, state, and federal income taxes also mean that local taxes may not be considered in isolation. For example, the intergovernmental tax immunity doctrine has been interpreted to mean that states may not relieve only state and local employees of taxes on retirement income while taxing all other retirement income including that of federal employees. The nature of the local or state income tax system's possible relationship to the federal system may raise delegation questions, and has led to mixed repercussions as a result of the 1986 federal tax act. The federal constitution's Privileges and Immunities Clause includes as fundamental for its purposes a right to be free from discriminatory taxation. Judicial deference accords to states the greatest freedom of classification in taxation but courts will more carefully scrutinize state classifications of nonresidents.

Retroactivity of Invalidation

Where state or local taxes are invalidated pursuant to intergovernmental tax immunity statutes, the Commerce Clause, or any other relevant statutory or constitutional provision, taxpayers may seek to recover taxes paid prior to the challenged year. Dollar amounts have been significant, and states have attempted to avoid the retroactive impact of tax invalidations. Several, but not all, of the questions have been answered by the U.S. Supreme Court. A remedy must be provided at least for taxes paid under protest within existing statutes of limitations, whether that remedy be refund or adjustment of other taxes. Unless the Court expressly reserves the question of retroactivity and remands for further proceedings on that point, a ruling invalidating the tax will be deemed retroactive; it will apply to all matters "in the pipeline," and all taxes that are subject to refund within the statute of limitations. States that create pay-and-complain processes may not after invalidation assert the earlier availability of generic declaratory judgment processes as the necessary pre-deprivation due process. In a case upholding a taxpayer challenge to one such process, the Court analogized these post-hoc argument to "bait and switch" tactics.

Corporate

As was discussed in the earlier analysis of the Commerce Clause, income taxes imposed upon domestic and foreign corporations present many questions under the dormant Commerce Clause. They also raise other complex problems which are largely beyond the scope of this text. Many issues involve combined reporting requirements, data beyond the "water's edge," the appropriate classification of sales transactions, the situs of property, and the effects of unequal weighting of formula components. States, and perforce their municipalities, may not be suitably equipped to compile the data necessary for effective tax administration. One method of assisting states in determining the necessary information is the work of the Multistate Tax Compact Commission. The compact has been upheld as not impermissibly enhancing individual state power at the expense of federal commerce supremacy.

C. NON–TAX REVENUE RAISING DEVICES

§ 1. General Considerations

Most local governments are authorized to use a number of revenue raising techniques that are more narrowly targeted than taxes. Understanding the non-tax techniques depends on a clear identification of the ways in which they differ from taxes, both in terms of their general methodology and computation, and also in terms of their underlying rationales. As noted earlier, taxes are general charges assessed against all who are within the scope of the government's taxing authority. They are levied to raise revenue for the operational costs of government Taxes are imposed without consideration of whether the individual taxpayer will benefit from the services to be funded by the tax. Thus, taxes collectivize the cost of service and spread it across the taxpaying population, either at a flat rate, or prorated on the basis of ability to pay or other indicia of wealth. In fundamental contrast to taxes, the non-tax devices to be considered in this section depend crucially on the relationship between the payer and the purpose for which the revenue raised will be spent. That is, these techniques are based on a computation of the benefit received by the payer or on a calculation designed to offset the cost imposed on the general population by the payer's activity. Thus, and again in contrast to taxes, these techniques have a privatizing effect on government services. They treat the government service or regulatory program like a market transaction in a consumer economy: the payer is legally entitled to receive a benefit in exchange for the levy imposed or to stand in direct relationship to the reason for which the levy was charged. In the absence of such a benefit or nexus, the non-tax charge is invalid.

The range of which revenue devices are available to local governments varies from state to state, yet some generalizations are possible. Most states authorize, for instance, user fees for the use of government owned facilities and equipment (city bus fares, e.g.), regulatory fees designed to offset the negative impact of private sector activity on the public welfare (lead abatement fees impost on paint producers, e.g.), fees for government services (marriage license fees, e.g.), and special assessments levied against property owners to pay for a locale-specific capital improvement (sidewalks, e.g.). Though the states employ a wide variety of implementation techniques and computation formulas, and though their validity depends on a number of device-specific legal tests, the underlying premise is the same. These devices may be used only if the person or property being charged stands in direct and substantial relationship to the reason for which the charge has been assessed. Moreover, the amount of the charge must be directly related and proportionate to the cost of the service provided; if the primary purpose of the charge is to raise revenue, it cannot be upheld as a fee, assessment or other user charge. Thus, the government is required to account to the payer in ways that do not apply when taxes are involved.

Assuming appropriate enabling authority, the local government's choice of revenue raising device will depend on a number of factors. Taxes will be more appropriate if the service being funded is seen as providing an important community-wide benefit or if there is a high correlation between users of the service and the local taxpaying population. In contrast, more narrowly targeted revenue raising devices may be more appropriate if a government service is used by many who are not subject to the local government's taxation powers (nonresidents, e.g.) or if the service is used only by a narrowly defined subset of the local government's residents (municipal golf course, e.g.). Non-tax devices may also be appropriate if, for instance, the government wishes to encourage conservation. If the cost of a service is directly related to usage, the government can reasonably expect to see greater self-imposed limits on consumption than would occur if the service were financed through general tax revenues and provided "free of charge" to the public.

Over the past several decades, the use of non-tax revenue raising devices has grown substantially. Local governments everywhere resort to an increasing number of fees, assessments, and other user charges. The increase can be traced directly to the growing number of limitations on state and local revenue raising powers, as discussed in this chapter's earlier treatment of taxpayer revolts. Starting in California with Proposition 13, and spreading to a large number of states, local governments have confronted stringent limits on their taxation powers. In some jurisdictions, the taxation authority is limited to a particular dollar amount or percentage; in others, no new taxes may be imposed without a supermajority vote of the legislative body or vote of the taxpayers themselves. Governments' response to these caps has been characterized by increased creativity in looking for ways to raise revenue without taxing; in nearly all states, the non-tax devices considered in this section are exempt from the tax limitations. As a result, fees and assessments have become increasingly popular for local governments that would otherwise be unable to raise revenues for services they deem important.

§ 2. Fees—Regulatory and User

Fees have long been a part of local government finance. As a general matter, they fall into one of two categories: regulatory fees and user fees. User fees consist of charges levied by the government in exchange for citizen use of government services or property. Regulatory fees, which include licensing and inspection fees as well, are based more broadly on the government's police powers and are imposed on a regulated individual, entity, property, or business in order to offset the cost of the regulation. The breadth and frequency of local fees have increased substantially since their early days. From the typical nineteenth century user fees for use of publicly owned facilities and licensing fees for the privilege of operating a business within city borders, the parameters have expanded enormously. Recently, user fees have been extended to levy charges for things like the residential use of local streets, or fire and flood protection. Similarly, regulatory fees have been imposed on an increasing number of activities, such as a fee on apartment owners to pay the cost of a rent control mediation system or a fee on paint producers to fund a broad governmental effort to treat and prevent lead poisoning.

Classification of fees is much more than an academic exercise. For one thing, some single purpose local government units have no taxing power and are authorized to raise revenue only through fees. In other contexts, the distinction between fees and taxes is crucial because the local government's taxation power is strictly limited or requires additional layers of voter approval, whereas fees can be imposed directly by the local government itself. Sometimes the state taxation principle of uniformity is key: though a particular charge would be invalid as a non-uniform tax, the fee label makes uniformity irrelevant. In other circumstances, whether for purposes of determining the scope of another entity's exemption from the charge, or for determining the applicability of federal statutes, the distinction is also crucial.

As a legal matter, courts have traditionally identified three requirements for valid fees. First, the party being charged must benefit from the service being funded or the regulatory program being implemented. Second, fees are voluntary. And third, the charges must correspond to the cost of the governmental activity being funded rather than reflect a general government desire to raise revenue. Although each of these criteria has been expanded, rejected, or restricted by some state court opinions, in their totality they outline the general parameters within which fees are analyzed by state judiciaries.

In the context of fees, the benefit criterion is potentially enormous in its breadth. If fees may be levied to recoup the cost of a government service or to pay for the implementation of a governmental regulatory program, it is not clear that much local government activity falls beyond the reach of fees. After all, what does local government do beside provide services and regulate activity? Moreover, because the range of permissible local government regulation has increased substantially with the abolition of Dillon's Rule and the narrow limits it imposed on local government activity, the potential scope of government fees is further increased. Though most state courts defer to local designation of benefit, some have invalidated fees on the grounds that the benefit alleged was so attenuated as to create an impermissible "tax in fee's clothing." On that basis, courts have invalidated user fees to finance local roads, service fees to cover the cost of criminal prosecution, and a stand-by sewer charge on undeveloped property.

Voluntariness, the second fees criterion, reflects the origin of government fees as payments by those who willingly used services or products provided by the government. Though some courts have tried to massage the voluntariness standard as applied to regulatory fees, by concluding that the payer can be said to have voluntarily undertaken the activity being assessed by the fee, the definition is stretched to its logical limits when the court concludes that a fee is voluntary because the individual complainant can avoid the fee by ceasing to engage in the activity being assessed Other courts have simply abandoned the voluntariness criterion, noting how it has gradually faded from the judicial analysis and recognizing the relentless increase of mandatory user fees across the country. For some courts though, the voluntariness criterion remains an important mechanism for restricting governmental enthusiasm for fees.

In its application of the third criterion, courts must determine whether the primary purpose of the challenged charge is to raise revenue, in which case it will be invalidated as an impermissible tax. In contrast, if it is limited to recovering the cost of the government activity for which it is levied, the fee is proper. As with the other criteria, the distinction is by no means clear cut. All fees raise revenue; in fact, local governments strapped for cash frequently adopt fees to fund projects or provide services that were previously paid for by tax revenues. One North Carolina city, for instance, hired an accounting firm to identify the cost of regulatory services and to recommend possible fees, presumably to shift the revenue source from tax to fee. As a result of the study, 22 new fees were imposed, such as, for instance, a driveway permit review fee and an erosion control review fee. Though the court upheld the fees, other courts have been less approving of fees that they characterize as blatant attempts to generate revenue in the face of anti-tax limitations.

Undoubtedly, the proliferation of fees is in large part motivated by local governments' perceived revenue shortfall in the face of increased service demands, heightened mandates imposed by state and federal governments, and deferred maintenance requirements that have reached crisis proportions. The judicial response to that reality is by no means uniform. Some courts have adopted a rule of strict construction of the anti-tax measures, resulting in generous and deferential interpretations of local revenue raising attempts. In this approach, the courts appear sympathetic to the government's plight and supportive of the perceived importance of the governmental purposes being funded by the revenues. For other courts, the underlying tax evasion motive is seen as a somewhat slippery governmental practice, an end run around clearly articulated anti-tax sentiments; the result is a heightened judicial scrutiny and invalidation of many attempts to levy non-tax fees.

Utility Fees

Though they are generally subject to the same basic rules as those described above for municipal fees, some different considerations arise when local services are provided by municipally owned utility companies. Because they may be a possible source of substantial revenues for general budget purposes, utility customers may seek protection against otherwise unchecked municipal monopoly status. Privately owned utilities are generally subject to state regulatory oversight, with agency approval required for rate hikes and other important decisions about the scope of utility service. Municipally owned utilities may not be subject to that regulatory scheme because of residents' ability to vote the governing body (the local city council) out of office. Courts have not been receptive to the argument that profits constitute unauthorized taxes, reasoning that utilities are proprietary activities. While some non resident rate differentials have been found to be unreasonably discriminatory, others have been upheld as supported by demonstrated cost differences. The continued revenue capacity of these utility distribution entities will be watched closely given federal efforts to permit user cogeneration of electrical power and state efforts to deregulate the electricity markets so that distributors may purchase from whatever producers offer the least price.

As we have seen above, user fees, tolls, assessments, and service charges may not exceed relevant costs and/or the calculation of benefit provided by the activity funded by the charge. Our city of Bigville's airport would offer numerous opportunities for challenge of user fees. Challenges have been brought to the U.S. Supreme Court, unsuccessfully, asserting that user charges at local airports violated the Commerce Clause, both dormant (unfair apportionment), and express (Congress' preemption of airplane head taxes). As the user fee concept is extended to what had been previously been provided "free" from general tax revenues, it raises questions of service availability to those who cannot afford to pay. Increasing reliance on non-tax devices is thus linked to the policy debates underlying privatization (as state permission to build and operate a private toll road may illustrate). Nevertheless, in jurisdictions with tax ceilings and elsewhere, use is dramatically on the increase and new proposals abound. For example, while regulatory and franchise fees may not exceed the costs of inspection and regulation, some municipalities attempted to impose user charges (rental fees) to franchisees for their use of public property. In some cases, however, the state courts invalidated the fees as an impermissible charge for use of a public right of way.

§ 3. Special Assessments

Of longstanding vintage, the special assessment allows local governments to provide an improvement to some residents or property owners and then send them the bill for it. Early judicial opinions routinely upheld special assessments as deriving from government powers of taxation but not bound by state requirements of uniformity. The rationale behind the practice is quite straightforward. In some instances, the government, or residents themselves, seeks to construct an improvement for which the benefitted group can be narrowly and precisely drawn. If, for instance, one neighborhood requires new sidewalks, or if a group of property owners petitions for neighborhood street lights, the government may decide that using general tax revenues would unfairly single out one subset of the taxpaying population for preferential treatment. A special assessment allows the government to recoup the cost of some government projects directly from those who benefit, thus leaving tax revenues to be spent more generally for the community welfare.

In most jurisdictions, special assessments must satisfy two court-imposed criteria. First, they must provide a special benefit to the properties assessed. By special benefit, courts typically mean that the assessed property will be "benefited by the improvement over and above the ordinary benefit which the community in general derive from the expenditure of the money." Second, the amount of the assessment imposed can be no greater than the value of that special benefit to the payer. Courts have consistently applied these standards to prohibit the use of special assessments when the improvement's benefit redounded to the community as a whole rather than to individual landowners, as well as to restrain municipal zeal to impose on abutting landowners the full cost of improvements that also have a general community benefit.

Authority

In order for a municipality to determine that the cost of some or all of an improvement such as street construction, lighting, repaving, sidewalks, sewers, water drainage, etc., should be borne by the properties specially benefitted thereby, it must have both the power to make the improvement and the power to impose special assessments to pay for it. Benefit districts created under state legislation and local general governments customarily possess such powers, many of the latter under the general grants of home rule. In fact, much legislation has been enacted to broaden the concept of special assessment improvements and general improvement districts to include parking facilities, pedestrian malls, downtown business improvement districts, condemnation of nonconforming uses, and other projects reflecting more refined and subtle views of what may constitute factors affecting property values and responding in part to the revenue restrictions of property tax ceilings adopted by the voters. Special assessments have been used in intergovernmental, cooperative projects to provide a participatory government's share of the cost while the rest is provided by a participating public authority's issuance of revenue bonds. Because property owners, and perhaps their tenants, will have to pay the assessments, special assessments have proved a far less useful technique for improving areas with low property values.

Special assessment authority cannot be implied from taxing delegations because such assessments are not viewed as general taxes. The imposition of two or more assessments on one property does not therefore violate constitutional bans of double taxation and assessments are not subject to other taxation clauses such as those mandating uniformity of taxation.

Procedures

Special assessments and the procedures incident thereto are for the most part quite specifically dealt with in constitutions, statutes, charters and local ordinances. Such procedures are commonly viewed as requiring strict compliance. While local law must therefore be consulted, there are common elements which may best be set forth in the context of a chronology of the process, a brief discussion of the likely challenges by affected property owners, and considerations applicable to all interests.

In viewing the chronology of the process, it is important to note that in particular jurisdictions, the initiation of the project, the city engineer's cost estimate, the scheduling of hearings, and the completion of the improvement itself all precede the assessment bill to the property owner and may affect the property owner's later ability to challenge the necessity for the improvement, to seek court review and to make certain arguments in seeking to overturn the assessment. Unfortunately, the first time many think to begin their protest is upon receipt of the assessment bill.

(i) The process will frequently be initiated by petition of a specified percentage of property owners directly affected by the improvement, followed by notice to all potentially affected of the proposed resolution declaring the necessity of the improvement.

(ii) Alternatively, the municipal council or the board statutorily authorized to do so may initiate the process by enacting a preliminary resolution of necessity or intention. This action occasionally requires the approval of an extraordinary majority of the body charged with initiating the process.

(iii) Often at this time, the cost estimate will be prepared. The project's ultimate assessments may be limited to this amount with little if any allowance for increase.

(iv) Local procedures will customarily require an opportunity for protest of the necessity of the improvement by those who did not petition therefor. In some jurisdictions, if more than one half or two thirds of the affected property owners protest, the plan must terminate.

(v) Before a determination that the improvement will be constructed, hearings may be required by federal and state due process concepts unless the state or local legislature itself has created the improvement district. When government acts directly, it will be assumed that the legislature has evaluated the need for the improvement; then, no hearing will be required.

(vi) Plans, maps, specifications and cost estimates will be filed and open to public inspection, as notice to the public will have indicated.

(vii) After the above steps have been completed, the council or board will enact an ordinance or resolution ordering that the improvement be constructed and defining the bounds of the improvement or assessment district where such is authorized by law. This action will sometimes require enactment by an extraordinary majority.

(viii) Administrative personnel will then begin the construction process, advertise for bids, and let the contracts.

(ix) Construction of the improvement will occur, and after necessary inspections to ensure its quality, the improvement will be accepted for the local government entity. Payment may be made to contractors from improvement moneys borrowed from banks in return for city improvement certificates or warrants. The contractors may themselves be paid with improvement certificates which they in turn will transfer to investor companies. Often, the government will borrow to finance the improvement. In some cases, funds will be obtained through the issuance of general obligation bonds; more generally, revenue bonds will be used. The differences between the two types of bonds has to do with the borrower's commitment to repayment and will be discussed later in this chapter.

(x) Administrative personnel and assessors will then determine the amount of the individual assessments. They will prepare a plat and schedule setting forth the various lots subject to assessments, the names of the owners and the amounts of the assessments. Sometimes caution will dictate that some portion of the total cost be borne by the general treasury. That is, the government may use general revenues to pay the amount that reflects the improvement's incidental general benefit to the city at large. Sometimes, such cost sharing will be required by statute or by the courts. The proposed individual assessments or the more formal assessment roll, if required to be filed by law, will be confirmed by the council or board statutorily authorized to impose assessments.

(xi) Notice will be given to listed owners announcing the assessment and indicating the time fixed for filing objections thereto.

(xii) A hearing will customarily be afforded on objections to the individual assessments. An opportunity to protest before the individual assessments become final is generally thought to be a due process requirement, although the method of accomplishing this result may vary. For example, court confirmation is required in some jurisdictions, and the opportunity to seek judicial review is available at this juncture in some others.

(xiii) When the opportunity to protest has been afforded, the council or board will then adopt a resolution levying the individual assessments as corrected after protest, and will certify the levy to the municipal official charged with collecting the assessment.

Challenges

A property owner who wishes to resist the special assessment will have a number of possible claims for relief. For instance, the owner may challenge the improvement itself, as conceived and as constructed; the power specially to assess therefor; adherence to mandatory procedures; the inclusion of the property in a defined improvement district; and the alleged excessiveness of the assessment in relation to the property. It should be noted that local procedures will indicate the manner of challenge including judicial relief, and that unjustified failure to follow legitimate procedures will be fatal to the property owner's case.

(i) Generic challenge to the power of the municipality to make improvements or to levy special assessments is customarily unavailing in the face of universal state authorization.

(ii) Nevertheless, it is possible to challenge the improvements, as conceived, as unnecessary. Necessity is a discretionary determination of the local body, and it will be overturned only when it is clearly arbitrary, unreasonable and oppressive. The ordinance will be presumed valid and the challenger's burden will be very heavy. There has been successful attack where, for example, the property owner established that the existing utility system clearly met current state standards and, therefore, that the proposed improvements were unnecessary.

(iii) In almost all jurisdictions special assessments can only be used to fund local improvements. To be local, the contemplated improvement must specially benefit properties in a local area in a manner and degree different from any incidental benefit which may accrue to properties in the community at large. The presence of some general benefit will not be problematic as long as it is not deemed primary. The judgment of the local body is almost foolproof, but courts will listen to the challenge. Special assessments avoid use of scarce (or nonexistent) general tax revenues. It is not inconceivable then that cities' attempts to perform their functions by means of special assessments will occasionally be attempts to achieve general benefits (bridges, libraries, e.g.) and will be disapproved by the courts.

(iv) The procedures set forth by law will, for the most part, be deemed mandatory. Failure to comply will invalidate the assessment process. Such procedures may include hearings on the cost estimates and necessity of the improvement, and on the individual assessments. Notice of pending resolutions or hearings must be sufficient to disclose to persons of ordinary intelligence what is proposed, including the nature of the improvement and the property to be affected. Notice must also stipulate how, when, and where citizen protests may be heard. Unless

the property owner is contending that the entire
process is void as unauthorized, or can rigorously
justify failure to do so, the property owner must
have exhausted all appropriate procedures for protest before seeking the aid of the courts.

(v) The property owner may contend that the
property should not have been included in the improvement district or on the assessment rolls because it will receive no benefit or because it is not
subject to assessment. In many jurisdictions, property owned by other governments, particularly federal and state, may not be subjected to special
assessments. In some states, however, the courts, in
measuring benefit by envisioning future property
uses, conclude that even county and state highway
property within the local jurisdiction may be assessed. Property which is exempted by law from
taxation, whether on governmental, charitable or
religious grounds, is not by that fact necessarily
exempted from special assessments.

(vi) In directly challenging the amount of the
assessment, the property owner may contend that
the amount of the assessment exceeds the special
benefit received by the property. While there is
occasional statutory language affirming the finality
of municipal determinations in the area, the power
to determine that certain properties have been benefitted and by how much is subject to judicial review.

A special assessment can be levied only to the
extent the property is benefited specially by the

local improvement. In addition, some courts require that the property bear only a fair share of the cost of the improvement, which may be less than the extent of the benefit. Where such further ceiling is not imposed, and where there are no statutory limits, assessments exceeding even the preexisting market value of the property have been upheld.

The special benefit is measured by comparing the value of the property before and after the improvement, taking into account not only its present use but any use which might reasonably be made of it, including its probable zoning status. The reader should recall the discussion of market value in eminent domain cases in Chapter IV of this text.

The assessment must be distributed among the benefited properties in accordance with the benefits each receives, but the courts frequently indicate that precise accuracy is not required. Where there is a substantial disproportion, the courts may conclude that there has been a taking of property without compensation under the guise of taxation, or that there has been unreasonable action amounting to a "fraud at law." Where there is a statutory method of allocating the improvement cost to be borne by the properties, it must be followed. Where the choice of the method of apportionment is made by the municipality, it will generally be presumed correct. Such methods include using a formula that calculates the assessment on the basis of the parcel's total number of frontage feet (sidewalks, e.g.), by the lot's total square footage (storm sewers, e.g.), or by a calculation that reflects the value of the benefit to the parcel. The courts will disapprove the use of any method which results in substantial disproportion between allocation and projected benefit. Disproportion arguments will not rise to federal equal protection status unless there has been manifest, invidious or unreasonable discrimination.

Additional Considerations

There are additional considerations of importance to the city, the property owner and the businessperson who deals with the municipality in financing or constructing the improvement.

(i) Many objections can be dealt with before the expense of construction has been incurred. Local procedures provide for publication of a notice to property owners and for subsequent hearings at which the owners may argue that the improvement is unnecessary, that their property will be unlawfully included in the improvement district, that their property would not be benefitted, or that they would bear an unjustly burdensome share of the total being assessed. Accordingly, one who has notice and nevertheless fails to attend the hearings and to protest, or who sits by while the work is completed, so that contractors have accepted certificates of payment, will not be permitted to object (estoppel or laches) in later court review.

(ii) Those who originally petitioned for the improvement and who in the allotted time did not withdraw their names will be estopped to deny at least the necessity for the improvement if not the validity of the assessment itself. Successors to their titles, provided they have notice, will be similarly estopped. Notice to successors is accomplished by filing the special assessment information in the required public repository, usually the Register of Deeds or City Tax Collector Office.

(iii) Typically, once the individual special assessment has been levied, there is a lien on the property for the amount of the assessment and collection may authorize foreclosure. Such liens will have priority over private contract liens but not over tax liens. The right to enforce the liens may follow the assignment of certificates or the revenue bonds in some jurisdictions or may be retained by the municipality to be enforced on behalf of appropriate creditors. If the property owner fails to pay the assessment, there will be publication of default followed by a brief opportunity for the property owner to pay the debt in full, known as the period of redemption. If the assessment remains unpaid, the property will be sold as it would be for taxes. Due process requires that the sale notice include posting, publication, and mailing to owners and reasonably ascertainable mortgagees.

In a growing number of jurisdictions, in addition to the above in rem liability, there may be personal liability sometimes extended to nonresident owners. Of course, personal liability will attach for failure to pay under contracts permitting payments to be spread over a longer time.

(iv) In most states, installment payment contracts are authorized. But the owner who takes advantage of this opportunity will typically assume personal liability for the debt, and the contract is likely to contain clauses waiving any and all objections to the improvements, procedures, and amount.

(v) The property owner may resist enforcement of a lien to compel payment by showing lack of substantial compliance by the contractor. The property will also escape liability upon a showing that the improvement was not made or was made so improperly as to give no benefit. Success in this contention is rare and the burden on the contender is very heavy.

(vi) Where the original assessment is insufficient to cover the costs of the improvement, municipal reassessment is frequently authorized by state law. Reassessment is not permitted where the inadequacy is caused by the failure of some to pay the original assessment. Reassessment statutes are sometimes construed to permit reassessment where the original assessment was defective, although the new assessment must conform to all mandatory requirements. Occasionally, curative statutes will validate defective assessments.

(vii) In determining the total cost of the improvement, the city may include construction costs, and such incidental costs for services performed by city employees or others as the cost of plans and estimates, determining the assessment rolls, levying the assessments and sale of warrants, and attorneys' fees. There is some authority for including the cost of sale of municipal paper at discount (below par), brokers' commissions and the interest to be paid on improvement certificates.

(viii) The existence of the assessment lien and the cost of any required connection to improvements present problems in the sale of property. While liens may be recorded, assessments about to become due may not appear in the customary title search unless the search includes the city tax collector's office. After the improvement is constructed, the city may by law require connection to it (sewers, e.g.). The requirement may not be enforceable by lien and thus may not be discoverable in a title search. These matters should be carefully handled in the contract of sale.

(ix) Other matters of significance include: the manner in which contractors are to be paid; the negotiability of city paper; whether payment is limited to revenues acquired by the special assessment; whether this municipal debt is affected by a constitutional debt limitation clause; and what statutes of limitations apply to challenges to the process. The availability of other municipal resources may be significant. If the city fails to reserve revenues from the special assessment solely for the creditors who hold the payment certificates or warrants, or fails to undertake the necessary efforts to ensure full payment of the individual assessments, creditors may seek relief from the municipality itself. A number of avenues of relief exist to compel city adherence to its contracts or to obtain recompense from other city funds.

Special Tax Benefit Districts

Over time, special assessments have been defended as an appropriate means of recouping the cost of government improvements and services that redound to specific parcels of land within the jurisdiction. Thus, in many major urban areas, groups of taxpayers may organize to seek the imposition of additional taxes to pay for lacking services, or for localized increases of sanitation, public safety, and transportation services that enhance the value of their properties. State laws have permitted the creation of such special tax districts, frequently called business improvement districts. They have used the structure of the special assessment to create community benefit tax districts in which fees to support private community achievement of public purposes are imposed as taxes by the local government after its approval of the submitted private budget. Finally, states have used the concept to approve large, even multijurisdictional, special districts (for theme parks, e.g.) with taxing and, perhaps, other powers.

Development Exactions

Illustrating characteristics of many of the above non-tax devices are subdivision and development exactions. Originally adopted as a response to the increased impact of subdivision and development, exactions were first limited to requirements that the developer provide immediate, basic safety requirements. Our discussion in Chapter III described how development exactions have evolved from those original parameters over the past three decades.

They expanded to include land set-asides for education and recreation facilities, subsequently to fees in lieu of such set-asides (for smaller developments), and then to impact fees reflecting more sophisticated understanding of the impact of the development on the approving community. Finally, in some jurisdictions, the availability of increased development density was tied to development-caused exacerbation of the need for low and moderate income housing and approved upon the provision of such housing or payment of linkage fees to a fund for that purpose. These in lieu, impact, and linkage fees had as their nexus the reasonable connection, or the rational relationship between the development and the exaction. Some states were stricter; the exaction had to be specifically and uniquely attributable to the impact of the development. The U.S. Supreme Court has said that, to avoid invalidation as a taking without compensation under the federal constitution, the exaction must be individually determined to be roughly proportional, related both in its nature and extent to the impact of the proposed development.

There remains the question of authority for the exactions. Some courts continue to see them as manifestations of the regulatory authority because that is how they began, or because some legitimate regulatory goal such as housing is thereby being achieved. Other courts analogize them to user fees, charges for the use or benefit causing the impact. Still others see the localized benefits for which the fees are paying as the sort of benefit for which special assessments might be imposed. Finally, and relevant to our study at the moment, some courts classify the monetary exactions, especially impact and linkage fees, as taxes and demand the customary authority therefor. It is important to note that in many instances, legislatures have in fact expressly authorized impact and linkage fees.

D. BORROWING

§ 1. Short Term Notes

If authorized to do so, local governments may engage in short term borrowing to regularize their cash flow for current operations and to have funds available for expenditures at times that do not match the timing of expected revenue collections. As borrowers, the governments issue notes, which are essentially promises to repay the money borrowed to the noteholder. In the case of short term borrowing, the notes are often called tax anticipation, revenue anticipation or bond anticipation notes, names that indicate the source from which the debt will ultimately be repaid. Under many applicable laws, if expected revenues in the year of issuance do not suffice, the short-term debt may be rolled over into the next budget year, and that process may be repeated one or more times up to a specified limit. The aggregate effect of repeated underestimation of expenses, overestimation of revenues, and multiple rollovers of short term debt inevitably leads to a financial crisis for the borrowing government.

§ 2. Bonds

All local government borrowing, whether authorized pursuant to a specific state grant of authority, home rule status, or implied authorization, must satisfy the public purpose standard. Bonds are the instruments that reflect the government's promise to repay the money transferred to it by the bondholder. Some states limit local bond issues to "municipal" or "corporate" purposes, terms that generally signify that the borrowing must redound to the particular benefit of the local inhabitants. Some states may impose by constitution or statute such additional restrictions as those limiting issuance to capital expenditures and excluding internal improvements.

State and local government bonds are generically referred to as "municipals," and they fall into one of two major categories. First, some are general obligation bonds, payable from all revenues, and backed by the full taxing authority and full faith and credit of the borrowing unit of government. The second type are revenue bonds, debts that are repayable only from the revenues of one or more designated enterprises. The distinction is crucial, as we shall see, because the latter type of bonds typically avoids being characterized as "debt." In many states, local governments cannot incur debt without following specified procedures, such as, for instance, the requirement that voters approve of the debt, or heightened, supermajority legislative approval requirements. Similarly, many states have constitutional, statutory, or charter limits on the amount of debt the government may incur. Classification as a "non-debt," then, makes the financing of many projects easier to accomplish. In addition, to offset the fact that revenue bonds are not backed by the government's full taxation authority, local governments frequently enter into covenants agreeing to use the facilities being funded, to charge adequate and uniform user fees, or to take other measures designed to assure that the revenue source will be productive. Such covenants have been sustained as authorized by revenue bond delegations and as valid in the face of challenge as improper delegations of governmental powers, although an occasional covenant to use the police power in a predetermined way has caused difficulty. Subsequent, mid-payment, statutory attempts to modify bondholders' contractual expectations of revenue and project realization and completion will raise serious impairment of contract questions under the federal Contract Clause. Another indirect method of reducing the risk of "non-debt" borrowing involves government recognition of a moral obligation to repay bonds if the revenues from the project being funded fail to cover debt services. Although moral obligation bonds are not generally characterized as debt for purposes of state constitutional debt limits, they may be quite attractive to prospective bondholders. Bondholders correctly assume that, although only morally obliged, the governments will want to avoid the repercussions of default.

Issuance

As in the case of other municipal actions, the issuance of bonds everywhere involves constitution-, statute-, charter-, or ordinance-required procedures, many of which will be deemed mandatory. Illustrative are the bond referendum provisions governing publication of the resolution authorizing the bond, notice of the issuance, and possibly elections to approve the bond. Failure to comply substantially with directory procedures or to adhere strictly to mandatory procedures renders the proceedings for the issuance of the bonds invalid, provided, of course, that the challenge is a timely one.

The process of borrowing through bond issues depends on the marketability of the bonds. Underwriters will bid upon advertisement therefor and will offer to purchase the issue at a sum reflective of the face amount (par) less the discount (below par) or spread (underwriter profit) where and to the extent that discounts are allowed. The underwriter will also give an opinion on the lowest interest rate the borrowing government can reasonably offer in light of the source of payment, the length of time until maturity, and the credit rating of the city. At many times bids may not be required and the terms of the sale will be the result of negotiation. Negotiated arrangements are increasingly common, especially for revenue bond issues.

The Interest Rate

The interest rate is a composite of many factors in addition to the ultimate source of payment and city credit: the narrowness of the tax exempt municipals market (the changing nature of the market to accommodate mutual funds has affected the nature of borrowing instruments and the availability of derivatives); the tax deductibility of the interest (the federal tax laws have also changed the nature of the instruments and prompted the use of derivatives, as we shall see); revenue certainty; additional backing by the issuer ("double-barreled," revenues also backed by government obligation, e.g.); market ratings and issuer disclosure (raters often rate insurers or lessees of bond-financed property, and disclosure is to be increased in response to amended rules of the Securities and Exchange Commission and the Municipal Securities Rulemaking Board); the yield on existing and competitive issues; risk inhibitors (e.g., bond insurance, or bank letters of credit, the latter lately an especially troubled area for some foreign banks); and the purpose for which the money is borrowed. A bond issue with serial maturity dates for segments thereof will bear different interest rates for each such segment reflecting the length of time to maturity. Depending on the terms of the bond, interest will be paid electronically, upon the submission of payment coupons, or only at maturity (zero coupon bonds, e.g.). For interest to be tax exempt, the bonds must be issued in registered, not bearer, form. Investors may buy directly from the underwriters syndicate, or from the issuer itself (public offering program, "POP," bonds, unrated and, therefore, not tradeable), or may participate in mutual funds. Rated municipals are traded (as indeed are coupons) and there is futures trading. Other derivatives serve investment and hedging purposes. Interest to be paid by a new issue thus offers yield comparisons with existing issues and other investment opportunities.

The bonds of a local government may be negotiable if issuance of such negotiable securities is authorized. This may make both underwriter syndicates and potential investors skittish and hesitant. Under negotiability statutes (UCC § 8–202) questions may be raised concerning governing constitutional provisions such as debt ceilings, the nature of the consideration, extent of compliance with governing legal requirements, and the authority of the municipality. Accordingly, a number of steps in addition to the opinion of bond counsel may be available to enhance the issue's marketability. Constitutions and statutes often dictate that municipalities must establish in advance of a bond issue that they have annual taxes or other revenues sufficient to pay the principal and interest. Frequently by statute or pursuant to the terms of the bond contracts themselves, local governments may be required to make regular payments into a sinking fund that will be protected against diversion or inadequacy and available ultimately for the redemption of the bonds. In a number of states, local government bond issues require, either automatically or upon citizen protest, approval and supervision of issuance and sale by state administrative boards or officers.

There are other protections for investors (diversion-of-funds rules, estoppel-by-recital doctrines, impairment-of-contract protections, receiverships, e.g.) and for taxpayers (allowance of taxpayer suits, often by statute, e.g.). One method, protecting both interested parties, is the statutory provision for pre-issuance or immediate post-issuance judicial bond validation procedures. How the procedures are invoked, whether by the local entity, state officers or taxpayers, whether they must be invoked, and whether they are exclusive are matters for local law.

Fiscal Crises

Municipal or special district default on bond issues is not impossible, and indeed has happened. Default has widespread repercussions in the bond market. Its causes have included lack of authority to covenant assured payment, overestimation of revenues, inadequate disclosure, and investment in derivatives for purposes of return, not just hedging (distinguish among a municipality's lowering costs of issuance by using derivatives, a municipality's investment in derivatives, and a municipality's issuance of derivatives).

State and federal regulators and industry participants have attempted to augment financial market bond ratings with more elaborate and systematic municipal disclosure of financial information, akin to that required of corporate borrowers. Municipalities may be required to make disclosure to the securities markets, to planned national depositories, and, in specified instances, to the Municipal Securities Rulemaking Board, in order to enhance potential bondholders' knowledge of the risks associated with their investments. Such disclosure is required by the federal Securities Exchange Commission, and by the Municipal Securities Rulemaking Board (MSRB), or has been prompted by voluntary organizations (the Governmental Accounting Standards Board, the National Federation of Municipal Analysts, and the Government Finance Officers Association, e.g.). The MSRB has also proposed to bar underwriter contributions to campaign funds of elected issuing officials (the "pay to play rules," challenged by some as having a detrimental effect on newly appearing minority-and women-owned investment firms).

A lack of sound fiscal management has resulted in a number of cases of local fiscal difficulty. As a result, many observers have urged states to adopt reforms such as uniform accounting standards for all local units and controls on budgetary practices (to prevent capitalization of current operating expenses, e.g.). In addition, they have endorsed schemes that compel the bond issuer to make periodic financial reports and that create state agencies to provide technical assistance.

In some fiscal crises, local governments have attempted to stave off default and the breakdown of city services. The courts have looked with disfavor upon local government attempts to ameliorate financial crises by such steps as: suspension of repayment and unilateral extension of the time span of short term, tax anticipation notes (notes' repayment constitutionally guaranteed); delay in making

required payment of tax revenues into a tax-antici-
pation-note retirement or sinking fund (mandamus
lies to require payment); and unilateral alteration
of bondholder protections set forth in the debt
instruments (possible violation of U.S. Constitution's Contract Clause). Bondholder trustees have
sued the issuers, the local governments that may
have pledged to pay (e.g., for nuclear-produced elec-
tric power even if not available, in order to make
the project feasible), and the attorneys and other
professionals instrumental in the issuance. The U.S.
Supreme Court has ruled that attorneys, accountants, and other professionals, in the absence of
their own fraud, may not be sued for aiding and
abetting under the securities laws.

Bankruptcy

As noted, revenues may not be available to repay
the debt that underlies the bond, either because the
project has failed, or because it relied on unauthorized sources of revenue. Fiscal crises have also
resulted from improper investment strategies,
sometimes accompanied by risky borrowing to
achieve unprecedented, and eventually unrealized,
returns. In the event that such crises cannot be
resolved, federal law, 11 U.S.C.A. § 902 et seq.,
provides the possibility of municipal bankruptcy at
the behest of the municipality without advance approval of creditors. A stay of ancillary actions
against the petitioning governmental unit is envisioned. The petition to the court must be accompanied by notice to the federal Securities Exchange

Commission, the state, and all creditors. The court is empowered to issue certificates of indebtedness to maintain essential city services, and to confirm a proposed plan binding both the bankrupt government borrower and creditors.

Derivatives

State and local government borrowing and investing has joined the explosion of derivative use in the private market. This is the result of several factors. In part because the market for municipals has been expanded and changed by the dramatic increase of more easily accessible mutual funds that need to serve varied investment objectives, and in part because issuers wanted ways to reduce the cost of taxable borrowing when, as we shall see, federal law made that their only course, derivatives have become more attractive investment vehicles. The term "derivative" covers a broad array of items since it means anything derived from a basic bond or security. Full exploration of this complex topic is beyond the scope of this text. It is important to note, however, that derivatives have enabled municipal issuers to engage in interest rate swaps, which provides the assurance of fixed rate interest obligations at a slightly lower cost because it is paired with adjustable rates. It also allows for currency swaps enabling borrowing in a foreign currency whose investors demand slightly less interest for taxable bonds than do American investors. Swaps envision some derivatives as issued by the municipal issuers or created by the underwriters. The use of these "hedging" (hedging against interest rate increases and currency increases) devices has enabled municipal issuers to reduce their cost of borrowing by a few basis points (a basis point is .01 of one percent), saving perhaps millions of dollars over the life of the bond issue.

Derivatives as investment devices, however, are much riskier than they are as hedging devices. The investor "bets" on, for example, the direction of interest rates in a complex swap transaction involving international indices and mutual obligations dependent upon the interest-rate direction of the "bet." In one famous case, if the interest rates (the complex of indices) had continued to go down, the government investor would have gained unparalleled returns. But if, as happened, rates in the indices rose, and the government investor stayed too long with its bet (did not arrange at the beginning for downside protection and a time for termination), the returns, and indeed, much of the invested principal would be lost, not to mention the fact that to "play" with more funds, the government investor had borrowed at higher interest rates.

§ 3. Debt Limitations

State constitutional provisions that prohibit government borrowing for private investment, that prohibit lending municipal credit to private enterprises, and that require a public purpose, circumscribe somewhat the flexibility of municipal borrowing. Such provisions were repeatedly raised, with little lasting success, in challenges to urban renewal programs. One of the most persistent constitutional and statutory problems involving government borrowing, however, has been the prevalence of clauses governing municipal debt. In some states, constitutional or statutory debt limits are not applicable to home rule cities (although their charters may contain similar provisions) and their applicability to special districts and authorities is a matter of interpretation.

The type of limit or ceiling varies. Some impose a ceiling based upon a percentage of the value of property within the local entity. Others limit debts to income for the year or require approval of the electorate, perhaps up to a specified maximum amount of permitted debt. Some apply one type to the state and another to local government. How property is valued differs. Some limits are interpreted not to bar certain debt purposes or debts necessitated by emergencies. Earlier debts within the limits will not be invalidated by subsequent excesses. While involuntary obligations may be included in computations to determine whether the limit has been reached, ceilings will most likely not be applied to bar assumption of involuntary obligations such as those imposed by state authority (unfunded pension liability, e.g.) and tort judgments against the municipality. Bonds issued to refund existing debt do not create new debt. The reader should recall that the Supreme Court has held that the bond referenda electorate may not be limited to property taxpayers, whether the bonds be general obligation or revenue.

Avoidance

If a particular bond issuance has been invalidated as impermissibly exceeding applicable debt limitations, attempted municipal "ratification" of the debt will not authorize municipal repayment. Similarly, and although results are predictably inconsistent, quasi-contractual relief may not be available to holders of the invalid obligations. Municipalities have, however, found ways to avoid the impact of debt limitation, and their efforts have frequently found judicial approval. Illustrative of the means used to escape the label of "debt" are long term lease arrangements with options to purchase (and sale-and-lease-back), bonds payable from special funds or revenues, and creation of special districts or authorities. Combinations of these methods are frequent. For example, in order to obtain the revenues necessary for construction and operation of the airport and domed stadium, our cities may issue bonds with repayment limited to the revenues of the projects. Alternatively, they may avail themselves of state legislation permitting creation of special authorities, which in turn may lease the stadium and airport to the cities, or after construction thereof, may operate them. In both cases, the special authorities will finance the projects through bonds payable from their own revenues; thus, the amount of their borrowing is not included within the sponsoring cities' limited debt.

At the outset, it should be noted that a few state court decisions have held that a municipality's decision to assume a long term lease obligation or to issue special fund revenue bonds constitute debt for purposes of applicable limitations. The majority of courts feel that installment payment purchase arrangements, where the city receives the property at the beginning of the contract, should be computed at the full amount eventually to be paid and considered debts to which the ceilings are applicable. Finally, when the courts conclude that a city's general faith and credit in some manner stand behind what purport to be bonds payable from special funds or revenues, the debt limits will apply to such obligations. There is room, nevertheless, in the vast majority of jurisdictions for avoiding the appearances of installment purchasing or general faith and credit obligations.

Lease

If a local government enters into a lease arrangement in good faith and creates no immediate indebtedness for the whole amount but confines liability for payment to consideration actually furnished in a given year, the full projected cost will not be computed as debt in determining whether the limit has been reached or exceeded. If the court finds evidence that seems to allow no conclusion but that the arrangement is a subterfuge, in actuality a conditional sale with installment payments, it will conclude that debt subject to the limit has been assumed and, if the limit has been

exceeded, that the contract is void. Such evidence
may include immediate indebtedness for the aggregate of rentals, "options" for eventual purchase
from a profit making lessor whereby, for little or
no additional consideration or less than depreciat-
ed value, the property will be conveyed to the city
upon completion of the "rental" payments for the
term of the lease, or annual payments in excess of
reasonable rentals.

Some courts are extremely deferential to so-called
lease transactions whose primary purpose appears
to be nothing other to avoid the label of debt. In one
New York case, for instance, the government owner
of vacant land entered into a 25–year lease on a
building to be constructed by a private developer on
that land. Rental payments covered the full cost of
construction of the building, with title to the building to transfer automatically to the government at
the end of the lease. While recognizing that the
transaction bore many similarities to an installment
sales contract, the court concluded that the crucial
element was not whether the deal was more similar
to a purchase than to a lease, but rather whether
the transaction was theoretically defensible as a
lease. The "theoretically defensible" standard
stands as an invitation to creative lawyerly drafting,
with the end result being avoidance of the dreaded
debt label.

Certificates of Participation

Issuance by a public entity created for that purpose of "Certificates of Participation," signifying

investment, treated as municipals for tax purposes, is designed to obtain funds, perhaps for a "consortium" of municipalities, permitting the investment repository to construct facilities then leased to the municipalities. Again, judicial approval may turn on the ability of municipalities to treat the lease as terminable after each year. Not surprisingly, the threat of a Florida county to do just that caused nervous repercussions among investors and other governments relying on the investment device.

Revenue Bonds

The debt limitations are not ordinarily held applicable to bonds or other obligations that are payable from special funds such as the revenues from municipally owned utilities and other facilities or from special assessments, as long as creditors can only look for repayment to the special fund or the revenues of the specified undertaking, and not to the general credit of the municipality. As noted earlier, city covenants to assure successful revenue production by the undertakings, including agreements to maintain sufficient rates do not convert revenue obligations to general credit obligations. Municipal revenue and special fund obligations are authorized in almost all states.

There are matters of some difficulty for which the cases supply inconsistent answers. There is authority permitting several undertakings to be financed by the revenues which only a few of them will produce. A few courts insist that the revenue producing entity be a new or at least a related one.

These courts look with disfavor upon the pledge of revenues from enterprises already in existence to support new endeavors. When either the property being financed or other municipal property is encumbered as security for the obligations that are payable solely from special revenues, the courts may conclude that because general city credit may be called upon to satisfy liens in the event of default, the mortgages convert what would otherwise be a non-debt special fund arrangement into a general obligation debt subject to the limitations.

Authorities

Normally, the debts of coterminous or overlapping special districts, authorities, boards or commissions created under the plethora of state authorizations will not be added to that of the coexisting city to determine whether its debt has exceeded constitutional or statutory limits. To the extent that the debt limitations are applied at all to such special districts, debt within the limit will be available to each as an individual quasi-municipal corporation, so long as each was properly created in the manner permitted in the unquestioned wisdom of the state legislature for a proper purpose. As a result, separate authorities have enabled sponsoring cities to achieve many goals including housing, sports facilities, public buildings, sanitation, recreation, transportation and flood control. But this ever-proliferating limit-avoidance technique is not foolproof. In addition to the few jurisdictions which do not subscribe to the independent-debt conclusion, courts in some other jurisdictions have occasionally been receptive to the contention that creation of a special authority to perform a vital public function, one long within the province of local general governments, must be justified on grounds other than financing (ease and efficiency of management, separate accountability, isolation from politics, professional expertise, e.g.) to escape rejection as a subterfuge to evade the debt limit.

§ 4. Practical Considerations; Borrowing Restraints

The amount of the debt owed by local governments is massive. In 1996–97, the total amount of outstanding local debt was $643 billion. Rapid evolution of the public purpose concept and governments', lawyers', and investment bankers' ingenuity have led to the ever expanding use of municipals in assisting private enterprise to achieve such government objectives related to economic development as jobs, housing, pollution control, sports facilities, student loans, mortgage financing, and urban redevelopment.

Economic development is important. Borrowing is often necessary and is the way to ask future generations to share the cost of intergenerational benefits. That is, if the benefit of an improvement will extend to future generations of residents, long term borrowing becomes a way to force those who will ultimately be benefitted by the government expenditure to share in the cost.

But history shows that local governments may borrow excessively (albeit often secured by private enterprise) and may borrow to achieve objectives not as necessary as others which go unattended. Attractive ideas may drive out more necessary ones. Restraints are few and ineffective and the complexity of modern municipal finance is very challenging.

Political restraint is sometimes a factor. The mobility of populations, desire of present generations for present improvements with costs to be "postponed," and frequent public apathy are such that municipal borrowing may not be subject to much political scrutiny as to its real cost, its real benefit, and its real importance to the community. The electorate is at best an inconsistent superintendent, venting its wrath in financially difficult times upon proposed bond issues for education and sanitation while funding dreams such as major sports facilities which may turn out to be nightmares of wildly inflating construction costs and minimal annual revenues. In fact, political restraint and reluctance to raise taxes may promote borrowing. As the politically tolerable levels of municipal taxation have been reached, major cities have issued general credit bonds to pay the daily expenses of government or at least to fund what should be paid for by taxes in the year in question.

The constitutional and statutory restraints typified by the debt limitations are ineffective because the inflexibility of their somewhat archaic ceilings and standards has been met by the avoidance methods previously described. Repayment of special district and revenue bonds is limited to the undertaking's revenues. Although the quality of revenue bonds varies widely, they may be a somewhat riskier investment, given the speculative nature of some nuclear power, turnpike, bridge and stadium endeavors. Accordingly, in order to attract investors, they may have to offer a higher interest rate than general obligation bonds, which are subject to debt ceilings. Municipal borrowing has intensified because tax revenues may have reached a political ceiling, because creative ideas for providing local growth capital have been developed, and because the borrowing objectives of one locality necessarily cause competitive reaction in another, even if its local priorities are distorted. Interest rates necessarily reflect not only the risk inherent in the revenue source, but also the competition for investors that is fueled by the proliferation of massive borrowing in a narrow market. Thus the result of debt limitations and their avoidance techniques is frequently not less borrowing but more expensive borrowing, hardly the desired objective.

The market itself has changed; more individuals participate through mutual funds, the varying objectives of which demand issuance or subsequent creation of a variety of municipal investment opportunities, including derivatives. The lowering of federal rates of taxation also necessitated increased interest cost so that investment in tax-exempt municipals could compete with investment in taxable corporate bonds and other taxable investments.

§ 5.   Practical Considerations—Federal Taxation

Because interest on municipals was for many years exempt from federal income taxation, the proliferation of municipal borrowing constituted an ever increasing federal tax expenditure. Indeed, revenues from municipal borrowing were arbitraged for returns higher than their interest cost through reinvestments in such devices as guaranteed insurance contracts. The long and fascinating history of the "partnership" between Congress and state and local government, in part the result of now rejected interpretations of intergovernmental tax immunity and asserted tenth amendment limitations on federal powers, would unduly enlarge this text. It resulted in Congress' gingerly, spasmodically, and creatively indirect approaches to taxation of the interest. In the Tax Reform Act of 1986 (Internal Revenue Code of 1986, §§ 103, 141 et seq.), Congress used approaches developed in earlier laws to define an area of tax-exempt government borrowing while limiting the loss of federal revenues. It excluded from gross income the interest on state and local bonds issued for essential purposes, reclaimed the "profits" from arbitrage bonds, and taxed the interest on state and local unregistered bonds. It adopted a less privileged status for so-called "private activity" bonds, the term used to describe bonds with a specified percentage of bond proceeds and funds to secure the debt coming from private, rather than governmental, entities. Tax exempt status for private activity bonds now requires strict adherence to exceptional definitions and qualifications; a statutory volume cap on private activity borrowing has also been imposed. The tax exempt exceptions were rather strictly defined and have in some cases been subject to sunset provisions. Indeed, some of the debate since the Act's passage has involved "stays of execution" on the one hand and efforts to recapture tax expenditures on the other (mortgage bonds, e.g.). A bond is a private-activity bond if a specified percentage of the bond proceeds and of funds to secure it are used for or derived from private entities. The Act also stringently limited issuance costs, ended the deductions related to bank purchases of municipals, and used the interest from even most exemption-qualified, private-activity bonds in computing income subject to the alternative minimum tax. Subsequent federal legislation has, inter alia, altered the rates of taxation and added to qualified private activities the concept of empowerment zones.

The 1986 Tax Act was followed by the U.S. Supreme Court's determination that neither intergovernmental tax immunity nor tenth amendment considerations barred Congress from taxing municipals' interest. Neither event, however, has triggered much of a reduction in municipal borrowing. Intervening reductions in overall interest rates buoyed the borrowing statistics, as many borrowers sought to refinance. Refinancing a municipal bond issue is not done lightly; Congress has strictly limited refinancings to one for issues after 1986, and to two for issues prior to 1987. Any possible dampening effect of the 1986 Act may also be lessened by government issuers' increasing familiarity with taxable borrowing and ways to reduce its cost. Taxable issues may still be attractive because they remain exempt from the issuer's state and local taxes, though not those of other states. Governments may mix taxable and exempt issues, and may use such hedging derivatives as currency swaps involving bonds issued in foreign currency and interest-rate swaps to reduce the costs of taxable borrowing, as has been noted earlier.

E. SOME ADDITIONAL CONSIDERATIONS RELEVANT TO MUNICIPAL EXPENDITURES

§ 1. Constitutional Restrictions on Expenditure Objectives

Local governments must have authority to spend for particular purposes. As we have seen throughout this text, the expenditure authority will be restricted to a public purpose, and in some jurisdictions to a corporate or municipal purpose. Again, if there is any distinction between public and corporate or municipal purposes, it is that the local government action or expenditure must reasonably promote the public health, safety, morality or general welfare of that municipality's citizens somewhat more substantially than it does other residents of the state. Recall that other constitutional restrictions include those prohibiting the lending of municipal credit to private enterprise, barring gifts to private individuals and corporations, forbidding investments, and banning the payment of additional compensation to municipal officers and government contractors.

In the face of such constitutional prohibitions, would the courts uphold expenses incurred by officials of a port authority for meals and entertainment of shippers designed to promote increased shipping use of the port facilities in the face of heavy competition? Would courts uphold municipal expenditures by our illustration cities designed to persuade voters to approve any bond issues necessary for the airport and stadium projects?

§ 2. Expenditure Method Restrictions

We have noted that in many states, local government fiscal procedures are somewhat lacking in detail and sophistication. While much improvement is needed, localities do not operate totally without controls. In order to foster taxpayer knowledge of proposed expenditures and resultant taxation, and to insure that the priorities determined by the political process are observed, constitutions, statutes and charters set forth mandatory, specific restrictions governing expenditure methods. The requirements may include statutory limits upon annual spending increases; presentation of revenue and expenditure estimates and budget recommendations by an administrative or executive officer; adoption and publication of annual and biennial operating, capital, and special, earmarked fund budgets and appropriation ordinances by the local governments after notice and hearings; reasonably clear disclosure in the budget of the purposes for which money is to be expended; and post-spending audits and published annual reports. There may be lump sum categories or line item requirements. Like many states, local governments may be subject to a balanced budget requirement. Enforcement of the restrictions includes such methods as voiding expenditures in excess of, or in violation of, the prerequisite steps; forbidding enactment of interim taxation ordinances increasing the taxation during the year; and prohibiting intrabudgetary, permanent transfer or diversion of funds for purposes other than those for which they were originally budgeted.

The restrictions may not be totally inflexible, however. Some jurisdictions permit intrabudgetary, temporary borrowing of funds. Some charters permit appropriation and budget amendments by ordinance during the year. Some courts will uphold emergency appropriations, although in such emergencies approval of the electorate or of a state agency may be needed. Moreover, judicial agreement that the emergency was real is not a foregone conclusion. There will be mandatory expenditures (court ordered, e.g.) that cannot be avoided. In some localities, unexpended and unneeded funds in one budget category may be diverted to another purpose.

A number of certifications and permissions may be necessary prerequisites to municipal spending.

For example, spending may have to be preceded by the comptroller's certification that appropriately budgeted funds exist, or an expenditure above certain levels may require specific approval by the local governing body. In some states, in addition to state prescribed procedures, there may be state administrative supervision, review and final approval authority over borrowing and expenditures and state authority to supplant local administration in fiscal crises.

§ 3.   Officer Liability for Unlawful Expenditures

Municipal officers who are responsible for the loss of public funds or who make illegal disbursements may be civilly, or even criminally, liable for their conduct. Reimbursement may be required, either by the individual officers or their sureties. Personal liability for the loss may depend upon negligence or upon value received by the city. Personal benefit by the officer or by an employee will result in personal liability for the return of the funds.

The management of invested special, earmarked, perhaps off-budget funds, pension funds, and the like, either directly by city officials or by delegation to trustees illustrates some of the underlying dimensions of officer responsibility. It also serves to remind the reader that the determination of officer liability may first depend on the illegality or impropriety of the action under standards and requirements set forth throughout this text. Illustratively, compare important investment and divestment decisions involving social or environmental objectives, where many argue for some room for legitimate policy decisions, with high-risk, high-return or high-failure investing, for which many seek stricter state controls.

CHAPTER VI

CONSIDERATIONS PERTINENT TO CITIZEN LITIGATION WITH LOCAL GOVERNMENTS

The questions discussed throughout this text reach the attention of the courts in a variety of ways. Challenges to local government actions or failures to act are raised by individuals, groups, government entities, and classes affected by ordinances and administrative implementation thereof. These challenges may be raised directly or through attorneys general in actions quo warranto, questioning the authority by which an officer or a government entity purported to hold or create office; in court reviews following upon the exhaustion or denial of administrative review procedures, either by "certiorari review" upon the administrative record or by such procedures as mandamus to compel the performance of an allegedly non-discretionary duty; in declaratory judgment actions; in individual actions seeking injunctive relief or damages; in taxpayer suits on behalf of or against the local government seeking to recover illegal expenditures, compel or restrain action; and in defenses to the proceedings brought by the local government to assert its contractual or other rights or to enforce its ordinances and regulations. Often, suits will add either the local government or its officers as defendants to avoid the restrictions of the respective immunities. Sometimes, relief will be denied because another remedy is adequate and more appropriate. Indeed, the area is so circumscribed by local procedures that no summary can adequately substitute for consulting state and local laws.

Nevertheless, there are some aspects common to citizen litigation with local government which deserve brief consideration in this chapter. Municipal immunity, restrictive statutes of limitations, and notice and claim-filing requirements will be viewed in the context of citizen suits in tort against the municipality. The evolving liability of local governments in actions under 42 U.S.C.A. § 1983 will be discussed. The chapter will conclude with some observations on standing in individual and taxpayer actions against the local government, primarily in state and local courts.

A.   CITIZEN TORT CLAIMS AGAINST THE LOCAL GOVERNMENT

Our purpose here is not to review tort theories of recovery. Rather, as noted above, our focus is upon those matters that are peculiar to a tort case against a municipal corporation.

§ 1.   Ultra Vires

Where the local government is engaged in ultra vires activities in the sense that the activities are beyond its powers under all circumstances, it will not be liable in tort for injuries caused by those actions. Despite the apparent injustice to the injured party, the ultra vires doctrine's protection of the taxpayer's interest in proper use of municipal funds will predominate. Perhaps because of the unfairness of the doctrine, some courts have narrowed its application to allow recovery when it is determined that the municipality's activity was not barred in all circumstances, but was, rather, undertaken in an improper manner.

§ 2. Statutes of Limitations

Tort actions against municipalities are frequently governed by limitation periods significantly shorter than those governing actions between private individuals. (The statutes of limitations governing other actions against the city will also involve much shorter time periods.)

§ 3. Notice Requirements

Except for suits to enjoin municipal torts, tort actions against municipal entities are customarily barred unless the claimant has met detailed notice requirements imposed by statute, charter or ordinance. Such notice requirements are generally upheld by the courts, even against constitutional, equal protection challenges. Some legislation has attempted to ameliorate possible harsh results, while retaining the requirements' valid objectives, by providing that actual notice of sufficient facts reasonably alerting the government or its insurer to a possible claim be construed as compliance, or that no claim be defeated by lack of post-injury notice unless the government shows substantial prejudice thereby. Generally, such notice requirements are of three classes:

Notice of Defect

The city's liability may be alleged to result from breach of a duty imposed upon it to exercise due care so that persons are not injured by defects in property supervised by the city, such as streets. In order to impose municipal liability, the city must have received actual notice of the defect's existence, or the circumstances must amount to constructive notice. In addition, the city must have foregone a reasonable opportunity to take remedial action before liability will be imposed.

Notice of Injury

The injured party must give notice of the injury to the appropriate government officials within a specified time so that the municipality may investigate while the facts are fresh and may make appropriate budgetary plans. Some courts allow the notice period to be tolled because of the unsupervised infancy or comatose condition of the injured person or permit such conditions to be raised in defense to a charge of notice failure.

Notice of Claim

The claimant must submit the claim either to administrative entities or to the city council itself in order to afford an opportunity for settlement before suit is filed. Denial of the claim or failure to act at this level does not serve to bar or delay suit and attempts by ordinance to add that suit can only be filed with permission of the city have been ruled invalid.

§ 4. Municipal Immunity

Until statutory and judicial abrogations of the doctrine, municipalities had enjoyed immunity for the results of at least some of their torts. There have long been exceptions. Where municipal liability has been founded in trespass and in nuisance, the courts have been loathe to uphold any claims of immunity even if the municipal function is classified as governmental. So too, cities have traditionally been held liable for injuries caused by defects in streets and sidewalks at common law and by statute. The tradition of liability is not without its exceptions, however, as decisions immunizing cities where injuries were caused by "trivial defects" or by snow and ice attest.

With respect to torts other than trespasses, nuisances and those involving street defects, the history of municipal immunity has followed the classic course of the various immunity doctrines. It began in response to the inability of English unincorporated "citizens associations" (Hundreds) to respond in damages to tort suits. The rule was carried into the jurisprudence of this country on the strength of overeager subservience to debatable precedent. Soon, the weakness of its origins and the demands of justice compelled modern justifications. First, some courts justified municipal immunity with the rationale that local governments should be entitled to a "sharing" of the protection afforded to the state under its sovereign immunity, particularly when they were operating in their governmental capacity. Later, a new justification emerged–judicial recognition of the financial disruptions which increasingly large damage awards would cause. Many jurisdictions distinguish between the terms "sovereign immunity" and "governmental immunity", using the former to apply to state immunity and the latter to describe the immunity of the state's political subdivisions.

Exceptions inevitably developed. If the activity could be classified as "governmental," the municipality remained immune where that activity caused the injury. If not "governmental," the causative activity was termed "proprietary." In general, the term proprietary referred to those functions of particular benefit to the corporate member-citizens, which perhaps earned profits, which perhaps could be performed by private enterprises, and desire for which may have constituted motivation for the city's initial incorporation. There would be no immunity for torts resulting from proprietary activities. While the dichotomy neatly fit the theory on which immunity for sovereign governments was based, its application has been and continues to be difficult and unpredictable. What determines whether an activity will be labeled "proprietary" may include the profit and private enterprise factors mentioned above, precedent, and, some may argue, the justness of the plaintiff's cause.

Other judicially created exceptions that have removed municipal immunity include liability for active but not for passive tortious conduct, liability for voluntary activity but not for duties mandated by law, and liability for ministerial functions but not for those determined to be discretionary.

State legislatures enacted a number of statutes abrogating immunity for specified types of municipal activity (fire and police vehicles, e.g.) and more rarely for broad categories of claims (mobs and riots, safe places, torts and contracts, e.g.). Judicial reaction to the latter served at times to limit the impact by strict views of the scope of municipal duty, or by interpretations permitting immunity for quasi-legislative and discretionary activities. Litigants strained to label as nuisances injurious circumstances for which government liability could not otherwise be imposed.

Criticism of the immunity doctrine grew. Courts moved from the way-stations of exception to abrogation. They recognized that the judicial origin of the municipal immunity doctrine meant that courts, rather than the legislatures, had the duty to remedy what they had come to believe was an unnecessary and unjust rule. Several courts relied upon the availability and acquisition of municipal liability insurance to decide that immunity was ended or had been waived. Some states enacted liberalizing legislation. As a result of this broad judicial and legislative repudiation, the piecemeal liability provisions mentioned earlier were in part overtaken by events.

Apparently, government immunity is retained in its classic formulation (governmental-immunity, proprietary-liability) in some states. The fact that at least one state permits waiver in the home-rule charters of its counties and independent cities illustrates the enormous variety that still pervades the area. Quasi-municipal corporations such as counties, townships and special function districts will not be immune if immunity of the state of which they are "agents" has been abrogated. Even if state immunity is retained, however, abrogation of municipal immunity will commonly include the quasi-municipal entities as well. Different treatment of states and their political subdivisions is not uncommon, as we have seen in other contexts (unavailability of the federal eleventh amendment, state protection for municipalities; no automatic state action exemption from federal antitrust laws for municipalities, e.g.).

Limit Costs

Legislatures in the vast majority of states have now enacted responsive statutes. The laws can best be understood as reactions, on the one hand, to the reality of citizen injuries and, on the other, to the enormous explosion in government exposure to damage awards. In addition, the insurance crisis has played an important part in the policy deliberations. Widespread unavailability of, or steep increases in, the premiums for reduced insurance coverage, has motivated contemporaneous and overlapping legislative efforts to limit liability and to increase damages predictability. The resulting government immunity statutes used one or more of the following approaches:

(i) restored immunity and listed exceptions;

(ii) abolished immunity but (borrowing from long existing antecedents) retained it for certain activities and categories;

(iii) restored immunity that could be waived by, and to the extent of, insurance (one state permitting only a direct action against the insurer); or abolished immunity but;

(iv) prohibited punitive damages (recently allowed by some courts that rejected prohibiting precedent);

(v) limited damages to the government's percentage of comparative fault;

(vi) imposed caps or ceilings on overall judgments sometimes increased by insurance;

(vii) imposed different caps on different types of tortious conduct;

(viii) imposed different caps on certain classes of damages; and

(ix) authorized participation in self-insurance risk pools.

Challenges to the contours of municipal immunity have asserted federal and state due process, equal protection, takings, and privileges and immunities clauses, the right to jury trial, and such state clauses as those providing a right to a remedy, separation of powers, open courts, and justice without delay. Most have been rejected. Rulings in a few cases have invalidated damage caps as an improper classification, sometimes as the result of heightened or strict scrutiny (deeming jury or remedy rights fundamental). The eventual extent of adverse judicial reaction to the legislated damage limits in the medical malpractice and other general torts areas may have a bearing on cognate limits to government liability, although classification rationales differ.

Limit Scope

The judicial and legislative efforts effectively repudiating or limiting government immunity have raised not only the question how to limit the cost of government liability, but also the questions whether, and if so, how, to limit its scope. Because respondeat superior applies, liability for public officers, employees, and agents is also involved. Several overlapping answers have been given in disputes over the scope of municipal liability:

(i) The government is not liable for legislative and quasi-legislative or judicial and quasi-judicial activities;

(ii) It is not liable for functions that are discretionary rather than ministerial, although liability may be found if the injury resulted from the government's failure to exercise its discretion under its own processes. The difficult line drawing accompanying the discretionary-ministerial test has led several courts to adopt a "planning-operational test," under which decisions that rise to the level of planning or policy making are deemed discretionary acts while those that are operational are not so characterized and do not give rise to immunity;

(iii) The public officer (not employee or agent) who is exercising discretionary (or planning or policymaking) functions also ought to be shielded. Courts have had some success in limiting immunity for individual officers to recognized policy objectives. Immunity removes the threat of litigation from functions that are closely related to the core operations of government. It may provide absolute protection to officers for particular functions (judicial, e.g.), thus requiring close examination of the circumstances when officers serve in multiple roles. It shields officers (without prescribed status hierarchy) who exercise personal judgment without malice. It also protects policy choices that include, to more than a minor degree, the manner in which the sovereign or government power (the police power, e.g.) should be exercised;

(iv) The government is not liable for governmental activities;

(v) The plaintiffs must show a breach of some duty owed them as individuals, not merely of an obligation owed by the government to the general public (public duty).

In many states, the public duty doctrine is a governmental defense to liability. It is not an immunity doctrine; rather it provides a substantive defense on the merits. The public duty doctrine is based on the principle that the local government generally owes a duty to the public at large, not to particular persons, and therefore cannot be liable to individuals for failing to fulfill that public duty. Some courts have abolished or rejected the public duty doctrine as a backhanded way of resurrecting sovereign immunity; others have rejected the labels as reflecting no more than standard tort doctrine. Some define the scope of liability by one or another of the above; others commingle the factors to produce a highly differentiated scope of immunity. For some courts, immunized governmental functions seem to be taking on the contours of public duties or even discretionary activities. For some, the discretionary-ministerial test is applicable only to public officers. Government and public officer immunity are not coterminous. For some, there cannot be discretion if there is a duty to act. But the duty that makes the matter ministerial may be a public duty thereby preventing liability to the plaintiff. The plaintiff then must show that, while the policy choice was discretionary, negligent implementation thereof caused the harm.

When government's failure to act has produced a detriment for the plaintiff, or when the government has failed to protect the injured party from harm by a third person, the plaintiff may raise a special relationship exception to the public duty rule. The special duty may arise in a variety of situations, and results in the conclusion that the government entity has assumed, through promises or actions, an affirmative duty to act on behalf of the individual plaintiff. If that standard is met, and if the plaintiff has relied to her detriment on the government's promises or actions, the public duty defense will be overcome by the existence of the special duty. The concept is evolving in varied ways among the many jurisdictions that accept it. Even within one state, inconsistencies may be found. Judicial responses are moving from negative to mixed in such areas as safety inspections, emergency calls, child abuse statute administration, and duties to discovered drunken drivers or their subsequent victims or to the victims of those with known, violent, criminal propensities (prevent or warn).

§ 5. Some Notes Concerning Damages, Execution, Contribution and Indemnity

If the person suffering special injury seeks to enjoin municipal tortious conduct, traditional equity principles will apply. In actions seeking damages, it was traditionally likely that only compensatory damages would be imposed. A series of arguments had been persuasive in avoiding the imposition of punitive damages in the absence of authorizing statutes. It was felt that their twin goals, punishment and deterrence, would not be furthered by applying the concept to government actors. The citizens would bear the burden of the award and are the same who would benefit from its deterrent effect. The size of the award, if related to the wealth of the tortfeasor, would perforce be based on the unlimited taxing power of the municipality. A large award against the city would not necessarily deter city employees who would not have to pay it, and the compensatory award would probably motivate city deterrent disciplinary procedures in any event. While for these reasons, some courts have held that public policy precludes punitive damages, others in the absence of statutory prohibition have concluded that punitive damages should be available against the city where in similar circumstances they would be warranted against a private defendant. As we have seen, some statutes have prohibited punitive damages. Punitives are also under general attack. An eighth amendment challenge has failed, and difficult due process challenges have at least succeeded in developing standards for judicial review of punitive awards.

When a judgment is obtained against the city, we have seen that recovery will not be barred because the judgment debt exceeds constitutional or statutory debt limitations. It will be included in determining the total debt of the city in evaluating other borrowing, however. When funds are borrowed to pay the judgment, the bond issue or other form of borrowing does not constitute a debt additional to the original liability under terms of the debt limits, although both are in a sense "outstanding" after borrowing and before payment of the judgment is made.

In some jurisdictions, attempts to obtain satisfaction of judgments by execution upon municipal property or the garnishment of funds in the hands of debtors and depositors of the city will be met by rulings that the only available remedy is mandamus against the appropriate city official to obtain the necessary funds by the appropriate taxation methods. In many jurisdictions, where no constitutional or statutory provision prohibits, attachment and execution may be had against proprietary assets of the government entity, although its governmental assets may not be reached. The courts adhere to a more inclusive concept of what assets are governmental than is common in other uses of the dichotomy.

Where the municipal entity and a private individual are co-tortfeasors, customary principles of indemnity, contribution and comparative fault sharing may allow eventual recovery by one against the other of all or some of the tort judgment, subject to the usual difficulties. Contribution may have been abolished as comparative negligence doctrines have evolved. The private tortfeasor may face the additional difficulty of governmental immunity. Indemnity awards against the city on behalf of officers and employees in several jurisdictions may result from laws requiring or authorizing the municipalities to indemnify specified employees against whom tort liability has resulted from actions in the performance of their duties. Indemnity awards for the city have been more likely (the general adoption of comparative negligence may obviate the necessity) than in private co-tortfeasor situations in cases where duties, such as the prevention of street defects, are imposed upon the city. It will then more likely be found "passively" or "secondarily" negligent within the meaning of indemnity doctrines, warranting recovery against the defect-causing co-tortfeasor deemed "actively" or "primarily" negligent. Indemnification of the city by its co-tortfeasor contractors is also more frequent because many municipal contracts will contain clauses providing therefor.

B. CLAIMS AGAINST THE LOCAL GOVERNMENT UNDER 42 U.S.C.A. § 1983

In 1978, the U.S. Supreme Court held that local governments were among those persons to whom the Civil Rights Act of 1871, now 42 U.S.C.A. § 1983, applies. Since then, the Court and other courts have attempted to define the contours of the increasingly complex theories of liability spawned by this ruling in the atmosphere of tension and uncertainty that inevitably accompanies massive local government exposure to liability for damages and extensive attorney fees.

Section 1983 is a remedial statute for violation of federal rights created elsewhere. While a full treatment of the rights and developing remedial doctrine is not possible within the confines of this text, a brief summary may be helpful.

§ 1. The Statute

42 U.S.C.A. § 1983 provides:

"Every person who, under color of any statute, ordinance, regulation, custom, or usage, of any State or Territory, subjects, or causes to be subjected, any citizen of the United States or other person within the jurisdiction thereof to the deprivation of any rights, privileges, or immunities secured by the Constitution and laws, shall be liable to the party injured in an action at law, suit in equity, or other proper proceeding for redress."

§ 2. Application of Statutory Terms

"Every Person"

The Supreme Court has held that state agencies, the states, territories, and their officials acting in official capacities were not intended to be persons to whom § 1983 applies and are not subject to suit thereunder for damages. Other political subdivisions are different—the Court has held that local governments are within the intended scope of "persons" for purposes of liability under § 1983. The Court has also held that respondeat superior, which imposes automatic responsibility on the employer for the acts of employees, does not apply. Thus, vicarious liability will not apply to extend liability beyond that of the the person who actually inflicted the injury. Only when the execution of the government's policy or custom inflicts the injury, when that policy or custom is the moving force, the cause, will the local government be held liable for damages. Included with such customary evidence of government policy as its laws and regulations are: policy choices made by the government's authorized decisionmakers (deliberate choices among alternatives by one not just exercising discretion but responsible for establishing final government policy); failure properly to train employees who then engage in unconstitutional conduct (for which there will be no respondeat superior liability) provided the failure to train itself amounts to deliberate indifference to protected rights of citizens; and a custom not formally approved by an appropriate decisionmaker that is so widespread as to have the force of law.

"... Under Color of ..."

The dimensions and permutations of this requirement are the same as those for state action under the fourteenth amendment and thus may extend to conduct beyond that of government officials. Illustratively, a Public Defender is not acting under color of law for § 1983 purposes when acting as defense attorney, but may allegedly be acting under color of law if bargaining with prosecutors amounts to a conspiracy in violation of defendant's rights. A person is traditionally said to be acting under color of state law if he or she exercised power by virtue of state law, was clothed with the authority of state law, and abused the position given him by the state. 'Under color of' law can be read to mean 'under pretense of' law, however a court will find state action only where the actor intended to act in an official capacity, not where action was in further-ance of personal pursuits.

". . . *Subjects or Causes to be Subjected* . . ."

Customary standards of fault and causation ap-ply. For example, a training failure alone may not be sufficient because the agent's shortcomings arose from other causes, because a sound program was negligently administered, because ideal perfection was not achieved, or because the agent made a mistake. Proof must relate to the adequacy of train-ing for the task the agent must perform and the deficiency must be closely related to the injury.

". . . *Deprivation of Any Rights* . . . *Secured by the Constitution*"

Analysis begins by identifying the specific federal constitutional right allegedly violated (excessive force used to arrest invokes the protections of the fourth amendment and its "reasonability" test, not the eighth amendment or the more generalized tests under substantive due process, e.g.). Other examples of claims that implicate federal rights include those of false arrest, abuse of process, mali-cious prosecution, interference with a person's right to pursue an occupation (but no right to a specific job), bad faith delay in decisions regarding zoning and land use, deprivation of an individual's proper-ty, racial discrimination in the provision of services, and sexual harassment.

Upon identifying a specific federal right allegedly violated, the analysis turns to the question whether the action deprived the plaintiff of that right. Section 1983 is a remedy, not for mere negligence, but for the deliberate deprivation of guaranteed constitutional rights. Thus, for example, a failure to train must amount to deliberate indifference to the constitutional rights of persons with whom the trained personnel would come in contact. The Supreme Court has ruled that "deliberate indifference" is established only where adequate scrutiny of an applicant's background would lead a reasonable policymaker to conclude that the plainly obvious consequence of the decision to hire would be deprivation of a third party's federally protected right. Nonetheless, action taken or directed by the municipality or its authorized decisionmaker that itself violates federal law satisfies the requirement that municipal action was the moving force behind the injury, without further state-of-mind requirement. [Board Cty. Com'rs v. Brown (S.Ct.1997)].

It is important to note that the demonstrated "deliberate indifference" links the city to the injury. But, as noted above, the constitutional injury must also be shown. If substantive due process is asserted, for example, the plaintiff must establish that the interest said to have been violated is among the life, liberty, or property interests protected by the constitution. Among the due process issues are whether the Due Process Clause is violated by every act or failure to act that affects life, liberty and property and whether § 1983 is a federal alternative to common-law tort actions.

As we saw in our torts discussion, inaction in the face of danger to persons not caused by the city, or caused by a third party, raises the question of a duty arising from a special relationship. While the government may not selectively deny its protective services to disfavored minorities, it will not be liable under § 1983 for failing to provide protective services to one whose injuries could have been thereby avoided. The special relationship and resulting government liability arise when the government takes an individual into custody thereby making that person dependent on the state for protection, or when the government itself creates a dangerous situation, for example by affirmatively acting to create an opportunity for an individual to be harmed by a third person. The compelled custody aspect has led many challengers to offer largely unsuccessful arguments that government should be liable for in-school and school-based-activity injuries to students who attend because of compulsory education laws. The theory is also limited by cases holding that an individual is not constitutionally entitled to emergency and rescue services. The states may develop special-relationship duties that they will enforce under tort law, but the Due Process Clause does not transform every government tort into a constitutional violation.

"... and Laws"

Section 1983 is available as a remedy for violations of federal statutes by local government unless Congress has foreclosed such enforcement in the underlying federal statute or unless that statute did not create enforceable rights, privileges and immunities within the meaning of § 1983. (Indeed, the Supreme Court has held that Congress intended that the explicit remedial provisions of § 1983 be controlling in damage suits against state actors for violation of rights set forth in 42 U.S.C.A. § 1981.) Courts asks a number of questions designed to reveal Congress' intent to foreclose enforcement of the statutory right under § 1983. Is plaintiff one of a class intended to be benefited by the statute? Does the provision create obligations binding on the government unit or only express congressional preference for certain results? Does the statutory language or legislative history indicate that Congress intended to create a remedy in that act or to deny one? (Courts looks for Congress' intent to deny a cause of action, but do not require a showing of intent to create a private cause of action.) Is such an implied remedy consistent with the statutory scheme? Is the "primary right" that the statute purportedly creates sufficiently specific and definite to enforce? Is the matter so traditionally relegated to state law that it would be inappropriate to infer a cause of action based on federal law?

Although it is an unusual result, a court may find that Congress denied a private right of action, or the remedial devices provided in the underlying statute may be held to be so comprehensive as to demonstrate Congress' intent to preclude the § 1983 remedy. For example, decisions have found such a statutory scheme in Title VII and in the

Education For All Handicapped Children Act. (It should be noted that plaintiffs may in these proceedings establish an independent statutory or constitutional basis for § 1983.) The fact that the federal statute is preemptive under the Supremacy Clause is not determinative. Preemptive statutes may also create rights enforceable under § 1983 (rights of labor and management against government interference, e.g.).

". . . Action . . . for Redress"

Section 1983 actions may be brought in federal or state court. Unlike states and state agencies, municipalities cannot assert eleventh amendment immunity as a defense to § 1983 actions. Nor can a municipality assert the good faith of its officers as a defense to municipal liability. Remember that the U.S. Supreme Court has ruled that the eleventh amendment bars federal court actions for monetary relief against the state, and that neither the state nor state officials acting in their official capacities are "persons" to whom § 1983 applies. Neither theory bars action for prospective declaratory and injunctive relief, and at any rate, the states' eleventh amendment immunity in damage actions is of no moment in actions against municipalities. Still, the classification by state law of subsidiary entities into either state agencies or local government units remains important because neither the eleventh amendment nor the Supreme Court ruling confirming immunity of states and state officials applies to local government units.

Individual officers acting in their individual capacities (suit against them in their official capacities is suit against the government) may have absolute or qualified immunity from § 1983 suits under a functional test that examines the nature of the functions an official performs and the effect of exposure to liability. Absolute immunity may be the conclusion where a historical or common law basis existed granting the official absolute immunity in performing a particular function, where performing the function involves special risks of vexatious litigation, and where sufficient safeguards exist to prevent abuses of power. Some officials, therefore, have absolute immunity for acts within the scope of their protected responsibilities (legislators, judges, prosecutors, when acting in those capacities, e.g.). They, when not acting in the absolutely protected capacities, and others, who may be subordinate, unelected officials charged with discretionary responsibilities (parole officers, police, e.g.) may have qualified immunity, i.e., may be shielded from liability for civil damages insofar as their actions do not violate clearly established constitutional or statutory rights of which a reasonable person would have known.

The existence of plain, adequate, and complete state remedies plays a § 1983 role, although the Supreme Court has held that § 1983 does not require plaintiffs to prove that they have exhausted their remedies. Some statutes explicitly require plaintiffs to seek administrative and state law relief before resorting to a suit under § 1983. If such remedies exist, under the federal Tax Injunction Act, 28 U.S.C.A. § 1341, and principles of comity, federal courts will not hear attacks on the validity of state and local tax systems. Similarly, the Prison Litigation Reform Act requires exhaustion of administrative remedies in suits challenging prison circumstances or occurrences. Exhaustion of remedies is distinct from the requirement of ripeness; thus if remedies exist, the unconstitutional takings and, perhaps, due process violations allegedly resulting from land use regulation are not complete until alternatives have been pursued and (at least in takings cases) compensation has been sought. Random, aberrational (rather than systemic) government actions will not be deemed due process violations if adequate state remedial procedures exist.

In developing the contours of this federal remedial action, the courts have answered a number of procedural questions. For example, the applicable statute of limitations will be that for personal injuries in the state where the action was held to arise. In the event that the state has multiple statutes of limitations for personal injury actions, § 1983 actions will be governed by the residual or general, personal injury statute of limitations. In addition, there is no heightened pleading standard in § 1983 suits against municipalities. Whether the § 1983 action is brought in federal or state court, the state notice-of-claim statutes applicable to government torts, and state law that immunizes government conduct otherwise subject to suit under § 1983, are preempted by federal law because they conflict with its purpose and effect. State court judgments and decisions made by state administrative agencies acting in a judicial capacity must be given both issue and claim preclusive effect in actions arising out of the same situation brought subsequently under § 1983. Failure to pursue federal claims arising out of the same situation as the state claims has the same preclusive effect. Among other due process issues are whether the Due Process Clause is violated by every act or failure to act that affects life, liberty and property and whether § 1983 is a federal alternative to common-law tort actions.

Punitive damages are available, when appropriate, against public personnel acting in their individual capacities, but may not be awarded against the government or public personnel acting in their official capacity. Compensatory damages, as in tort cases, include financial harm and expense and such injuries as impairment of reputation, personal humiliation, and mental and emotional distress, but may not include the jury's perception of the abstract importance of the offended constitutional right in our system of government. A state statutory cap on general damages and prohibition of punitives in tort actions are inconsistent with § 1983's deterrent intent and, hence, are preempted under the Supremacy Clause. It would appear that if a bargain involving withdrawal of criminal prosecution in return, inter alia, for a waiver of a § 1983 civil claim, survives an ad hoc examination balancing competing public and individual interests affecting covenants not to sue, it will be upheld if the covenanting party was knowledgeable and advised by counsel and if there was no prosecutorial misconduct.

Attorney's Fees

An area of potentially enormous expense to local governments, attorney's fee awards in § 1983 actions by virtue of 42 U.S.C.A. § 1988 (amended by the Civil Rights Attorney's Fees Awards Act) have spawned numerous challenges. The statute provides that "[i]n any action or proceeding to enforce a provision of sections ... 1983, ... the court, in its discretion, may allow the prevailing party ... a reasonable attorney's fee as part of the costs." An exhaustive list of issues, perhaps apparent from the terms of the statute, is too extensive to be detailed in this text. Illustrative are such questions as whether: a plaintiff who wins nominal damages constitutes a prevailing party for purposes of attorneys fees; (yes, where plaintiff obtains relief on the merits which materially alters the parties' legal relationship and modifies defendant's behavior); the defendant qualifies as a prevailing party (yes, stringent standards as to claim's frivolousness); expert witness fees can be recovered (yes, by virtue of the Civil Rights Act of 1991); attorney's fees can be higher than underlying damage award (yes); attorney's fees at the prevailing market rate in the area can be enhanced by exceptional success, and by risk of non-or delayed payment (yes, prevailing rate is the lodestar and enhancement is possible); contingent fee arrangement is a ceiling on the award of attorney's fees or the converse (no); the prevailing party must prevail on all issues (no), on the § 1983 issue (yes), in court (yes); and status of fees (and, if awarded, of market rates for paralegals and law clerks) as costs, not damages subject to limitations (yes, eleventh amendment would not bar award or enhancement of attorney's fees in an action against state officers for prospective injunctive relief, e.g.).

C. STANDING

§ 1. The Requirement's Rationale

We have seen a number of challenges which might be raised in appropriate actions attacking the city of Allgood's domed stadium, Bigville's airport and Hearing's public disclosure ordinance. Before the challenger can raise the substantive arguments, however, each faces an initial hurdle: does the plaintiff have standing to bring the action? A number of general policies are served by the requirement that the suing plaintiff have the necessary standing to bring the action and will be vindicated by the relief sought. Among them is the policy that legal rights should be presented by parties whose well-defined interests and stake in the outcome will ensure that there will be the "specificity," "adverseness" and "vigor" of advocacy needed for proper dispute resolution by the courts. The standing requirement is also intended to serve the public interest by restraining what would otherwise be an inundation of litigation which saps the courts' abilities to give reasoned, considered resolution to important legal and social problems. Thus, the objective of judicial administration or convenience is an important consideration in standing disputes. Insistence upon proper standing is intended to isolate and provide a forum for parties specially aggrieved, and to prevent the creation of a platform for voicing a multiplicity of grievances common to the public at large. It is intended to protect significant interests without causing dissipation of judicial energies upon a host of challenges to government activity which do not rise to this level.

The challenges here discussed may be raised by individuals, groups or classes who claim standing because they suffer the adverse effects of government action, and because they seek to uphold personal, property or contractual rights alleged to have been violated. Or they may be raised in a taxpayer representative action either because taxpayers are suffering an injury peculiar to taxpayer status or because they are serving as a watchdog to see that important legal rights and protections are not bypassed by otherwise unchallenged municipal activity.

§ 2. "Adverse" Effect of Government Action; Illustrative Questions

Where standing is to be based upon the alleged adverse effect of the municipality's action upon persons and groups, the courts will insist upon a personal injury in fact, a direct impact, one that is special to them. This direct and personal injury, when applied in connection with the relevance of the remedy to the plaintiffs, gives them a "personal stake in the outcome" that assures the desired adversity in the litigation process. Are their personal, property and contractual rights such that the common law, the statutes or the constitutions provide that they shall be free from this type of injury?

Standing might be relevant to determining the scope of the following potential lawsuits. May one who is injured by construction at the stadium site sue to recover from Allgood (prescinding from questions of indemnity or immunity)? Does a property owner who lives one half mile from the stadium site have standing (come within the statutory label "aggrieved") to challenge the rezoning ordinance permitting the site to be used for a stadium or the surrounding area to be used for the inevitable commercial satellites? Does a nearby property owner have standing to assert that stadium access and traffic regulations have damaged the owner's right to ingress and egress? May an unpaid contractor sue to recover money allegedly owed under a contract to construct the airport? Does an association of surrounding landowners have standing to challenge the airport plans because the eventual construction on land created by filling in wetlands will disturb important breeding grounds for animals, fish and birds? May one who has submitted the lowest bid for construction of the airport challenge the award of the contract to one whose bid was higher? Do citizens or candidates or public officers have standing to contend that the public disclosure ordinance constitutes an unreasonable intrusion upon the right of privacy, an unjustifiable limitation upon the right to seek or hold public employment and an ambiguous and vague affront to the dictates of due process?

Whether any or all of these challengers have the necessary standing will depend on whether the courts conclude that the law on which the claim is based establishes the right to be free from the injury alleged (the low bidder, e.g.); whether, in light of the nature and gravity of the municipal action and the degree of its impact upon the plaintiff, the courts are receptive to the asserted interest sought to be vindicated (rezoning effect one half mile away, e.g.); and whether the courts see the injury as special, different in kind and degree from that which affects the general public interest in the outcome, and capable of vindication by the relief sought (the wetlands challenge; invalidation of the award of a construction contract, e.g.).

It should be noted that in addition to the broader recognition of protectible legal interests resulting from liberal standing decisions, statutes will often promote judicial review of particular municipal actions by according "standing" to (giving legal recognition to the interest of) specified individuals. For instances, some state bidding statutes explicitly authorize the disappointed low bidder to challenge the bid award.

§ 3. Taxpayer Suits

The balancing process that weighs the importance of the legal right's vindication and the significance

of the societal interest against the desire for the
honing process of adversary advocacy and the goal
of restricting excessive use of the judicial system
has led the jurisdictions to inconsistent results in
deciding whether taxpayers have standing to bring
representative actions in connection with municipal
activity. Is it more important to allow general citizen oversight of municipal activity? Or should concerns about overtaxing judicial facilities, and about
the inconvenience and expense of municipal defense
limit citizens to remedies at the polls and the rights
in question to review only where such is sought by
someone adversely and specially injured?

May one or more taxpayers of our illustration
cities bring representative actions to enjoin payment by the City of Allgood of extra compensation
to the construction contractor at the stadium, or to
recover from the airport contractor extra compensation wrongfully paid by Bigville? May a taxpayer
sue to require Bigville to zone the area around the
airport to avoid unsafe conditions for residences?
Does an Allgood taxpayer have standing to seek on
behalf of all taxpayers to enjoin the city from entering into an ultra vires contract to build the stadium? May a taxpayer suit be brought to compel
recalcitrant officials of the City of Hearing to enforce the public disclosure ordinance?

On Behalf of the Municipality

Courts have struck different balances between
the interests of judicial convenience and citizen
vigilance. In many jurisdictions, a taxpayer has

standing to bring a taxpayer suit on behalf of the municipality if taxpayers in general would be exposed to financial harm because the city failed to bring the action itself. Where such standing is recognized, the right being vindicated (recovery of funds and property wrongfully disposed of, or of funds wrongfully retained by public officials, e.g.) is deemed to outweigh the fact that the plaintiff has suffered no special injury.

Against the Municipality

Similarly, in many jurisdictions a taxpayer may bring a representative action against the municipality and its officials, when the class of taxpayers would be exposed to financial loss (increased taxation), to enjoin illegal expenditures or contracts which would have such result, illegal disposition of property, waste, assertedly illegal levy of taxes or creation of tax exemptions (even though ending the exemptions would not affect plaintiff's taxes). These courts insist, though, that the municipal action result in actual financial loss to the taxpayers. Some other courts insist on a greater interest before the plaintiff and the class have standing, viz., special injury different from that suffered by taxpayers in general. A few courts are wary of any of these actions. Yet others would allow them only with respect to funds derived from general taxation (insisting that actions involving water revenues be brought by ratepayers, e.g.).

A sizeable body of authority supports the proposition that municipal nondiscretionary duties imposed by law are of such significance that standing should be accorded to a citizen or taxpayer who invokes mandamus to compel performance of such duties. This concept of citizen vigilance and the importance of deciding significant legal questions and matters of public interest has been extended by some provisions in constitutions, statutes, and charters and by some liberal judicial standing determinations to permit representative actions by residents or taxpayers, even if the class will not suffer financial harm, seeking to require power exercise or to restrain waste or illegal expenditures, disbursements, and contracts.

§ 4. Note on Federal Cases

Because the rights invoked against municipal action so frequently flow from the federal constitution and from federal statutes and administrative implementation, the challenges are frequently brought in federal court. The specific details of standing requirements in the federal forum are beyond the scope of this text. It is important to note, however, that they are designed to achieve the same goals as those described above, with the special underpinning of the federal constitution's case or controversy requirement, the doctrine of separation of powers, and principles of federalism.

Individual

Individual standing in federal court requires that the plaintiff have personally suffered actual or threatened injury which is fairly traceable to the challenged action and is likely to be redressed by a favorable decision. The alleged injury must be to personal or property rights which are federally protected. Such plaintiffs may sue if a private right of action can be implied from a federal statute, because they are one of a class for whose special benefit the law was enacted, because there is legislative intent to create or no legislative intent to deny such a remedy, and because the cause of action is not one customarily relegated to state law and the private remedy is consistent with the purposes of the legislative scheme. Recall the evolving § 1983 jurisprudence allowing claims of deprivation of federal statutory rights where Congress has not denied the availability of this remedy.

Prudential considerations may be significant in federal standing determinations as well. Thus, courts will, except in some first amendment contexts, require a party to assert his or her own legal rights, not those of third parties. Although prudential considerations weigh in favor of standing, the Article III (case or controversy) requirements must nevertheless be met; and although Article III requirements are met, prudential considerations may move the court to avoid adjudicating "abstract questions of wide public significance" amounting to "generalized grievances."

Taxpayer Representative Suits

A taxpayer representative action and a class action are both representative actions. The taxpayer suit is not technically a class action and need not conform to the class action rules. It must meet specific standing requirements, however. Taxpayer standing to bring representative actions in federal court varies according to the target government.

Taxpayers who seek to enjoin federal actions must either allege the palpable, fairly traceable, remediable injury described above or, in order to meet the required adversity, must meet the two aspects of federal taxpayer nexus, namely, a suit to enjoin actions that are exercises of Congress' taxing and spending powers and that exceed specific constitutional limitations imposed on those powers.

Municipal taxpayers' relation to municipal taxes is more direct and immediate. Injunctive relief is not inappropriate. The taxpayer must show that the challenged activity or transaction will probably result, directly or indirectly, in an increase in that taxpayer's taxes or would in some other manner cause irreparable or great injury to that taxpayer.

When state taxpayers seek to enjoin state actions, some federal courts apply the federal taxpayer injury test and others use the more liberal municipal taxpayer standard in deciding whether the plaintiff has standing.

INDEX

BORROWING
    Generally, 408–430
Bankruptcy, 416–417
Bonds, 409–418
    Authority to issue, 409
    Default, 414–417
    Derivatives, 417–418
    General obligation vs. revenue bonds, 409–410
    Interest Rate, 411–414
    Investor protection, 413–414
    Issuance, 411
    Marketability, 411
    Referenda, 411, 419–420
Debt limitations,
    Generally, 418–425, 425–427
    Applicability, 421
    Avoidance of, 420–421
    Debt ceiling restrictions, 423–425, 425–427
    Tort judgments, 447–450
"Double barreled," 412
Interest,
    Exclusion from federal taxation, 428–430
    Federal taxation, 429–430
        Private activity bonds, 429–430
        Tax Reform Act of 1986, pp. 428–429
Interlocal cooperation, 96–103
Long term borrowing, 408–418
Long-term leases, 423
Moral obligation bonds, 410
Notes, 408
Political restraint, 426
Short term borrowing, 408

BUILDING CODES
See Land Use, this index

CHARTER POWERS
Optional charter laws, 21–22

CITIES
See Government Units, this index

CIVIL RIGHTS
Americans with Disabilities Act, 118
Civil Rights Act of 1991, 118, 122, 461
Comparable worth, 137–138

EQUITABLE RELIEF—Cont'd
Contracts improperly bid,
    Estoppel, 272, 283
    Measure of relief, 293–294
    Unjust enrichment, 271–272, 293
Ultra vires, 270, 294
Unjust enrichment of municipality, 293
Where both parties claim, 293–294

EXPENDITURE CONTROLS
Authority to spend, requirement of, 430
Contracting controls, see Public Contracts, this index
Expenditure method restrictions, 431–433
    Certification, requirement of, 433
    Intra-budgetary diversions of funds, prohibition of, 432
    Purposes of, 431
    Spending increases, limits on expenditure controls,
        Officer liability, 433–434
Interest,
    Federal taxation, 428–430
        Private activity bonds, 428–429
        Tax Reform Act of 1986, pp. 428–430
Officer liability for unlawful expenditures,
    Pension funds, 433
Public purpose restrictions, 430–431
State constitutional limitations, 430–431

FEDERAL AID
See Federal–State–Local Relations, this index

FEDERAL–STATE–LOCAL RELATIONS
    Generally, 50, 58, 63
Annexation, constitutional challenges to, 94–96
Boundary alteration, constitutional implications, 90
Campaign contribution disclosure laws, 111–113
Commerce clause,
    Foreign commerce, 284, 353
    Regulation, 182–183
    Taxation, 350–355, 368
Competence, 48–49
Constitutional limitations, 68
Contracts,
    Clauses,
        Affirmative action set-asides, 286
        "Buy American," 284
        General Agreement on Tariffs and Trade, 284

MUNICIPAL PROPERTY INTERESTS—Cont'd

MUNICIPAL RESTRUCTURING

†